LATINA/CHICANA
MOTHERING

LATINA/CHICANA MOTHERING

edited by

Dorsía Smith Silva

DEMETER

TORONTO, CANADA

Published by:
Demeter Press
140 Holland Street West
P. O. Box 13022
Bradford, ON L3Z 2Y5
Tel: (905) 775-9089
Email: info@demeterpress.org
Website: www.demeterpress.org

Demeter Press logo based on Skulptur "Demeter" by Maria-Luise Bodirsky <www.keramik-atelier.bodirsky.edu>

Cover Photo: Antonio Silva Rosario
Cover Design/Interior Design: Luciana Ricciutelli

Printed and Bound in Canada

Library and Archives Canada Cataloguing in Publication

        Latina/Chicana mothering / edited by Dorsía Smith Silva
Includes bibliographical references.
ISBN 978-0-9866671-3-8

        1. Hispanic American mothers — Social conditions.
2. Mexican American mothers — Social conditions.
3. Motherhood — Social aspects — Cross-cultural studies.
I. Smith Silva, Dorsía

HQ759.L37 2011   306.874'308968073   C2011-906515-0

To Tony and the Little One

Table of Contents

Acknowledgments
xi

Introduction:
Conceptualizing Latina/Chicana Mothering
Dorsía Smith Silva
1

I: Telling Our Tales: Testimonios

Are Hunters Born or Made?
Ana Castillo
21

My Mother's Memory
Mayra Santos-Febres
28

How (In a Time of Trouble) I Discovered My Mom
and Learned to Live
Junot Díaz
38

Journey to Motherhood
Dorsía Smith Silva
46

Learning the Hard Way
Angie Cruz
51

Mi Madre, Mi Hija y Yo:
Chicana Mothering Through Memory, Culture and Place
Michelle Téllez
57

**II: Counting the Ways to Mother:
Communities and Resources**

Life, Death, and Second Mothering:
Mexican American Mothers, Gang Violence,
and *La Virgen de Guadalupe*
Richard Mora
71

"No hay nada tan mala… (There is Nothing So Bad)":
Latina Mothering Across Generations
Laura Ruth Johnson
87

Transformational Caring:
Mexican American Women Redefining Mothering and Education
Gilda L. Ochoa
104

**III: Scenes of *La Familia*:
Facing Challenges**

Latina Teenage Mothering:
Meanings, Challenges, and Successes
Elizabeth Trejos-Castillo and Helyne Frederick
125

CONTENTS

Motherhood Unbound:
Homeless Chicanas in San Francisco
Anne R. Roschelle
141

Surviving Warfare and Trauma:
Consequences for Salvadorian Mother-Daughter Relationships
Mirna E. Carranza
161

**IV: The Ties that Bind:
Literary and Cultural Representations of
Latina/Chicana Mothers**

Counternarratives in the Literary Works of
Mexican Author Ángeles Mastretta and Chilean Author Pía Barros
Mary Lou Babineau
177

Contesting the Meaning of Latina/Chicana Motherhood:
Familism, Collectivist Orientation, and Nonexclusived Mothering
in Cristina García's *Dreaming in Cuban Yolanda Martínez*
194

The Telenovela *Alborada*:
Constructions of the Latina Mother in an
Internationally Successful Soap Opera
Petra Guerra, Diana I. Rios, and D. Milton Stokes
209

Malinches, Lloronas, and Guadalupanas:
Chicana Revisions of *Las Tres Madres*
Cristina Herrera
224

About the Contributors
239

Acknowledgements

I AM EXTREMELY DELIGHTED TO HAVE HAD THE OPPORTUNITY to work on this book and receive the generous assistance and support of several people. It has been a great pleasure working with them and seeing the book develop from abstract ideas to concrete essays to publication.

Thank you to the contributors to this collection. I appreciate their effort in meeting the deadlines and their receptiveness to my comments. Their essays were a joy to shape and I am grateful for their trust in the process. I must give a special thank you to Mayra Santos-Febres who offered her essay for this book without a second thought. Her willingness to share such a personal story amazes me; I thank her for sharing her truth. I am also grateful for her courage and selflessness. I owe another special thank you to Ana Castillo and Junot Díaz who took time from their hectic schedules to respond to my e-mails and thought of the perfect essays for this collection. *¡Mil gracias!*

Thank you to the agent of Ana Castillo, Krista Ingebretson of the Anne Edelstein Literary Agency. I also thank the agents of Junot Díaz, Jim Hanks and Christie Hauser of Aragi, Inc. I appreciate their assistance and prompt response to my inquiries.

I am full of gratitude to my dear friend Velma Pollard. I thank her for encouraging me and giving me feedback when I felt like I was losing my focus. Her words kept me going, "Press on. Push on." I am fortunate that I have her to lean on and that she always reminds me to trust myself.

Thank you to Andrea O'Reilly at Demeter Press and the Motherhood Initiative for Research and Community Involvement (MIRCI) for being open to the project and for embracing me as the editor. I appreciate. her receptivity to examining motherhood in a full spectrum and for giving the project a big green light. I also thank her for her patience with the publication schedule and for her assistance with the minute details. I thank Renée Knapp at Demeter Press and MIRCI as well for her positive demeanor and keen attention to keeping me informed of the publishing developments. I thank her also for responding swiftly and kindly to what seemed like my endless stream of questions. Thanks also to the staff members at Demeter Press for attending to all of the necessary, but mundane, issues. The book shines even brighter because of their hard work.

Thank you to my family for encouraging and supporting me. I am particularly indebted to my husband, Tony, who has cheered me on from day one with this project. I thank him for understanding when I was typing away, sending e-mails, and fretting about grammar and punctuation. He never once complained when the office saw more of me than he did or when I babbled on about Latina/Chicana motherhood. I am also grateful that he understood my reasons for sharing our story. I owe him a world of heartfelt thanks.

Finally, I am grateful to the Little One. I thank you for this opportunity to be your mother and for reminding me of the spirit of motherhood. This pregnancy could not have come at a more opportune time and I appreciate everything that you are teaching me.

Introduction

Conceptualizing Latina/Chicana Mothering

DORSÍA SMITH SILVA

> To survive in a society that considers us dispensable utilities and
> yet, to care for and lovingly raise generation after generation,
> expect and even demand love in our lives, work under sometimes
> arduous conditions and yet find it within ourselves to appreciate
> flower and song, despite endless degradation to put on our red
> lipstick and walk down the street with our heads high like Queen
> Nefertiti, in my estimation, makes us quite formidable.
> —Ana Castillo, *Massacre of the Dreamers: Essays on Xicanisma*

LATINA/CHICANA[1] *MOTHERING* PROVIDES A GLIMPSE INTO THE
journey of mothering within the diverse spectrum of the histories,
struggles, and stories of Latinas and Chicanas. Here, the Latina/Chicana
mothering experience emphasizes the need for various conceptualizations of mothering, especially in regard to the conditions which shape
the lives of Latinas and Chicanas, such as race, gender, sexuality, culture, language, social status, religion, kinship, location, and migration.
By having a broad definition of mothering, the text builds upon and
extends Teresa Arendell's observation in "Mothering and Motherhood:
A Decade Review" that "mothering is neither a unitary experience for
individual women nor experienced similarly by all women" (15) and
Vicki L. Ruiz's reflection in her book *From Out of the Shadows: Mexican
Women in Twentieth-Century America* that motherhood must take into
account the different paths and cultural influences:

> People navigate across cultural boundaries and consciously make
> decisions with regard to the production of culture. However, bear

1

in mind that people of color do not have unlimited choice. Race, gender prejudice, and discrimination with their accompanying social, political, and economic segregation have constrained aspirations, expectations, and decision making. (16)

Latina/Chicana mothering also calls for an inquiry where the maternal body is neither a utopian space nor site of oppression:

Mothering can confer both maternal power and an immense burden of responsibility; the life-giving aspects of mothering may be undermined by the rage and aggression it inevitably elicits; the isolation it may impose on a woman can coexist with her invitation into a maternal community; the desexualization it may imply may go along with a new element of maternal sexualization. (Oberman and Josselson 344)

It means asking how do we feel as mothers? How are our lives affected by motherhood? How do we negotiate and renegotiate our identities as mothers? How do we claim our bodies as mothers? How do we begin to answer Ann Snitow's essential question: "To what extent is motherhood a powerful identity? ...To what extent is it a patriarchal construction that inevitably places mothers outside of the realm of the social, the changing, the active?" (49). By challenging these boundaries of the institution of motherhood and by extending the context and form of what it means to be a Latina/Chicana mother, this book interweaves multiple approaches to mothering, contributes new critical perspectives on the state of motherhood, and brings into the fold new generations of Latina/Chicana mothers.

African American feminist theorist and law professor, Patricia Hill Collins refers to the mothering experience as "inextricably linked to the socio-cultural concerns of racial ethnic communities" (47). The influencing factor of oppression becomes even more pronounced for Latina/Chicana mothers who migrate and cross the various cultural and territorial borders, leave family members, and forge new paths to integrate their new lives with or without their children. Writers such as Oliva M. Espin, Roberta Villalón, Juanita Heredia, Virginia Sánchez Korrol, Denise Segura, and Patricia Zavella explore the many reasons Latina/Chicana mothers migrate: to have access to jobs, education, economic security, and medical care; to escape trauma, war, and violence; and to experience freedom.[2] Yet in their new homelands, Latina/Chicana mothers may face pressure to adopt new accents and customs. They may also feel like chameleons—undergoing transformations with every crossed border—and experience hostility and discrimination. In addition, they may become vulnerable to being emotionally and financially dependent on others while handling the numerous obligations to their family within and across borders. On their journey to establish their lives in new lands, many Latina/Chicana mothers show resiliency, hope, and power; and confront the scars of prejudice, distress, and resentment. They represent those mothers who overcome complex tensions and reconcile migration as a blurred dimension of nations, languages, and traditions.

Latina/Chicana mothers transform the concept of mothering by becoming transnational mothers who are mothers that live and work in a new homeland while their children remain in their countries of origin. These mothers usually dedicate their lives to working hard and finding systems of support to assist with the rearing of their children in other territories. Sometimes their stories are ones of frustration due to constant traveling; limited social networks and support systems; insufficient economic resources to visit their children; and societal enforcement of cultural gender ideologies, especially in regard to perceptions about "bad" transnational mothers who "abandon" their children. All too often their experiences are rendered invisible in societies that only recognize them as economic commodities—nannies, domestic workers, and migrant helpers;[3] and in some instances due to their social class status, level of education, and ethnicity, they become accused of defying "traditional" mothering practices. As Pierrette Hondagneu-Sotelo and Ernestine Avila explain:

> Latina mothers are improvising new mothering arrangements that are borne out of women's financial struggles, played out in a new global arena, to provide the best future for themselves and their children. Like many other women of color and employed mothers, transnational mothers rely on an expanded and sometimes fluid number of family member and paid caregivers. Their caring circuits, however, span stretches of geography and time that are much wider than typical joint custody or "other

mother" arrangements that are more closely bound, both spa-
tially and temporally. (567)

Maxine Schwartz Seller in the text *Immigrant Women* (1994) further
illustrates that since "many immigrant mothers brought from their
homelands distinctive patterns of child rearing" (133), their forms of
child rearing present different lifestyles and values. The proliferation
of texts on transnational mothering also addresses the mixed emotions
of transnational mothers; many feel guilty and sad for leaving their
children, but must cope with the reality of having to earn a living and
fulfill economic responsibilities.[4] These works represent an attempt to
formulate the visibility of Latina/Chicana transnational mothers and
to draw attention to the many challenges they endure: separation from
their children, alienation and loneliness, anti-immigrant laws, xeno-
phobia, lack of educational opportunities, and cultural and language
denigration.

   Another part of Latina/Chicana mothering is about forming a strong
connection to family, which transpires into significant mother-child
relationships. Esmeralda Santiago and Joie Davidow in the book *Las
Mamis: Favorite Latino Authors Remember Their Mothers* (2000) note
the importance of the Latina/Chicana mother-child relationship. This
collection features the essays of several Latina and Chicana writers, in
which they honor their mothers. The experience of celebrating Latina/
Chicana mothers also encourages reflection on the process of mothering. Beneath the image of Mami as the giver of life, fierce warrior, and
preserver of cultural heritage, Latina/Chicana mothers struggle with
contradictions. Chicana theorist and writer Gloria Anzaldúa evokes in
her work how mothers communicate a variety of gendered ideas:

   Through our mothers, the culture gave us mixed messages: *No
   voy a dejar que ningún pelado desgraciado maltrate a mis hijos* (I'm
   not going to let any lowlife mistreat my children). Gendered
   messages that promoted gender roles are contested by the
   Latina daughters. *La mujer tiene que hacer lo que diga el hombre*
   (the woman has to do what the man says). Which was it to
   be—strong, submissive, rebellious or conforming? (18).

Chicana feminist and writer Ana Castillo further asserts in *Massacre of the Dreamers: Essays on Xicanisma* (1995) that the internalization of gendered patriarchal concepts often relates to how Latina/Chicana mothers "discipline" their children on sexuality:

> We will sometimes find it impossible to escape a sense of shame, regret, violation after expressing our sexual desire, so long have we [as women] been taught that sex is an unforgiving crime against divine mandates. In the past, an admittance of our sexuality demonstrated, at the very least, a lack of dignity and self-containment. (141)

By conforming to these patriarchal frameworks, some Latina/Chicana mothers also replicate traditional gender roles by teaching their daughters the ideologies of *marianismo*[5] and their sons about *machismo*.[6] However, the recognition of these images as stereotypical and oppressive has led many Latina/Chicana mothers to challenge the patriarchal instruction of motherhood and move across and between the spectrums of gender roles. They strive for Latina/Chicana mothering to "stop the chain of events" and "free the daughter to love her own daughter" (Moraga, *Loving* 34).

The mother-daughter relationship and mother's role in the cultural identity of her daughter is a prevalent issue in Latina/Chicana mothering as well. Writers such as Esmeralda Santiago, Isabel Allende, Cristina Garcia, Nicholasa Mohr, Judith Ortíz Cofer, and Julia Álavarez are noted for examining Latina/Chicana mothers who perpetuate the patriarchal institutions and traditional cultural and social codes while raising their daughters. Thus, the figure of the Latina/Chicana mother usually becomes linked to a repressive construction, especially in regard to controlling her daughter's sexuality and autonomy. Yet, these writers also show that not all Latinas/Chicanas act as a "castrating matriarch" or engage their daughters in the virgin/whore binary (Iglesias 509). They reveal that Latina/Chicana mothers can become victims of living in a sexist, classist, and racist society, a circumstance, which according to feminist, psychoanalyst, and social activist Jean Baker Miller is replicated in the mother-daughter dyad:

> It is easier to blame mothers than to comprehend the entire system that has restricted women. It is true that mothers have interacted most with daughters and, thus, were the most direct

agents of an oppressive system. But mothers were themselves victims of the system. (139)

As Latina/Chicana mothers engage in identity negotiation with their daughters, they begin to dismantle the systemic mechanism of alienation and repression in mother-daughter relationships. And in this process, they create chinks in patriarchal motherhood and inequalities of patriarchal culture.

Latina/Chicana mothering also represents an exploration of the female archetypes as described by Gloria Anzaldúa in her essay, "Entering Into the Serpent," where she writes about the "good mother" La Virgen de Guadalupe, "treacherous mother" *La Malinche,* and "bad mother" *La Llorona*:

> *La gente Chicana tiene tres madres.* [The Chicano people have three mothers]. All three are mediators: *Guadalupe,* the virgin mother who has not abandoned us, *la Chingada (Malinche),* the raped mother whom we have abandoned, and *La Llorona,* the mother who seeks her lost children and is a combination of the other two. (30-31)

In some traditional Latina/Chicana households, mothers are pushed to emulate the chaste and sacrificing *La Virgen,* repudiate the evil and sexually submissive *La Malinche* who is called the mother of the "bastard" race of mestizos, and reject the immoral and selfish La Llorona who has children out of wedlock and kills them. Latina/Chicana writers such as Gloria Anzaldúa, Cherrie Moraga, Sandra Cisneros, María Meléndez, Maria L. Figueredo, Sandra Messigner Cypess, Maria Herrera-Sobek, Cordelia Candelaria, Denis Lynn Daly Heyck, Norma Alarcón, Adelaida R. Del Castillo, and Domino Renee Pérez challenge how these figures are used to teach Latinas/Chicanas the "correct" way to mother. By critically examining these archetypes, they show that mothers can embrace sexuality, privilege, power, and reject cultural and ideological practices which oppress them. In other words, they call for Latina/Chicana mothering to reject this traditional dictation of "good" and "bad" mothers and "good" and "bad" mothering.[7]

Latina/Chicana mothering is foregounded not only in changing the ways the institution of motherhood is oppressive to Latinas/Chicanas, but also in challenging cultural and traditional prohibitions on queer mothering. Texts such as those by Cherríe Moraga, Carla Trujillo, Adriana Ortiz-Ortega, Achy Obejas, María Dolores Costa, and Gloria Anzaldúa are central to reconfiguring Latina/Chicana lesbian motherhood and contesting the subjection of the Latina/Chicana lesbian mother figure in patriarchal and colonial cultures.[8] Their work has paved the way for the surge of lesbian Latina/Chicana writers (including Terri de la Peña, Ibis Gómez-Vega, Monica Palacios, Alicia Gaspar de Alba, Emma Pérez, and Sheila Ortíz Taylor) who situate lesbian mothering in the intersection of cultural identification. In so doing, these fresh voices examine the strong cultural roots of Latina/Chicana lesbians, confront sexuality in Latina/Chicana culture, and battle against internalized homophobia when Latina/Chicana women identify themselves as lesbian. Such issues are reminiscent of Moraga when she asserts: "[F]reely … yes, should I pass on, this baby goes to you alone, unequivocally. Es la cultura. There is no denying that I had this baby that he might be a Mexican, for him to know and learn of mexicanismo" (*Waiting* 91); "[L]esbianism, in any form … challenges the very foundation of la familia" (*Loving* 111); and "[E]ach of us in some way has been both oppressed and the oppressor.… I think of how, even as a feminist lesbian, I have so wanted to ignore my own homophobia, my own hatred of myself for being queer" (*Loving* 57). And like Moraga, they push the imposed boundaries on queer motherhood—especially in regard to the perceptions of "la femme" or "butch" mother.[9]

The field of mothering means an examination of the strength of Latina/Chicana mothers who view the act of mothering as a political act where activism and agency are intertwined with the politics of identity and social justice. For Luz del Alba Acevedo, the act of remembering how the personal is political becomes an essential part of engaging in mothering. In her narrative "Daughter of Bootstrap" in the book *Telling to Live: Latina Feminist Testimonios* (2001), she recalls how a visit to her mother's hometown in Puerto Rico was instrumental in understanding the various political dimensions of her identity as a woman and the differences with her mother. This recognition of mothering as a political site represents how Latina/Chicana mothering is situated from a position of social change, political purpose, culture, and autonomy. *Latina/Chicana Mothering* contributes to these spaces of agency by giving attention to the complex social and political dynamics that are part of the mothering experiences for Latinas/Chicanas—an area where further documentation is highly needed.

TELLING OUR TALES: *TESTIMONIOS*

In Part I of *Latina/Chicana Mothering*, writers share their personal narratives of single mothers, feminist mothers, mothers in the academy, "othermothers," mothers-to-be, mothers to parents, and mothers to adult children. Through their voices, they reveal multi-faceted Latina/Chicana motherhoods and the changing dynamics between mother and child. In the first chapter, Ana Castillo writes of this shifting relationship when her son's transformation into adulthood challenges her life as a feminist mother. As she tries to reconcile her son's behavior with her feminist practices, Castillo reveals that Latina/Chicana mothering calls for a confrontation of machismo and patriarchy. Through her humor and realistic tone, she explores how mothers can influence their children and help them integrate their identity and principles of feminism.

Mayra Santos-Febres reveals the complicated journey of becoming a mother to a parent. Her story describes her attempt to balance her life as a professor while taking care of her mother who has Alzheimer's. With great candor, she explores the issues many Latinas face: how to be responsible for family matters (the family backbone) and still be faithful to one's own needs and desires. Santos-Febres articulates that there are no easy answers with mothering and that a part of motherhood is making difficult choices and defying cultural expectations.

Junot Díaz's essay draws from his experiences of being raised by a hardworking, single Dominican mother while living in an impoverished environment. Exploring how his mother sacrificed for him and his brother and tried to instill in him a sense of pride and knowledge of cultural traditions, Díaz confronts his callousness, anger, and love as a son who struggles to understand his mother. He uncovers the problematic layers between mothers and their children and how the frictions can give way to irresolvable silence and then great intimacy.

My essay reveals the struggles of becoming a "mother-to-be." Too often, women are bombarded with the pressures of starting a family and fulfilling other obligations. As I mention in my narrative, when we do decide to start a family at a later age, we run the risk of having problems with fertility and feeling inadequate for failing to conceive a child. Even after conception, the issues continue when women endure pregnancy-related health problems. I argue that the process of mothering must look at these factors and end this problematic silence.

Angie Cruz articulates her first-hand experience of giving birth to a child, while still being firmly engulfed in the world of academia. By confronting the myth of the "Supermommy Complex," she explores the obligations mothers feel to build their careers and raise their children—why many mothers feel the need to push themselves when their bodies and minds demand rest. As she challenges the myth that mothers can do it all without help and should feel ashamed to ask for assistance, Cruz also discusses the openness of Latina/Chicana culture to raise other women's children and embrace children in the public and private spheres.[10]

Michelle Téllez's essay interrogates mothering practices across the generations in her family. While arguing that propagating the ideals of marianismo and limiting biculturalism are deficient for effectively raising Latinas/Chicanas, she also addresses the benefits of ensuring children have strong ties to kinship and culture. In her frank writing, Tellez shows how her life and the life of her mother embody power and Latina/Chicana identity; her desire is to forge a new course of confidence for her daughter.

COUNTING THE WAYS TO MOTHER:
COMMUNITIES AND RESOURCES

The essays in Part II examine the relationship between Latina/Chicana motherhood and community as a site of empowerment, resistance, and oppression. Confronting the complexities between Latinas/Chicanas and society, the contributors illustrate some of the significant historical, political, and socio-cultural issues of Latina/Chicana motherhood and show the effects on transforming cultural images of Latina/Chicana motherhood. The section opens with Richard Mora's essay, which addresses how the problem of gang violence impacts not only gang members and their victims, but also affects the victims' families. In his study, he shares the interviews of ten Mexican American women who changed their definitions of mothering when their children were killed by gang-related violence. Inspired by La Virgen de Guadalupe, the mothers extended their mothering practices by taking care of the children in their barrios. The essay's poignancy comes from the souls of mothers who have lost their children and transform that grief to saving the community's youth.

Providing an alternate window on Latina/Chicana motherhood, Laura Ruth Johnson articulates the mothering strategies of women enrolled in the Family Learning Center (FLC), an educational program serving young Latina/Chicana mothers in Chicago. Their mothering practices often include following the advice of community members and using lessons from the stories and experiences of their mothers. Johnson argues that while many theorists and researchers have examined the ways in which familial knowledge and community support serve as resources for children, these "funds of knowledge" theories are usually limited and overlook the role that stories, experiences, and community involvement can play in imparting life lessons and developing morals in children.

Gilda L. Ochoa argues that there is a long history of programs aimed at Mexican American mothers, especially under the pretense that they are responsible for the educational outcomes of their children. Drawing on 44 in-depth interviews gathered between 1994 and 2008, her essay captures the everyday and collective strategies that Mexican American women in the Los Angeles area employ to enhance educational op-portunities for their children and for the community's children. These strategies include: (1) mothers teaching their children family histories, cultures, and languages; (2) community members pushing for bilingual education; and (3) K-12 teachers working to shield students from the hurdles and barriers that they encounter. These strategies, according to Ochoa, reveal a range of transformative caring and mothering practices that are occurring in homes, communities, and schools.

SCENES OF *LA FAMILIA*: FACING CHALLENGES

Part III confronts the entrenched struggles and tensions in Latina/Chi-cana mothering emerging from mothers who are teenagers, mothers who are homeless, and mothers who are migrants. Emphasizing the resilience and values of Latina/Chicana mothers when navigating the levels of friction, the contributors illustrate the complex dimensions of labeling motherhood as a continuum of hardship. Elizabeth Trejos-

Castillo and Helyne Frederick argue that despite the financial ordeals involved in supporting offspring as well as providing an adequate socio-emotional environment for children, there is evidence that suggests that being a teen mother for Latina girls can be a positive experience. By examining Latina adolescent mothers' strategies and values in parenting and the challenges and successes they attribute to the process, they explore how Latina mothering might be understood as a function of the deep cultural values and meanings that Latinas attach to pregnancy and child-rearing practices. The essay also engages in reviewing results from empirical research on Latina teenage mothers and exploring the greater implications of teen pregnancy among Latinas for social policy and teen pregnancy prevention programs.

Anne R. Roschelle's essay is based on a four-year ethnographic study of homeless Chicanas in San Francisco, California. By acknowledging these women from a race, class, and gender perspective, she proclaims that homeless Chicana mothers in San Francisco have traditional attitudes about marriage and motherhood, but delay marriage because of the exigencies of poverty. Roschelle also explains that resisting this "dream of marriage" before motherhood creates significant obstacles to fulfilling the traditional profile of "good mothers" for these homeless Latinas, pushing them further onto the margins of society. She calls for an honest confrontation of the narrow images of poor, homeless, and single Chicana mothers and critiques their depiction as threats to the moral fibers of society.

Mirna E. Carranza discusses how the experiences of loss due to migration and war impact the relationships of Salvadorian mothers with their daughters. Her research findings analyze the ways these mothers and daughters stay connected, while concurrently processing their individual traumas. Using the essay as a reconfiguration of mothering and migration, Carranza pays pointed attention to the links between the wounds of relocation and "tense" connection between mothers and daughters.

THE TIES THAT BIND: LITERARY AND CULTURAL REPRESENTATIONS OF LATINA/CHICANA MOTHERS

Part IV focuses on exploring the literary and cultural images of motherhood and mothering practices and how they defy the patriarchial models which have traditionally defined the "motherhood institution." Mary Lou Babineau looks at the counternarratives of motherhood in the literary works of Mexican author Ángeles Mastretta and Chilean author Pía Barros. These texts illustrate the psychological evolution of the protagonists during pregnancy and through the initial stages of motherhood, which are experiences marked by feelings of isolation, disgust, and alienation. In her examination of the aversion and dissociation that mothers experience in regard to their own pregnant and post-partum bodies, Babineau argues that this literature challenges and subverts the most prescribed social and cultural role for women and undermines patriarchal assumptions. She finds that the highly uncomfortable and yet very authentic experiences of these mothers make an invaluable contribution in giving recognition to the extremely diverse journeys of Latinas/Chicanas as they embrace—or endure—pregnancy and motherhood.

Yolanda Martínez's essay details the deviation from transnational motherhood models as presented in Cristina García's novel, *Dreaming in Cuban* (1993). Characterized by the complications which arise in the mother-child relationship and the experience of migration and adaptation to new socio-cultural values, the Latina/Chicana maternal experience can be a space of collective and individual change and renegotiation. As Martínez argues, the varied methods of mothering that defy the normative standard negotiate women's identities as mothers and discourses on motherhood.

Petra Guerra, Diana I. Rios, and D. Milton Stokes discuss the construction of Latina mothers in the genre of *telenovela*s (Spanish-language soap operas). They argue that this form of contemporary media has been effective in feeding and recycling several mother archetypes, especially in the soap opera entitled *Alborada*. In this program, viewers can find mothers who fit within the marianismo archetype of the emotionally martyred woman who will sacrifice anything for her children and suffer silently. There is also the image of the greedy mother who achieves prosperity, but damages the well-being of her offspring and manipulates them in the process. Moreover, *Alborada* features weak mothers who are powerless to withstand the injustices committed against them and their children. Noting the repressive nature of these mothering images in *Alborada*, the authors call for soap operas to challenge the gendered norms of society and redefine mothers as women who show means of resistance. They note that the role of telenovelas can move beyond their limited extent to create new dialogues on mothering identity and power.

Lastly, Cristina Herrera focuses on the confining binaries of the virgin/whore and good/bad mother as represented by the mythic and historical figures of La Malinche, La Llorona, and La Virgen de Guadalupe. She finds that these images have become so embedded in the Latina/Chicana culture that Latina/Chicana writers use this prominent theme in their literature to illustrate how this destructive binary of women inhibits women's self-realization. Yet, the three mothers of Latina/Chicana culture—La Virgen de Guadalupe, La Malinche, and La Llorona—are also re-constructed in the works of Latina/Chicana writers in ways that stray from traditional patriarchal representations that view women as "others." As Herrera proclaims, Latinas/Chicanas develop well-rounded, complex female characters and depict mother-daughter relationships outside of the good/bad dichotomy. She also contests the legends of motherhood and finds that it is this patriarchal-oriented perspective that is reinforced from one generation to the next and essentially responsible for placing the three mothers in an impossible binary.

CONCLUSION

The contributors of this text represent the wide range of experiences in the Latina/Chicana mothering process. We are mothers-to-be, mothers to parents, "othermothers," sons, daughters, feminist moms, mothers in academia, single mothers, mothers to communities, and mothers to adult children. We also come from various cultural, linguistic, political, and social backgrounds and recognize how these different spheres shape our connections to Latina/Chicana motherhood. Our work presents an important opportunity to acknowledge the intersections of Latina/Chicana cultural identity and motherhood with the changing dynamics of everyday life such as migration, employment, language barriers, classism, racism, sexism, violence, war, education, teenage pregnancy, homelessness, and poverty. In so doing, we explore the salient themes, images, disciplines, and perspectives on Latina/Chicana mothering, and critique the strategies of limiting Latina/Chicana mothering to set modes of mothering and particular experiences. As the essays unfold, they reveal new images of motherhood and offer ways to transform

Latina/Chicana mothering. This is a great beginning and takes us a major step forward.

[1]Latina refers to all women of Latin American heritage and the Spanish-speaking Caribbean. The term Chicana refers to women of Mexican descent (Ruiz and Sánchez Korrol 5). I recognize that Latina/Chicana is a broad term and note that others under this umbrella may have a more specific ethnic and cultural identity.

[2]For information on Latinas/Chicanas and migration, see Glenn; Espin; Heredia; Sánchez Korrol; Ruiz; Segura; Segura and Zavella; Villalón.

[3]Barbara Ehrenreich and Arlie Hochschild explain the situation: "Thanks to the process we loosely call 'globalization,' women are on the move as never before in history.... But we hear much less about a far more prodigious flow of female labor and energy: the increasing migration of millions of women from poor countries to rich ones, where they serve as nannies, maids, and sometime sex workers. In the absence of help from male partners, many women have succeeded in tough 'male world' careers only by turning over the care of their children, elderly parents, and home to women from the Third World. This is the female underside of globalization, whereby millions of ... women from poor countries in the south migrate to the 'women's work: of the north—work that affluent women are no longer able or willing to do'" (2-3).

[4]For a more detailed explanation on transnational mothering, see Dreby; Hondagneu-Sotelo; Kanaiaupuni and Donato; Kandel and Kao; Levitt; Parreñas; Schmalzbauer; Suárez-Orozco, Todorova and Louie; Tung.

[5]The ideology of *marianismo* teaches the Madonna/whore complex: a girl will either be a virgin (Madonna) or a sexually promiscuous person (whore). For a detailed overview, see Stevens.

[6]*Machismo* encourages a boy to be macho and usually sexually adventurous. See López-Springfield for different views on this issue.

[7]See for example Cordelia Candelaria who states that the tale of La Llorona is now transformed: "*Today* it tells me that the La Llorona legend survives as potent folk nourishment because it re/presents a hero who bravely exercises her active agency in order to will her own destiny by electing a tragic fate rather than passively allowing herself and her children to live under inescapable tyranny. Usually when men do that they're called heroes, especially if—like kings, presidents, and gener-

als—they kill thousands of *other* people's children on the battlefields. It is finally time to let go of a single, narrow understanding of the tale and to see La Llorona instead as an always evolving, freshly created emblem of gender, sexuality, and power" (97). See also O'Reilly who discusses "good" mothering within dominant patriarchal constructions.

[8]See also the texts by Sandoval, Rodriguez, Rueda Esquivel, and Ramos.

[9]Cherrie Moraga shares her physical transformation when she becomes pregnant and later a mother: "Ella tells me daily how much more feminine I look. I see it, too.... I like it and yet in bed feel a strong urge to reassert my butchness, my self as love-maker" and "Ella, ever observant, tells me on the sly how 'different' the dynamic is when I am pushing Rafaelito in the stroller and she is guiding her mother down the crowded main drag. 'Now that's interesting.... The butch mom and her kid, the femme strolling with her mother. That's a compelling couple'" (*Waiting in the Wings*, 45, 110).

[10]For a discussion on "othermothers" as women who raise children that are not biologically their own, see Alexander and Williams.

WORKS CITED

Alexander, Simone A. James. *Mother Imagery in the Novels of Afro-Caribbean Women*. Columbia: University of Missouri Press, 2001. Print.

Anzaldúa, Gloria. "Entering Into the Serpent." *Borderlands/La Frontera: The New Mestiza*. San Francisco, CA: Aunt Lute, 1987. Print.

Arendell, Teresa. "Mothering and Motherhood: A Decade Review." Center for Working Families Working Paper No. 3. Berkeley: University of California, 1999. Print.

Brown-Guillory, Elizabeth, ed. "Introduction." *Women of Color: Mother-Daughter Relationship in 20th Century Literature*. Austin: University of Texas Press, 1996. 1-19. Print.

Candelaria, Cordelia. "Letting La Llorona Go, or, Re/reading History's 'Tender Mercies.'" *Literatura Chicana 1965-1995: An Anthology in Spanish, English, and Caló*. Ed. Manuel de Jesús Hernández-Gutiérrez and David William Foster. New York: Garland, 1997. 93-97. Print.

Castillo, Ana. *Massacre of the Dreamers: Essays on Xicanisma*. New York: Plume, 1995. Print.

Collins, Patricia Hill. "Shifting the Center: Race, Class and Feminist

Theorizing about Motherhood." *Mothering: Ideology, Experience and Agency*. Ed. Evelyn Nakano Glenn, Grace Chang, and Linda Forcey. New York: Routledge, 1994. 45-65. Print.

Del Alba Acevedo, Luz. "Daughter of Bootstrap." *Telling to Live: Latina Feminist Testimonios*. Ed. Latina Feminist Group. Durham: Duke University Press, 2001. 139-47. Print.

Dreby, Joanna. "Children and Power in Mexican Transnational Families." *Journal of Marriage and Family* 69 (2007): 1050-64. Print.

Ehrenreich, Barbara, and Arlie Hochschild, eds. "Introduction." *Global Woman: Nannies, Maids, and Sex Workers in the New Economy*. New York: Holt, 2003. 1-14. Print.

Espin, Oliva. *Latina Realities: Essays on Healing, Migration, and Sexuality*. Boulder, CO: Westview, 1997. Print.

Glenn, Evelyn. *Mothering: Ideology, Experience, and Agency*. New York: Routledge, 1993. Print.

Heredia, Juanita. *Transnational Latina Narratives in the Twenty-First Century: The Politics of Gender, Race, and Migrations*. New York: Palgrave, 2009. Print.

Hondagneu-Sotelo, Pierrette. *Domestica: Immigrant Workers Cleaning and Caring in the Shadows of Affluence*. Berkeley: University of California Press, 2001. Print.

Hondagneu-Sotelo, Pierrette, and Ernestine Avila. "'I'm Here, but I'm There': The Meanings of Transnational Motherhood." *Gender & Society* 11 (1997): 548-71. Print.

Iglesias, Elizabeth M. "Maternal Power and the Deconstruction of Male Supremacy." *The Latino/a Condition*. Ed. Richard Delgado and Jean Stefancic. New York: New York University Press, 1998. 505-15. Print.

Kanaiaupuni, Shawn Malia, and Katherine M. Donato. "Migradollars and Morality: The Effects of Migration on Infant Survival in Mexico." *Demography* 36 (1999): 339-53. Print.

Kandel, William, and Grace Kao. "The Impact of Temporary Labor Migration on Mexican Children's Educational Aspirations and Performance." *International Migration Review* 3 (2001): 1205-31. Print.

Latina Feminist Group, ed. *Telling to Live: Latina Feminist Testimonios*. Durham: Duke University Press, 2001. Print.

Levitt, Peggy. *The Transnational Villagers*. Berkeley: University of California Press, 2001. Print.

López-Springfield, Consuelo. "Cuando Fuiste Mujer: Remaking 'Woman' in Latino Cultures." *Gender Mosaics: Social Perspectives, Original Readings.* Ed. Dana Vannoy. Los Angeles: Roxbury, 2001. 486-95. Print.

Miller, Jean Baker. *Toward a New Psychology of Women.* 2nd ed. Boston: Beacon, 1986. Print.

Moraga, Cherrie. *Loving in the War Years: Lo Que Nunca Por Sus Labios.* Boston: South End, 1983. Print.

Moraga, Cherrie. *Waiting in the Wings: Portrait of a Queer Motherhood.* Ithaca, NY: Firebrand, 1997. Print.

Moraga, Cherrie, and Gloria Anzaldúa, eds. *This Bridge Called My Back: Writings by Radical Women of Color.* Latham, NY: Kitchen Table, Women of Color, 1983. Print.

Oberman, Yael, and Ruthellen Josselson. "Matrix of Tensions: A Model of Mothering." *Psychology of Women Quarterly* 20 (1996): 341-59. Print.

O'Reilly, Andrea, ed. "Introduction." *Feminist Mothering.* New York: State University of New York Press, 2008. 1-22. Print.

Parreñas, Rhacel Salazar. *Children of Global Migration: Transnational Families and Gendered Woes.* Stanford, CA: Stanford University Press, 2005. Print.

Ramos, Juanita, ed. *Compañeras: Latina Lesbians.* New York: Latina Lesbian History Project, 1987. Print.

Rodriguez, Juana Maria. *Queer Latinidad: Identity Practices, Discursive Spaces.* New York: New York University Press, 2003. Print.

Rueda Esquivel, Catriona. *With Her Machete in Her Hand: Reading Chicana Lesbians.* Austin: University of Texas Press, 2006. Print.

Ruiz, Vicki L. *From Out of the Shadows: Mexican Women in Twentieth-Century America.* Oxford: Oxford University Press, 2008. Print.

Ruiz, Vicki L., and Virginia E. Sánchez Korrol. *Latina Legacies: Identity, Biography, and Community.* New York: Oxford University Press, 2005. Print.

Sánchez Korrol, Virginia E. *From Colonia to Community: The History of Puerto Ricans in New York City.* Berkeley and Los Angeles: University of California Press, 1994. Print.

Sandoval, Chela. *Methodology of the Oppressed.* Minneapolis: University of Minnesota Press, 2000. Print.

Santiago, Esmeralda, and Joie Davidow, eds. *Las Mamis: Favorite Latino*

Authors Remember Their Mothers. New York: Knopf, 2000. Print.

Schmalzbauer, Leah. "Searching for Wages and Mothering from Afar: The Case of Honduran Transnational Families." *Journal of Marriage and Family* 66 (2004): 1317-31. Print.

Segura, Denise. "Working at Motherhood: Chicana and Mexican Immigrant Mothers and Employment." *Mothering: Ideology, Experience, and Agency*. Ed. Evelyn Nakano Glenn, Grace Chang and Linda Rennie Forcey. New York: Routledge, 1994. 211-33. Print.

Segura, Denise and Patricia Zavella, eds. *Women and Migration in the U.S.-Mexico Borderlands*. Durham: Duke University Press, 2007. Print.

Seller, Maxine Schwartz, ed. *Immigrant Women*. Albany: State University of New York Press, 1994. Print.

Snitow, Ann. "Feminism and Motherhood: An American Reading." *Feminist Review* 40 (1992): 32-49. Print.

Stevens, Evelyn P. "Marianismo: The Other Face of Machismo." *Confronting Change, Challenging Tradition: Women in Latin American History*. Ed. Gertrude Matyoka Yeager. Pittsburgh, PA: University of Pittsburgh Press, 1994. 3-17. Print.

Suárez-Orozco, Cerola, Irene L.G. Todorova, and Josephine Louie. "Making up for Lost Time: The Experience of Separation and Reunification among Immigrant Familias." *Family Process* 41.4 (2002): 625-43. Print.

Tung, Charlene. "Caring across Borders: Motherhood, Marriage, and Filipina Domestic Workers in California." *Asian/Pacific Islander American Women: A Historical Anthology*. Ed. Shirley Hune and Gail M. Nomura. New York: New York University Press, 2003. 301-15. Print.

Villalón, Roberta. *Violence Against Latina Immigrants: Citizenship, Inequality, and Community*. New York: New York University Press, 2010. Print.

Williams, Norma. *The Mexican American Family: Tradition and Change*. Oxford: Altamira, 1990. Print.

I.
Telling Our Tales: Testimonios

Are Hunters Born or Made?

ANA CASTILLO

I WAS IN THE KITCHEN ONE LATE AFTERNOON LAST SUMMER when my son stopped by. Actually, he was moving back home.

The first year of college I had put him in the dorm. (That sounds as if I had him incarcerated. The truth is that I had suggested, in no uncertain terms, that he stay in a dorm.) Never mind that the university he chose is exactly two blocks from the high school he attended, and both schools are exactly five quick "L" train stops away from our place. It was time, his mother felt, for him to take the next step toward independence. His and mine. Just like when I weaned him from the bottle and potty trained him right after his second birthday. Now we do it, *Mi'jo. Y ya.*

You might say it has always been a matter of unilateral decision-making in our family of two. "Such a feminist having to raise a boy!" was the customary response to my status as a mother, as if there were a secret feminist agenda to procreate a race of Amazons. This was not true, of course. I raised my son much the same way that I would have raised a daughter, conscious not to fall into gender stereotypes. You monitor TV programs, reading materials, music, activities, and playmates.

While he was growing up I took writing residencies around the country. At the end of one school year and in receipt of a letter inviting me to join the faculty of some department in a university across the country, off we went. Mama packed, made arrangements, a trail of furnishings and personal belongings left in storage rentals strewn along the way; I sold and bought things as needed. I found new schools, encouraged friendships, signed him up for a basketball team at a boys club in one town, sent him off to basketball camp in another, taught him to ride a bike at five, drive at sixteen, slow dance, shave, do his own laundry from the age of twelve, and, once, when he broke my French espresso pot while doing the dinner dishes with an attitude, I made him pay me for it then and there. He never broke anything again.

We managed. He grew up; he's got about six inches on me now. In high school he lived in his bedroom. He never ate. I was certain that my gaunt, dark—in mood as well as in pallor—child had been bitten by a vampire. But even vampires need to learn independence. He took this particular stage with him to the freshman dorm.

He didn't care for the dorm that freshman year. He came home, he said, to shower. Apparently he didn't like sleeping in the dorm much either: more often than not when I'd get up and walk past his bedroom, I'd find the blankets on the bed making a much bigger, or more specifically, longer lump than *Mi'jo*'s little Boston terrier, who still slept there, possibly could.

What my son really wanted was his own apartment.

"That's why I am putting you through college," was the usual course of our brief exchanges that year. This way—or more precisely, *my* way—someday, with the right credentials, he'd get a job, and thereby support himself. Then he could afford his own place.

Nevertheless, the following autumn, at the start of his second year of college, he found a roommate with a job. They got an apartment in a neighborhood that I wish I could say would have caused any parent to worry—but then so would the neighborhood we have lived in for nearly seven years. Unlike the roommate's mother, who immediately set herself to the task of redoing her son's vacant bedroom in her own house and turning it into a sewing room for herself, I kind of lapsed into a period of domestic confusion. What now?

He'd left behind his bedroom furniture, taking only the bed, as well as a spare dresser and futon that had been in the guest room. During the following school year both my son's former bedroom and the semi-plundered guest room remained in a perpetual state of suspension, the absence of their defining accoutrements giving the term "empty nest" literal meaning in my home.

Even the little dog, with its year-round shorthaired shedding, had moved out. (Actually, the dog's departure had been upon my own insistence. One more opportunity for my son to learn responsibility, I believed.)

We had been separated many times during my son's lifetime. His father had maintained *Mi'jo* during all of his vacations and holidays. Weeks had passed during his childhood when I received no return phone calls.

But of course, this was different.

Have I mentioned yet that I teach at the same university my son attends?

He avoids my office. But not those of my fellow colleagues, from whom he'll take classes or to whom he'll look for guidance, at least with regard to his education. So I knew some things about his life during school that second year. Meanwhile, with each rare visit home, he showed increasing signs of intentional disregard for the hygiene and other regimens strictly enforced during his upbringing—even common-sense rules like wearing gloves in mid-winter in Chicago—so that one night he ended up in an emergency room with frostbitten hands. Most grating to a mother or to any other reasonable, mature individual, he continued to refine his contrariness toward any and all opinions and advice I offered.

His junior year of college was coming up, and he was moving back in. I made it look like it was his idea. That is, once his roommate announced he couldn't keep up with the rent and go to school, while my son, a full-time student, had a mother living all of a fifteen-minute train ride from campus, I did not have to point out the obvious.

Instead, I kept quiet. If the truth be known, I was starting to get used to prancing around in my *pantaletas* and skinny tees in the morning, once spring came and the gloom of a long, lonely winter was past me. Not that I didn't miss my boy. The Good Son, that is—the one with the jagged front tooth and traces of baby fat around the middle and the Buster Brown haircut; the one with a forgiving nature who never understood why the girl cousin who was exactly his age (as well as size and weight) was so free with the back of her hand. He had no more wanted to give his girl cousin the back of his hand in return (which was his father's advice on the telephone) than he wanted to receive one from her, or from anybody.

He had always been and, I assumed, would always be sensitive to others. We had never taken to yelling at home. He learned early on to respect my privacy and my property, as I always did his. For example, he would never have gone into my purse for lunch money. Instead, he would bring the bag to me, as he had been taught, so that I could dole out the dough. He grew up without paramilitary toys. (Prohibition of such gifts elicited some consternation on the part of the male family members, who obviously feared that the boy would miss an important aspect of his macho development.) Because I refused to pay for any toy with an implicit political dimension so counter to mine—meanwhile aware that out-and-out denial on my part would render my son an adolescent outcast—he had to buy his own PlayStation, which he got used from some other kid in a later stage of puberty.

He was, as I said, a person who was naturally sensitive, guided further toward being respectful, an independent thinker, responsible. Still, I noticed. It happened subtly: my son's definite and undeniable enlistment on The Other Side.

Not that he just became a man—a natural process—but he became one to the fullest extent of the sociological and traditional meaning of gender. How and when it happened exactly I cannot say. But by the time my son, about to start his third year in college, was moving back home, he had definitely become a guy, a dude of the highest rank. Public Enemy Number One for any girl looking for a steady beau and believing that in my sensitive, introspective son she might have found him. By the time it became clear that he had all the requisite traits to allow him full lifetime membership into Guyness, she'd realize she was in mined territory.

When a woman gets together with a man, she has to work with what's there, in terms of the taming process. But when she has issued him forth from her own womb, wrapped him in swaddling clothes, and waded down the river with him to find a place to raise him away from the Pharisees, a place where he might learn to value the gentler and more nurturing culture of women, where household chores are an equal division of labor, where men always put the toilet seat down, brush their teeth before to bed (if not take a shower), and not only listen with marked interest to their companion after the perfunctory question, "How was your day?" but actually care, she does not expect ever to stand in her kitchen and hear the following proclamation: "Oh yeah, no doubt about it. I'm a hunter."

My son was talking about the urban preying of the so-called "groomed male" on the opposite sex.

The specifics were the following and I put them to you, reader, now:

Should I not have been somewhat wide-eyed and speechless, at least momentarily, in response?

As I said, there we were, in the kitchen, when he shared with me how the girl he was "kicking it with" lately had stopped talking to him. We had been away for a weekend—one of those "family trips" on which I had successfully coerced my son into accompanying me to an event related to my public life. During this particular weekend he had intentionally not notified the girl he was seeing of his whereabouts. "I wasn't that interested in her, I guess," he admitted.

Ah. To have had the vantage point of a nineteen-year-old guy's honesty when I was a girl! How many hours on the phone with my girlfriends would that have spared me? "I thought you liked her!" I said, remembering the conversation when he said how beautifully she played the cello, the same instrument he had studied in high school. They seemed to have something in common, at least.

"I like her all right," he said, standing next to me like a poplar tree. (I got over the height disparity in relation to power dynamics between us when he was twelve and had passed me by. It took a few months, but I was determined.)

You can't push. You can't say too much. You mustn't show your eagerness to right their world, to fight off the dragons, to show them that the thirty years you have on them is worth something even if you lived those years way back in the Garden of Eden. I went about my business. All ears, I relentlessly wiped the counter like an obsessive-compulsive. I may have begun to whistle a little tune to really feign only the most casual interest in his big, fat, mysterious, juicy life outside the paltry world of my half-abandoned and orderly apartment.

He shrugged his bony shoulders. "I just wasn't into her, you know? Once she showed she was interested."

The blood left my brain. Would I faint or grab the nearest blunt instrument at this news, which was in such opposition to all the feminist principles I had ever tried to instill in him? Not by words. Not by lesson plans. I never said, "This is what a decent guy does and this is what a jerk does." Not outright. Not even to other members of the male gender when within his hearing range. Still one hopes, against the monolithic onslaught of society, that a mother gets her message across on an impressionable young mind.

Stay calm, I told myself, rubbing the sides of my pulsing temples.

"You getting a headache?" he asked.

"You mean to say," I asked, "that it's all about the thrill of the chase or else you lose interest?"

He nodded. Proudly. Confidently. Standing there with his hip-hop baggy pants and paint-stained hands from nocturnal graffiti activities, T-shirt with photos of Che, Subcomandante Marcos, and Malcolm X, with block letters underneath reading: WE ARE NOT A MINORITY.

"In other words"—I needed to paraphrase what he'd just confirmed to give myself a little time to absorb it—"if a girl goes after you, you are automatically not interested in her on principle."

"Oh, without a doubt. I'm a hunter."

"Okay, Bambi," I said. "As you go off to join the thundering herd, what do you expect from the girl now? You blew her off. You were rude. What do you want from her anyway?"

People say my son has my eyes. They are very dark. When he was a child, after someone made such an observation, he'd answer, not quite comprehending but already defiant, "No, I don't. I have my own eyes." I don't know about mine, but his get even darker when he gets pensive, like a mood ring, with black raven eyebrow wings-in-flight above them, set against the wind.

"I'd still like us to be friends," he said, sounding a tad remorseful, this confession maybe something he wouldn't admit to his crew. "I mean, it's awkward when we run into each other now. It would be nice to talk like we used to at least."

I don't think we ever discuss our sons losing their virginity the way the world observes the loss of sexual innocence in a girl. But I suspect I know at what point in his life and with whom it happened in the case of my son.

How quickly we learn, after that first rush of carnal passion, that sex isn't everything. He was going on twenty soon, on the autumn solstice; his teenage years about to disperse like countless memory motes floating around him for the rest of his life. To plague him. To cheer him in more complex times, perhaps, with their simplicity.

"So why don't you talk to her about it?" I asked.

"Whenever I see her, she's with her girlfriends and ignores me," he said. Perhaps as much as she knew, now, that he was a hunter, she knew she needed the protection of her pack.

"Call her then, *Mi'jo*," I urged. "Ask her to meet you somewhere for a cup of coffee so that you can explain things to her. More than anything, bottom line, women want to be respected as people. They're not pillage."

In the next few seconds, as this simple statement began to sink in and the racket of innumerable influences from all around that had been delivering the very opposite message was pushed aside, at least for the present, the black thunderbolts of his expressive eyebrows relaxed, as if a storm had just passed. His slightly slanted eyes brightened. He pulled out his cell phone, went to the living room to call her, and left a message. He was all smiles when he came back into the kitchen.

Now I remember what we were doing that day in the kitchen. We were having tacos, the kind we Mexicans enjoy, especially on Sunday—where you get meat already cooked at your local *carnicería* and you put each taco together yourself. A warm corn tortilla, chunks of *carnitas* or *barbacoa*, add on *salsita*, sour cream, and avocado slices—it's a cholesterol fest for the arteries. For some reason, both *Mi'jo* and I insist on eating standing up, just like at the taco stands in Mexico.

"You're great, Mom. I'm so glad I talked it over with you." He grinned, reaching out for a tortilla to start on another taco, thereby proving to me that he hadn't been bitten by a vampire after all.

"It's what a mother lives for." I smiled back, although, for sure, once he moved back in I would miss the prancing around in the last summer days in my undies, like Jill Clayburgh in *An Unmarried Woman*. But, then, there is no such thing as an "unmothered woman," which doesn't even make sense. Or maybe it could, if you really gave it some deep thought and were open to the concept. But not for me. Any feminist of my day worth her salt knows: The revolution starts with one man at a time.

Ana Castillo's "Are Hunters Born or Made" is originally from BECAUSE I SAID SO: 33 Mothers Write About Children, Sex, Men, Aging, Faith, Race & Themselves, *ed. by Camille Peri and Kate Moses. Copyright © 2005 by Ana Castillo. Published by HarperCollins. Reprinted by permission of Anne Edelstein Literary Agency.*

My Mother's Memory

MAYRA SANTOS-FEBRES
(TRANSLATED BY MARISOL PÉREZ CASAS)

ITINERARY OF A LOST MEMORY

SHE STARTED LOSING HER KEYS AND HER PURSE; AND FORGETTING important appointments, taking her medicines, and paying the bills. Little by little, she began forgetting the people that she knew, familiar places, and how to return to her own home. But she still remembered her name, her children and her sisters, at least some of them. She also remembered her ex-husband and that she had been a teacher for thirty years. That was back in 1995, the year we started to suspect that my mother had Alzheimer's.

But the warning signs began much earlier. Who knows how many years before? Who knows if it started that Christmas when my Aunt Cruz Josefa came from New Jersey to visit the family? She and her husband Teo used to stay at *Mami's* house for three or four weeks. All of Mariana's children had grown up; "*la Nena*" (meaning me) was already a professional. Mariana had finally divorced her awful husband and the only one that was still with her was the little one, Juan Carlos, who went about the streets trying to prove he was a real man, and was always getting into trouble.

Maybe it all began that Christmas…

It was nighttime. My mother, her older sister, and her brother-in-law had spent the day shopping, going to a Teacher's Association party, and fixing up the house for the New Year's celebration. They had to paint, fix the front door that got damaged every time it rained, and replace a few light switches and the closet door hinges in the largest room. That was the plan and it all got done. When it came time to rest, everyone went to their own rooms to sleep. Suddenly, Aunt Cruz Josefa heard someone walking in the still house. She got up to investigate, and bumped into my mother in the hallway.

"What are you doing in my house? Who are you? *La Nena*, what did you do to my children? Get out of my house right now!" screamed Mariana, my mother, with eyes that seemed not to focus. She was out of it. My aunt tried to calm her down and explained that she was her sister, the one she knew so well, Cruz Josefa, the oldest one; the one who knitted and taught math classes while she studied to become a lawyer, but my mother wouldn't stop screaming, "Get out of my house or I'll call the police."

My aunt and her husband had to go outside in their pajamas and wait on the street for my mother to calm down, return to her usual self, and go back to being the happy, generous woman she had always been. After a while, my mother came back. And that sudden disorientation did not return during the rest of the Christmas vacation. It was obviously the stress, we thought. It was obviously the result of everything that had happened to my mother lately with the divorce, the retirement, adjusting to a new budget, and the problems with my brother; everything had to do with it. It was an isolated incident. That's what it was, we all agreed. Yes, that was the logical explanation. That's what it was.

Or maybe it all began even before that, when my mother was still working. My Aunt Cuca told me that she insisted that Mami should retire because something was not right; she knew something strange was going on because they worked in the same office. So Cuca began correcting Mariana's reports, correcting her older sister, because her sentences would not end; they simply floated in the air, fluttering incessantly. It was as if the wind would take her words. They would not fit into the reports about the administrative status of schools in District IV. They would not fit into the evaluation sheets that Mariana Febres, graduate teacher, had to fill out and which were suddenly filled with strange words, of trains and honeysuckles, which wanted to say asbestos and lack of books; all of this was evidence of the confusing labyrinth that her mind was turning into.

And thin.... The sturdy, black woman with a ready smile that my mother once was wilted away, becoming a jumble of bones tainted with melancholy. But she was still beautiful. I took her to a doctor in naturopathy who explained this could happen to pancreatitis patients (my mother had suffered from a severely inflamed pancreas several times in her life). Once I returned home, with my Ph.D. in hand, I had to regularly visit my mother's house. I noticed that she was reed thin because she only drank coffee and ate bread. Coffee and bread, bread and coffee, my mother lived off this menu, as if all other menus had been erased from her mind. Her stewed rice, her pot roast, and her fritters were gone. I'm not going to lie to you. My mother was never a great cook. Her beans would always need salt. Salads and desserts would never show up at our table. We ate what was normal for many other middle-class neighborhood homes, rice with something, in front of the television and were always in a hurry. The exhaustion from a long day at work, picking up the kids from school, going by my grandmother's house, the stress of playing roulette with bills (let's see which one lady luck will let us pay this month…)—all of this would leave almost no time to engage in culinary delights. We did eat at home, without excess and simply, but we did eat. Then, why was it that the fridge was always empty, with only a few empty milk containers filled with water, the cooking ham slowly becoming a salty mummy in the back of the drawer? Not one piece of fruit, one potato, or one vegetable. Yet, the bank account was full. That was full, but our house was slowly becoming empty of life.

She began to call in tears, like that afternoon when *Mami* called in desperation because a thief had broken into the house and had taken everything. That day I had been obsessed with painting all my kitchen cabinets yellow. Christmas was getting near and I was set on decorating my tiny apartment. I just had to make it nice, now that I could, now that my college and graduate student days were over. I was no longer a starving student, teaching a class here and there. I finally had a full time tenure-track position at the University. Now, I had real money. I could even paint and fix my small apartment. So there I was, happy, on top of a table and covered in canary yellow paint (my taste has always been a bit loud, a bit out there, a bit Caribbean, the taste of a black woman, some may say, trying to insult what makes me proud).

The phone rang and rang, and it wouldn't stop ringing. I reluctantly got down from my small ladder. And there she was, my mother, in tears, begging me to come over, a thief had taken everything, everything, and had left her with nothing.

"Are you ok, *Mami*?"

"Yes, *mija*,[1] yes."

"But, what did they take?"

"*Ay nena*, come over."

I took the stairs two by two as fast as I could, ran to the car, without bothering to change my clothes, covered head to toe with yellow paint. The five-thirty traffic jam was getting between my mother and me. I ran over speed bumps, drove against traffic through back alleys. Whenever I could, I sped way over the speed limit, thinking about my mother and the fact that the thief could still be in the house. He could have tied her down, could be hurting her. A pool of blood would have already formed over the pristine tiles of the living room. It was my fault. I got distracted and I took too much time for myself, to work, to rent that apartment, to start having the life of a young professional who had just come back to the Island with a sack full of the future and the time to finally enjoy what I had postponed so many times. I just had to buy that stupid and superfluous can of yellow paint that was now propping the door open for the man that was killing my mother.

When I got home, in a state of panic, ready to face the catastrophe, my mother greeted me with a "*Nena*, it's so good to see you." She went looking for the keys to open the garage gate. I had to wait fifteen more minutes there on the street because *Mami* could not find the key, and she stepped into each room to check something, the light switches, a closed or an open window. I shouted from the gate: "But, what did he steal, how did he get in?" With a calm, serene voice she said, "*Mija*, what are you talking about?" "The thief, Mami, the thief." Her face revealed an effort to focus on something there inside her brain, a brain that would insist on hiding the clues of what was happening. My mother could not remember anything. Anything. The call she made in tears that had hastily torn me away from my yellow cabinets, her inconsolable tears over the phone, and the reason why I, covered in paint, was yelling at her so that she would open the gate, and do it quickly because we had to call the police.

Then the neighbors confirmed it. "Your mother can't live alone anymore. Ever since she retired, she has been a bit disoriented. We often find her walking aimlessly, trying to get to the store or the bakery, but she cannot find her way. And you know you can't count on your brother…." I focused on my brother for a moment: his eyes were red, angry; he slept all day, spent the night in the streets, and had constant allergies and erratic behaviors. My brother, always roaming the streets, had developed a drug problem. He was the problem, and the sleepless nights he made *Mami* go through. That was probably not helping my mother adjust to her new life as a retired teacher and divorced wife after twenty years of a grueling marriage. The paranoia about getting robbed and the things that would suddenly disappear from the house could only be explained by my brother's addiction. We called my Aunt Cruz Josefa, asked her for help, and she, with the seething responsibility of an older sister, and being a veteran of such predicaments, gave us her help. We just had to get my brother on the plane and she would take care of the rest. It was always she, the oldest aunt who would solve all our family's problems—paying the price for her family's mistakes, having to leave the Island to reclaim her life for herself, and not having to devote it to taking care of her mother, managing the clan's finances, making contracts for buying houses, lending money to sisters with unemployed husbands, rescuing her brothers, all of them alcoholics, and handling cases of addicted nephews. My Aunt Cruz Josefa was fear itself. Overbearing, loud, rough, and a nag. I hated having to call and ask for her help, but there was no other solution. Well, there really was one, giving up my recently decorated apartment, forgetting my private life, and moving to that middle-class home to take care of my mother, and fighting with my brother only to see him send his life (and ours) down the drain. I chose the first option. I called my aunt, the "Field Marshal."

My Aunt Cruz Josefa, with her tough, piercing voice, her stern face. Now that I can step back and look at everything from afar, I don't blame her for being that way. I don't blame her stubbornness, her commanding tone, always ordering, always dictating what needed to be done. How could she be any other way, when she had always been forced to solve everything for everybody? When even from her exile in New Jersey, she was called upon to take care of someone who couldn't take care of himself?

"Put him on a plane. I'll take care of this," she said, to get the whole thing over with. I did not realize at that moment that her offer was a great act of love. I only felt incapable and guilty. Incapable of owning my role as an older sister and deciding to put order in that house, in that family, the only one I had, as it was falling apart. My father, gone after a thousand infidelities, one of which led to the birth of a beautiful child who my mother took care of until she could no longer do it. My brother, addicted to drugs. I, having returned to my country, a professional, with a thousand plans in my mind. I had finally been able to escape that neighborhood. But life was asking me to go back no matter what, to my mother's house, to give up my house, work, and what I really wanted.

My brother was definitely responsible for my mother's strange behavior. Once he was out of the house everything would go back to normal.

But that didn't happen. Days before sending my brother to New Jersey, I called a psychologist friend so she could help me look for solutions. Maybe we could put Juan Carlos in some local program and not force the harsh detachment between my mother and my brother. There had always been a strange connection between those two. The relationship excluded me, it was a mysterious, corrosive link between a mother and her male child, which is the same as saying needy child, who depends entirely on his mother to cook, to iron, to buy his underwear, to serve him food, put it in his mouth and almost chew it for him, and then shout insults at him, with belt in hand, for being so inept, irresponsible, and insensible. I was left out of that web of endearment and claims; I was independent, responsible for my own acts and obligations, perfectly capable of arranging and administering houses, of proving myself a coherent and professional woman. How is it that a mother, the same mother, could raise two children so differently?

The psychologist asked me to allow her to visit the home. She spent several hours listening to Mariana's complaints. She spent a few more trying to get my brother to talk, but he kept closing up like a clam and would not answer any questions. I, not knowing what to do, allowed a stranger for the first time to look at the intimate world of my family. "We don't air our dirty laundry in public," I would say to myself over and over. "I'm airing our family's dirty laundry." The dictum would pound on my conscience: "a family's problems are solved as a family." I felt like a traitor.

"Your brother has a problem of addiction and your mother of co-dependence" was the final verdict. "But the one I'm really worried about is your mother, not your brother. It's for the best that he leaves the house and becomes independent. That way we can find out for sure what's wrong with your mother."

That day the catastrophe started. The psychologist left me with seven thousand questions and dozens of referrals. Appointments with the neurologist, the psychiatrist, the geriatrician, (my mother was a young woman, only in her mid fifties), the internist, nutritionist, laboratories … I ran from the classroom to my mother's house to take her to appointments, buy her medication…. My visits became more frequent and my calls constant. I asked the neighbors for help. I talked to Doña Victoria and Doña Lucy, my mother's closest friends. I ordered a home delivered meal service so *Mami* wouldn't have to cook or turn on the stove to avoid accidents. I disconnected the stove and put a lock on the electrical box. I continued asking for tests. Each doctor would interpret them differently, and I would be lost in a labyrinth of medical terms that did not explain why my mother was slipping through my fingers, because even with my brother gone, she could not sleep, and she would call me at strange times because she was scared. I did not have the peace and quiet to correct tests and write novels; this was consuming more and more of my time. Why did her eyes fill with tears every time I said goodbye? I was anxious to go rest and furious at her for making me feel guilty for wanting some time for myself. The doctor's faces were stern, professional; they never felt my pain, the terrible exhaustion that got a hold of me, and that strange rage against my mother. I grew madder and madder at her. I could not stand the way she walked all over the house before every appointment or outing, making sure that every door and every window was closed. Her lost keys would drive me crazy. She noticed my annoyance and said shyly, ashamed, "Don't come tomorrow, *mija*, rest. Come in two weeks." Yet, after two days she called me, hysterical, scared, roaming the hallways of a house that she did not recognize as her own.

The house was becoming as empty as my mother's memory. My brother was no longer there to take the blame. Pictures, paintings, decorative plates, everything disappeared from the walls and the tables. Vases, plants, diplomas, her children's medals, something always seemed to have vanished every time I came back. "*Mami*, where is my graduation photo that was hanging here in the hallway? And the painting that Miss Collazo, the art teacher, painted for you? *Mami*, what happened to the pastel portraits we did at Disney?" Everything that documented our lives in that house: our birthdays, wedding anniversaries, crucifixes, Catholic stamps, the Palm Sunday leaves that she always kept in her room, everything was disappearing. I searched the armoires to find strange boxes filled with newspaper clippings that had no meaning, and then at the bottom, unexpectedly, the paintings. They would be covered in plastic bags, along with two-week-old groceries, all rotten. There, at the bottom of the armoires, I would find canned food and the crucifix, clothes that had disappeared from the closet, books, and the retirement check that had been lost a month ago. Crumpled plastic bags would appear everywhere, with shoes, clothing, brassieres, diplomas. I found everything and put it back in its place only to find it again inside the invasive plastic bags the week after. "There are burglars in this neighborhood, *mija*," *Mami* would tell me, trying to give me some sort of explanation for her new craze. I, Sisyphus' daughter, returned to my duties, trying to make life return to normal. It was a losing battle. I finally understood that she stored in the armoires what she could no longer store in her memory. Those terrible burglars lived inside of her, in her brain, and from there they stole the diplomas, the wedding anniversaries, the books, the shirts, and her complete story as a living being on the face of the earth. How could I remove those burglars from my mother's head?

And then that terrible thing happened, which once and for all let me know that my mother's life, that my life, would never be the same again.

THE SUBSTITUTE HOME

One night I received an alarming call. My mother had decided to go shopping with my cousin; she went to the bathroom and never came back. She was lost in the middle of the city. Alone. Disoriented. The whole family went out looking for her. After seventeen hours of looking for her with no results, another cousin found her in front of a school talking nonsense. The suspicions were confirmed. My mother had Alzheimer's.

The family reacted in different ways. Some ignored it. Others offered support. There was some pressure for me to move to her house to take care of her full time. I did not want to do that. My nerves were already starting to feel the effects of the sudden races to rescue her, the huge amount of attention that my mother required, those changes in personality that turned her into a strange person, suspended in a remote place to which I had no access.

But I decided to move in with her for a while, until I found a solution for the dilemma. Two weeks after she got lost, she woke me up in the middle of the night screaming, ordering me to leave the house, asking who I was to be sleeping in her daughter's bed. Confused and still half asleep, I tried to make her come back, I called her name, screamed at her and then she came to her senses. She apologized, returned to her room, and fell asleep as if nothing had happened. I, on the other hand, spent the whole night trembling, hiding under the covers like when I was a child and heard my mother and my father scream at each other in the middle of the night. A great fear took hold of me. I knew that my whole life would become my mother's sickness, and that I did not have the knowledge, the training, or the emotional objectivity to deal with it. There were too many feelings colliding with each other in my head and between the walls of that house where I grew up. I could not go back.

In light of my uncertainty, Aunt Cuchira, the youngest one, decided to take care of her and took my mother to her house. She lasted a month taking care of her. She could not take it anymore. There was no other way. I sat down with my calculator. Adding the numbers, her pension and my professor's salary were not enough to pay for someone to come take care of her, plus food, mortgage, and monthly expenses. I talked to my aunts. We tried to take turns taking care of her. At first, my closest aunts offered to help. But then, the daily grind of their lives started to wear down their strength and enthusiasm. I was the one left with the whole weight of my mother's care. It was twenty-four hours of burden. I had unending nights of hearing my mother drag her sandals through the corridor; fighting with her so she would go to sleep, take her pills, eat her food, remember what she ate; fighting so she would not put my students' tests in the armoires, so that she would let me prepare my classes and write, so that she would not forget my name, forget who I was. Then, exhausted and desperate I had to make one of the hardest decisions I have had to make in my whole life—I put my mother in a nursing home. Even today, eight years after her death, I'm not really sure I made the right decision.

I don't remember what day it was. I don't remember the month or the week. I don't want to remember. But I still have nightmares where I see myself driving to the nursing home where I put her on San Francisco Street. I see myself signing papers, taking the bags out of the trunk. I see her, my mother, Mariana Febres Falú, sitting there. Waiting. A peaceful look on her face, looking at me with the eyes of a child. The signatures and admission talks were over. A nurse came through a door. She approached my mother and said, "Ma'am, let's go." I stood up to say goodbye. I hugged her, kissed her, took her hands in mine, and promised that when she got better I would come get her. And she, before going up the stairs and getting lost in that home full of senile, sullen, old people, bored from waiting so long for death, looked into my eyes, sad but determined and said, "*Mija*, what can we do. This is another stage of life." I saw her leave and collapsed into tears. I had never been so close to such an act of dignity in the face of fatality. It took me many years and many losses to learn that last lesson my mother taught me. In her final lucid moments my mother gave herself to me, relentlessly. She was there to comfort me, when I grieved *her* loss, and *her* sickness. I looked at her a bit surprised, a bit proud, but absolutely defeated. My mother appeared grand, once again. And I was left with the insignificance of my tears.

[1]This is an affectionate term for daughter; the word comes from combining *mi hija,* which literally translates to my daughter.

How (In a Time of Trouble)
I Discovered My Mom
and Learned to Live

JUNOT DÍAZ

1.

I SPENT MY SENIOR YEAR IN HIGH SCHOOL PRETTY MUCH fucking everything up. I stayed home when I should have been in class; I didn't do any work; I fought with my teachers; I fought with my peers; I had a wise fucking mouth. By the time October rolled around I'd gotten demoted out of the honors program—first nigger in, first nigger out—and put into the "regular" classes where I did nothing except stare at the walls and read Stephen King books. *It* was the last book I read in high school, which should tell you something about my state of mind. (*We all float down here.*) I was nineteen, having stayed back a year because of my Spanish, and was adolescent skinny and adolescent ugly. No pulchritude of face, no pulchritude of clothes. And man, our poverty. Ever since my pops had bailed, my family had become eighties-Reagonomics broke. Anybody who's lived through that period knows what I'm talking. Those were tough years to be a poor person of color, especially tough if you were an immigrant. You know it was hard because white folks weren't *even* trying to be us. Things were pretty desperate. There were mad mornings I cut school just because I couldn't bear the thought of wearing the same shit I'd put on three days before. So on those days, instead of heading to the bus stop (ever since my brother had checked into the hospital me and my boys had been forced to take the bus because none of us had the loot to keep his Monarch on the road) I walked out to the landfill and stayed in the woods as long as I could stand it. On rainy days I trooped down to the Sayreville library and poked around the stacks. I remember being especially enamored with Doris Lessing's *Canopus in Argos* series, the design and heft of those hardcovers. I'd found them one day while looking for something else to read besides King. I remember taking them down and wondering how the hell could this be science fiction. I was too intimidated to read the books themselves but I liked to keep them near me when I was in the library and reading something else. I think this was the only openly hopeful gesture I made in those days. You have to understand: I was in an emotionally "difficult" period. Blame it on adolescence, on poverty, on young person of color self-hate, on my father's departure, on whatever—I was the gloomiest kid around and there were times I couldn't imagine living past the age of twenty. Those books at my elbow were some sort of promise of a tomorrow when I might actually feel smart enough and confident enough to read the whole series. A tomorrow when I might actually feel *good* about myself. No doubt this was a ghetto nerd's tomorrow but it was the best one I had.

I was also angry. Almost all the time, so angry that after most of my days I fell easily into dark exhausted sleep. I was especially angry at my father for leaving and at my older brother for losing fifty pounds and only then being diagnosed with leukemia. Rafa was up in Newark, in Beth Israel, on the top floor of the hospital so that when you pushed your face against his window you could see the burned-out blocks, the scarred-over reminders of '67; and New York's skyline, a million brick middle fingers pointed at the world.

2.

My moms had her own problems. Because of my brother and because of the economy and because the locals weren't trying to hire non-English speakers, she couldn't work full-time. So we were Section Eight, *los cúpones*, AFDC all the way. She was still grieving over my pops. The nigger had pretty much shipwrecked her—abandoning her in a state where you needed a car to survive, where she didn't have any family nearby, in a neighborhood cut off from any economic tides whatsoever. And while I might not be the best judge of these matters, I believe this was one of the darkest periods in my moms' life. Years later, when I interviewed her for my book, she still claimed the Dark Age was 1965. The year of the Revolution. When I mentioned 198-, she got quiet. Yes, she said. Those were bad times, too.

My moms was a tiny woman—later, when I started weightlifting for real I'd be able to curl her—and she was as light-skinned as you could be without being able to pass for white. When my brother was still around we used to call her the Queen of the Bata because it seemed she never got out of hers. She'd come to the United States because of us, but I don't think the move had ever given her much happiness. She was a silent woman, never spoke of herself or her heart and for most of my life the only "facts" I knew about her were that she was my mother and that she didn't play around. (Once she'd mentioned that when she was little she'd won a jacks competition but the next time we kids brought it up she pretended like we'd heard wrong, said to us, I never won anything in my life.) My pops I knew a lot about but of my mother I knew nothing. All of my friends talked about their pops, we compared them like we compared everything about ourselves, but unless our moms cooked well or hit us they didn't get no public play at all. I felt like the girl in *Abeng*, but unlike her I accepted my moms' silences as a given, assumed that's all she had to give.

I watched my moms a lot, though, that last year of high school. I didn't have anything to do. I was tired of my boys, they were tired of me. Me and her spent a lot of time tranqueado in our apartment. Mornings she always got up at the same time and I listened to her moving around up above me. She washed up, made her coffee and then listened to Radio WADO, which in those days was our primary bridge to the rest of the Latino world. On the days she went to visit my brother she'd leave me an egg sandwich on the stove and then one of her friends or the taxi that the Medicaid paid for would pick her up and I'd slip out of bed and watch her from behind the curtains. She always waved at the driver; she might have been quiet and worn-out but my moms was a friendly woman and the niggers who knew her, liked her. She visited my brother three or four days a week and always on weekends. But before she left she would knock on my basement door and say Levántate, muchacho. Every damn morning the same thing. Levántate.

But some days I'd oversleep and when I woke up she'd be sitting on the edge of my bed, right next to me. Her presence never surprised me. As if, even in my sleep, I could feel her near me, and know not to be alarmed. Our basement was extremely dark and she'd be nothing more than some breathing and the dark cut of her hair but I'd know it was her. Señora, I'd say and she'd put her hand on my face.

She, I see now, was watching me too.

We fought a lot. As you can imagine. She'd have her rages over my father and our situation and I'd have mine over everything. Doors slammed, nights spent out with friends, TVs raised high. We were a couple of fuckups living in the ruins of our lives. There was a lot of shame too, more than I can discuss here comfortably.

In April I learned that I hadn't been accepted to any of the colleges I'd applied to, not even Rutgers Livingston, which in those days was us niggers' safety. Even though I'd fucked up my grades—I mean, I failed whole classes that year—I'd honestly thought I'd get in *somewhere*. I was, after all, smarter than my boys who *had* gotten into school. What arrogance. When those letters came, I don't think I talked to anybody for a week. Just locked myself in my basement for six straight days, and when finally my boys came for me one night, forced me to take a ride with them to the Shore just so that they could cheer me up and tell me that the world wasn't over yet, it had been so long since I'd been outside that I remember that the streetlights hurt my eyes.

When I told Mami about the rejections I said to her, Well, it looks like I'm fucked. I went on to blame her *and* my father *and* my brother *and* the school, while she watched me and said nothing. Finally, she went, You should have worked harder, which only sent me into a bigger louder fit. Neighbors banging on their walls, my mother retreating to her room, another night with my boys, drinking in the backseat of a car.

Graduation Day I refused to attend the ceremonies down at the Garden State Arts Center—which was where the rich-ass school that I was being bused into held their shit—stayed in bed despite my mother's anger. In the end she went without me. Caught a ride with somebody else and when they called my name, mispronouncing it as always, my boys told me she nodded once and put both hands on her purse. I still remember what a beautiful day it was—the sun was everywhere, driving deep and hard into the bricks. I took a walk down to the Sayreville library and stayed late. When I got back Mami was in her room, no longer dressed up, watching her novelas. She heard me come in, I'm sure, and I heard her TV. I went downstairs and waited for my boys to call.

She didn't talk to me, really talk to me, for a long time after that.
Such was our lives.

3.

I don't know how much time passed. Enough, I can assure you. I worked delivering pool tables by day and at night I took drives with the boys that remained. We headed out all over New Jersey and had the usual Parkway-Turnpike adventures. Saturdays I visited my brother, tried not to stare at his ravaged body. The rest of the time I was in my basement, trying out the new loneliness of my post-high school life.

Sometimes when I got off the M15 coming back from my job my moms would be getting off the bus coming from hers. She shaded her eyes with her hands, and said, Hijo, and I tipped my head and said, Señora. We walked home in silence, me between her and the road. Sometimes I'd get off the bus and she'd already be halfway up that long curve that was Ernston Road and I'd follow her at a distance. We both had crazy jobs but hers was worse, cleaning houses for professors and middle-class people, and when she got home she always cooked dinner while I sat in front of the TV and watched *Doctor Who*. Now that I didn't have to hide out I didn't go to the Sayreville library no more. (The next time I'd see *Canopus in Argos* I'd be in college and the tan spines of those books staring from the stacks would hit me like a right cross to the chest.) Whatever it was that was around my heart in those days—an armature of anthracite, a crust of gyprock—didn't feel like it was going to crack anytime soon. I decided this would be my life for the next couple years and was miserable because of it.

4.

I can't tell you how many times she tried to talk to me. It was hard for her, you know, to have one of those pat sit-down mother-to-son chats, the kind the TV was always insisting were possible; sit-down chats weren't a part of the family repertoire; we just weren't brought up that way. We were Dominicans and Dominicans, at least the ones I knew, don't really talk to their kids. Mami tried. She'd wait for me to be watching TV, usually at night, when she thought I'd be my calmest, and then she'd sit down at my side and I could see it coming a mile away because she'd have this serious look on her face. Look, she'd say, you have to struggle if you want—

I usually didn't let her get any further than that. I'd either put my hand up and tell her to leave it or I'd go downstairs without a word. It was easy to hurt her; after all, she was my mother. For some reason it felt good to leave her mid-sentence on the couch, to have her follow me onto the stairs and say things like, I didn't come to this country so you could quit. What about college? I used to shout at her. It's not like you even went to school! My moms certainly didn't need that kind of shit from me. She was barely keeping her own self above water. Money was mad tight and even with government help cancer medicine wasn't cheap. It was like we couldn't win; every time my brother got released from the hospital he caught a flu or an infection and had to be taken right back. Lots of nights I could hear her walking around upstairs when she thought I was asleep, could hear her moving from the bedroom to the kitchen to the porch and that never stopped her from dressing for work in the morning or from knocking on my door and saying, Levántate, muchacho.

5.

In the end it was just some words that did it.

Can't tell you nothing about that day except that I was coming back from another one of my useless nights out and my mother was sitting on the couch watching the main TV; the shit was so busted-up that we couldn't turn it off, had to lower the volume when we wanted to go to sleep. It was this huge horrible never sleep cyclops in the center of the room. My moms was still as a bone and her hair was dark and wet from the shower and as I headed down to the basement she said, with some bitterness, You know, I cried less when I lost my first son.

I heard her say it, but I didn't answer back. I sort of shrugged and headed downstairs, pretended like I didn't know what the hell she was talking about. The TV stayed on for another hour and then she headed back into her room for some more TV and finally sleep.

That night I lay in bed and stared at my walls. *You know I cried less when I lost my first son.* Like I said, I didn't know nothing about my mother. That I'd had another brother who had died was a huge shock even to hard cold me. That she'd never mentioned him in all these years was something else altogether. Said a lot about the kind of relationship niggers like me have with their moms. I always used to claim that I loved my moms, told everybody this, but how in the world can you truly love somebody you don't even know?

This is a short piece so it's not like I can fill in all shades or hit you off with crosshatchings galore but I'll tell you one thing: That night was the first time in my life that I had to deal with the possibility that my moms was a person and not just somebody who washed my under-wear and cooked my meals. She had a world inside of her, I realized.

A world. It was like suddenly finding yourself in a depth of water. It was an astonishment.

My mother had surprised me similarly once before, back in Santo Domingo. I didn't remember that earlier incident right then, but I do remember it now. This was back in our Villa Juana days. I remember we were on a bus going somewhere and my mother pointing at another neighborhood and saying, This is where my old novio used to live. She didn't say nothing else and even then I was taken aback by her statement. I'd always thought my mother had known my father her whole life.

The next day we had breakfast together. Avena and some toast. Radio WADO was on and so was the TV. Come out here and look at the birds, my mother said. She was sitting on the porch. I followed her outside and stared at the sparrows, those ubiquitous flying woodchips. When I was grown I'd hear about it—the first pregnancy, the Invasion, the bomb falling—but right then we didn't speak about my dead brother and we wouldn't for many, many years.

6.

I can't say our relationship changed much after that night. Our world still sucked and it continued to suck for a long time afterwards. We didn't suddenly become best friends. I can't even honestly say that it was her words alone that got me going again but when I look back on it now this assessment—that she was the one who helped me jump-start my life again—doesn't seem that wild or wrong. Because sometime in those next couple of months I started making small moves, nothing too radical, little changes that slowly began adding up. The first big obvious one was that I stopped lurking around in the basement so much. I stopped hating my boys for their hard work and their college acceptances and brought myself back into the fold. I bought a car and started taking night classes at Kean College. (Certainly, you say, words alone can't have this power. Somewhere in my heart I must have been ready for this change and Mami only facilitated the emergence of what was already there.) Eventually I was able to transfer to Rutgers—New Brunswick, a dream of mine. But by then a lot of the other shit had cleared up as well. I was still angry, still an emotional mess, but I'd learned to hide it somewhat, not to let it paralyze me as much as I used to. Sure, my pops never came back and the old brother

I'd known before the chemo never did, either, but after a couple of years I'd begin to talk to my mother seriously and a couple of years later, we'd even become friends.

Junot Díaz's "How (In a Time of Trouble) I Discovered My Mom and Learned to Live" was first published by Pantheon Books. Copyright (c) 2000 by Junot Díaz.

Journey to Motherhood

DORSÍA SMITH SILVA

WHEN I GOT MARRIED IN 2000, THE TALK OF *FELICIDADES* (congratulations) quickly turned into chatter of having children. My family in Puerto Rico started with the barrage: "Are the *niños* coming soon?" "You're not going to wait too long to start having a family, are you?" "When will you be ready to become a mommy?" I tried to smile politely and dodge the issue. These questions swirled around me as I was trying to enjoy the life of being a newlywed. I wondered if there was something wrong with having some time with just me and my husband and why I was the one getting hounded. Why weren't they asking my husband these questions? Surely, he was part of the equation when it came to having children.

Family members continued to push the topic. At a dinner for me and my husband, they asked Father Pepín who presided at our wedding to bless us with a baby on our one-year anniversary. I covered my astonishment with a joke that Father Pepín should delay that miracle. He thankfully got the message and wished us a beautiful long marriage instead.

My family still persevered with their baby-making campaign though and gave me hints on Mother's Day. They also placed random infants in my lap, so that I could "practice" taking care of children. The last straw came when they reminded me of becoming a mother during a Gerber commercial; the chubby bouncing baby on television started to melt my resistance. I gave way and told them that my husband and I would have a child in two years. They were pleased and smiled brightly.

Two years quickly passed, and then another two years went by, and then another two. It was unheard of. What kind of Puerto Rican couple did not have children early in their marriage? Many family members buzzed and wondered if we were ever going to have children. Others gave me a little break. They saw that I was trying to finish my Ph.D. and get a tenure-track position at the University of Puerto Rico. Surely, they told me, I would start a family when the merry-go-round of academia slowed down.

But things didn't settle down, not even when I received my Ph.D. and tenure-track position. I spent another year working feverishly—trying to prove that I was worthy of these new titles—by going to conferences, publishing, teaching, and organizing events. And when the end of the academic session came, my body called for rest. I surrendered to slowing down. I finally had some moments to listen to my thoughts and discover that I was ready to welcome a baby, welcome the process. I opened myself to beginning the journey.

A NEW PATH

My husband and I started trying to get pregnant around our ninth anniversary. To help us along, I read fertility web sites and pregnancy books. They all had advice about what to do and what not to do to conceive. I sounded off tidbits to my husband: we can only be intimate on certain dates; we have to make sure that I'm ovulating; there are also certain positions, which might help us; and I am supposed to rest my hips afterwards on a fertility pillow. It all sounded like nonsense to him. "My grandmother had fourteen children and I'm sure she didn't check the calendar and do any of those other things you mentioned," he stated.

Friends gave me advice too. "Just have a romantic romp on the beach. It will happen then," a friend said. Another told me about waiting until La Noche de San Juan to conceive. "On this night," my friend remarked, "you will frolic in the water and then come up a pregnant woman." "One guarantee," another well-meaning friend added, "is to say the prayer to St. Gerard to become pregnant: O glorious Saint Gerard, powerful intercessor before God, and wonder worker of our day, I call upon you and seek your help… It will bring you luck and you will be pregnant in no time." They had good intentions, but nothing worked. Months passed and I wondered if I had waited too long to have a baby. I was after all thirty-seven.

After several more months of trying, I grew desperate. I purchased an expensive electronic fertility monitor, which calculated my fertile days. My mother-in-law gave me a drink made of boiled sesame seeds to increase my fertility. I gulped the sour concoction and prayed that it would work. The Internet said that I should hold my legs up straight in the air for thirty minutes, while resting my hips. It was to help the egg get fertilized. I held my legs up for an hour. But, still there was nothing.

The doctor recommended that I take some tests to make sure that everything was okay. She assured me not to worry, but how could I not? I was surrounded by pregnancy everywhere; I saw pregnant women at the grocery store, young women at the University, and teenagers on television. And whenever I saw their baby bump, I doubted if I would ever have one. I had to blink away the tears several times and stir myself away from feeling like I had failed to live up to the image of the fertile woman of color. I knew it was a stereotype, but I still carried this sense of disappointment.

As I waited for the results of my tests, I received unsolicited advice from neighbors and colleagues. I was annoyed at their intrusion into what I considered a personal matter, but I had forgotten that the borders of privacy in Puerto Rico get crossed all of the time. Once something is told, it floats and is carried on so that everyone pretty much knows everything about everybody.

I was told "to just relax." It didn't work. A colleague informed me about fertility beads. It seemed like a waste of money. My hairdresser shouted to me that "there was no point in trying, because I just had to do it." "You have to DO IT, JUST DO IT!" she laughed and gyrated wildly. Needless to say, it was all useless. Every month my "friend" showed up and I sighed at seeing the streaks of red.

My husband and I decided to take a vacation—get some mental and physical space from the fertility suggestions—and celebrate our tenth anniversary in St. Martin. We lounged on the beach, ate well, walked into town, and rented a car to sightsee. We didn't get pregnant on this trip, but we discovered that we shouldn't try so hard. Wasn't baby-making supposed to be fun? We promised ourselves that whatever happened, we would be receptive to looking at our options.

I thought about adoption, but adoption was a foreign concept to my husband. He has a large extended family in Puerto Rico and there has always been an aunt, uncle, cousin, or grandparent who has taken care of a child of another family member. "How can someone give away their blood? It's unconceivable," he stated. The idea of going to a fertility doctor didn't seem the best way either. My Catholic upbringing had instilled in me that procreation should not include science or technology. Plus, I didn't want to subject myself to more tests, prodding, and quizzical looks. That pretty much left us being a childless couple. I felt like we were doomed to have the label freak tattooed on our foreheads. *Wasn't it rare to see a relatively young married couple in Puerto Rico without children? How would we bear it when people asked us about our children? How would we feel at age sixty without children or grandchildren?* I had no answers and my family, friends, neighbors, and colleagues could not give me advice this time.

We were navigating through this dilemma when I got pregnant. I couldn't trust my eyes. *Was the line really blue this time? Did one line mean that I was pregnant or was it supposed to be two lines?* I poured over the instructions until I saw spots. I was pregnant! I didn't know what had finally clicked—the prayers, beads, monitor, fertility pillow—or how it had finally clicked. All I knew was that the little one was inside of me and was finally calling.

A CHANGE IN DIRECTION

I sailed through the first three months of my pregnancy without morning sickness or any major problems. My baby bump started to grow and colleagues started noticing my "glowing" skin. Family members jumped with excitement; they showered me with tips on nutrition and offers to help. My students also started asking me questions—What's the sex of your baby? When are you due? Don't you feel nauseous? I took it all in great stride. The privacy boundary was crossed here too, but in Puerto Rico it was not unusual for professors to be friendly with students. And if we knew them well, we even hugged and kissed them like they were our own children.

At the beginning of my fourth month of pregnancy, I grew miserable. My breathing was off and my heart felt like galloping horses had taken over my body. The heat enveloped me. It was a chore to walk to my classes. I had no energy. The doctor on campus saw me and told me to get more rest. "Let me take your blood pressure," he said gently. The numbers on the machine skyrocketed. "You need to see your OBGYN right away," he warned. "You have tachycardia." "No," I protested weakly, "it's just the heat." "The heat can't cause this," he said while shaking his head. "Call you doctor right now and if you can't get through then go to the hospital," he urged.

The rush to the OBGYN's office started the maze of seeing cardiologists and sub-specialists in cardiology; taking a battery of tests; being monitored on machines; and making serious adjustments at work. I was placed on restrictive movement, given medication, and told not to travel for the remainder of my pregnancy. The old feelings of disappointment started to creep back. *Why couldn't I look like the pregnant women I saw at Plaza las Americas?* They were strutting around in high heels and make-up, looking fabulous. I looked frowsy in my ballet flats and I could barely take five paces without panting for air.

As I realized that I was again holding myself up to more stereotypes about mothering and motherhood, I started thinking about what it means to be a mother especially in Puerto Rican society. We all have our different paths to becoming a mother, which cannot and should not be narrowed into a single universal experience. My story of having difficulty conceiving a child and developing pregnancy-related health problems is not the only one, but is one that is often untold. We need to share more of our journeys and, in the process, open the space of mothering.

Learning the Hard Way

ANGIE CRUZ

WHEN I WAS PREGNANT WITH DANIEL, I WAS DETERMINED TO be the kind of mother who would have my son accompany me to lectures and conferences. I imagined he would sleep peacefully in a sling while I did my research in the archives. I thought I would be the kind of mother who would create space in her life, for her creativity and productivity and he, my son, would be proud of me for it. I thought I would be the kind of mother who despite the sleepless nights, despite my aching back from carrying him, despite my leaky breast from feeding him, despite the rumor or is it fact that I apparently had one third less of my brain to work with while breastfeeding, I would still be as productive, on-time, in the mix, working in the same way as I had been before he was born.

So when I received the invitation to present at a conference in New Orleans, I said yes. I had always wanted to visit NOLA because of its Caribbean history. I was eight months pregnant, still teaching at the university. Feeling strong and able. I told the organizers that I would certainly attend the conference in February. By then my son would be about two months old. Old enough to practically fend for himself. According to some of the books I was reading, if I was lucky, and I planned to be, my son at two months would be sleeping through the night. The conference would be an occasion for me to jump back into my work. Besides, I knew for a fact that at this conference there would be the loving arms of some colleagues and writer friends who had repeatedly offered to help care for Daniel.

When the time came to go the conference I wasn't ready to present or travel with Daniel. I felt vulnerable and my body was still recovering from an emergency c-section. One part of me wanted to cancel, another part of me felt that if I didn't go I was admitting to some kind of defeat. Besides I was my mother's daughter. She raised two children alone, put herself through college and managed to facilitate the passage of all her brothers and sisters from the Dominican Republic to the United States. She did this without knowing a word of English, because according to my mother, we Latinas do not have the luxury to be tired or to make excuses when we are called on to work.

So I went to NOLA determined to walk the city's uneven sidewalks, cracked from age, keeping pace with other conference participants. I reminded myself that other mothers, the women I witnessed before I became a mother, were able to lecture at a conference with their babies strapped on their bodies; mothers who told stories about writing and finishing their books between feedings in the dark hours of the night. Women who became stronger after the birth of their children, more productive, better writers, no-bullshit kind of women. While I was pregnant other mothers who were writers and academics assured me and told me repeatedly that once you have a child there is literally no time to waste so they became more productive, more efficient, as I will become more productive, more efficient with my time. I was told that once you're a mother you do what you have to do without excuses. Many women rubbed my large belly with confidence that it could all get done, the reading, the writing, the loving, the socializing, the cleaning, the caring for a child. You will see, they said. What they didn't say was that it would take me two years for me to be truly functional. Two years when I would be caught up with my body and sleeping six to seven hours without any interruption. So as a new mother with a two month old, I was tired, which is expected. But I pretended that I was just fine.

At the conference, during many of the panel discussions, in my sleep deprived state, I couldn't make sense of what anyone was saying. The academics slung words across the table, long multi-syllabic words, spoken so effortlessly, as if those of us (okay, me) who recently had a short hiatus (childbirth) from the academic jargon, were completely dumb not to be able follow up with something intelligent to say. And truthfully, as interested as I am about ideas and theories, at that moment it seemed so irrelevant. Instead, I was hyper aware that Daniel was sitting on my lap. I couldn't help but follow his eyes that darted from someone's curls, to the tip of their nose, then to their eyes. Like him I watched the way a presenter slumped over the table and another spoke with their hands. I wondered if any of them had children? Were they mourning something? Were they falling in love, out of love? And when Daniel smiled at the pen tapping against the large wooden table, the way he gasped at the loud street noises out the window, I had to be strong and restrain myself from calling out the names of things: *agua, lápiz, carro* in the same way I repeated *mama, papa, buenas noches* at home. I kept thinking back to my mother who put herself through college with my brother and me in tow. She would make me sit quietly in a desk next to her through her French and accounting classes. She would take notes while my brother was asleep on her lap.

When Daniel began to fuss, I snuck in and out of the conference roundtables, waiting for him to settle down again so I could again pretend that I wasn't a distraction to other participants. As soon as I tried to sit back down at the table, Daniel's soft gurgles, that I had thought to be soft and sweet at home, seemed loud and intrusive. When I looked for a pen in my bag I found a pacifier, a bib, and a ready-made bottle of formula. I anticipated Daniel's voice to cut through the conversation in the way children's voices do; in the way that would make everyone look at me in disdain. In the way I perhaps would've looked at myself before I was with child, wondering, couldn't she find a babysitter?

To avoid such looks but even more so as a preventative measure, I snuck out of the meetings, trying my best not to disturb the discussion and when people asked me about Daniel, I changed the subject to whatever topic was going on in the conference to stay on point. I didn't want to be one of those mothers who only spoke of her child. I took every opportunity to excuse myself and went back to the hotel just to put Daniel down on the bed, to rest my backpack on a chair, to undo and stretch my shoulders that ached. I didn't admit it to anyone that if I could snap my fingers I would give up being in vibrant New Orleans to go back home to lackluster, College Station, Texas, just so I could put on my PJs and curl up on the couch with a boppy on my lap and feed and nap with Daniel.

On the last day of the conference, a number of us participants decided to have beignets at Café Du Monde and finally see the Mississippi River.

"What a trooper," someone said about Daniel who was full of good humor.

As usual I was carrying my heavy backpack with wipes, diapers, a change of clothing, formula bottles, water, rattles, etc. Daniel was in a Bjorn facing forward, his back to me, his legs dangling in the air, his eyes open wide. We walked the aging New Orleans' streets, its complex and troubling history, exposed through the Spanish Architecture, French street names, bricks made with the hands of enslaved peoples. *This is where jazz was born*, I told him. *This is what parts of Santo Domingo look like.*

On the way back to the hotel to check out, I bought chicory coffee as souvenirs. I remember praising the Bjorn because it freed my hands to carry stuff. Daniel was hanging off my chest, his legs kicked in the air, his squeals responded to the noisy New Orleans morning.

"Can I carry something for you?" my friend Emily offered.

"No, it's okay," I replied. Because just like my mother, a strong-willed Dominican woman, I was sure I could manage. It didn't matter that I was packed like a mule.

"I just can't wait to put Daniel down in his crib," I confessed to Emily. His crib is one of the few places where I could leave him and then sit, relax and write, or shower, nap, or finish reading a book.

That's when I tripped. I tripped on one of those water hole lids on an uneven sidewalk, the same sidewalk I thought of as charming when I first arrived. I fell forward and imagined Daniel's head split open, my full body weight on him. A pack of tourists encircled me. Their faces filled with horror.

"Is there blood?" I asked my girlfriends and the tourists who surrounded me. Daniel cried. I cried. There was dust on his lips. No blood. He cried because he was startled or because I was crying. I cried because for a split second I thought that my fall had killed him. Somehow I managed to turn on my side and save him from getting hurt. I broke the fall with my knees. I pulled him out of the Bjorn and carried him close to my chest all the way back to the hotel. *I'm so sorry*, I said repeatedly to him and even to myself. I fell down because I was exhausted. Why hadn't I asked someone to carry my backpack when they offered to help? Why did I pretend that I could keep up the pace with everyone else? The women around me had offered their hearts and arms during the conference. Why did I resist their help?

If I was in the city of Santo Domingo, or even in Washington Heights, I would've had women with generous arms surrounding me much like

I did in New Orleans. The difference would've been that in the Caribbean, to share your children with the women around you is part of life. I would have not felt I was imposing on anyone when I asked them to watch Daniel. I would have not thought twice that they had their own work to do, or were too busy. I would have not tried to apologize for Daniel's presence every time someone looked at me wondering why I didn't leave him back home.

Just a few years before, a friend of mine had a baby and I offered to baby-sit. I offered with good intentions but at the same time I never did baby-sit. She never called me and I never found the time to volunteer. Now as a mother I understand why, because even I have not taken up the baby-sitting offers to care for Daniel. This makes me feel *Americanisada* (as my mother likes to say) in a way that I don't like. If I learned anything at this conference it is that, we as women should trespass on each other's lives with more frequency. Trespass into each other's homes and lives when we know the other is in need of help, and trespass when we ourselves need help. This is how a true community can be built.

When I was a child I remember having my cousins stay in my room, share a bed with me. I remember the bottles of milk on my bedside and how I would feed my little cousin in the middle of the night while his mother worked. No one asked me if I wanted to share a bed, and my aunts didn't ask my mother if they could leave their children. We were at home, therefore, they left their children so they could go out to work. In the same way, I remember being sent off to Dominican Republic as a child to my godmother, sent off to fly with any one of the trustworthy family members for the summer, for Christmas holidays, for Easter; that way, my mother, who was a single mother of two, could for a short while care for my brother, work and also finish her college accounting degree. My mother sent me off knowing I would be taken care of. I remember *las primas y los primos* that were tied to me, not blood tied, but family tied because they were *hijos de crianza*, children temporarily adopted by *mis tias*, that were dropped off for a number of years at our homes and then picked up when the mothers were ready to care for them. They would've never called it trespassing when they showed up at our door without calling first and sit at our tables for lunch, for dinner, for coffee; for a much-needed break.

With all this said, and in retrospect I have yet to attend a conference that accommodated mothers with their children. I know some that do provide daycare but not many, and when they do, it's expensive. Not so long ago I attended a conference in Dominican Republic. It was an academic literary conference centered around women scholars and academics, and a few select creative writers were invited to read. In the audience there were children. There were scholars with their children and even mothers who tagged along to the conference. There were random interruptions during our talks, referring to the sound of a child's voice and even the acceptance or recognition that as women scholars/writers we are often responsible for the well being of our families, our mothers, our grandmothers, our children, our girlfriends, our girlfriend's children, and of course let's not forget our partners. And we also do our work. Show up to conferences, write our books, and so on.

Now that I am a mother, I think often about what we can do to facilitate the participation of mothers inside and outside of academia so we can continue to do our work and also take care of our elders and children; to take care of each other as well. Since my trip to New Orleans, I have been better at asking for help when I need it. By honoring my motherhood I begin to dismantle the unspoken formalities in such professional contexts, maybe even inspire other mothers to bring their children. Most importantly, I try my best to remember that the mothers I know that seem to have superhuman qualities, because they appear to keep it all together, didn't achieve it alone. Even my mother, who I hold on a pedestal, relied heavily on family, friends, and neighbors to raise her children so she could finish her education and take care of us all.

Mi Madre, Mi Hija y Yo

Chicana Mothering through Memory, Culture and Place

MICHELLE TÉLLEZ

I HAVE ONE CHILD. MY PREGNANCY WAS SOMEWHAT PLANNED, I suppose, if you call dreaming and talking about creating a family with someone you're falling in love with family planning. Being alone during my pregnancy, being a single mother and, a year after my daughter's birth, fighting for custody of my first born, certainly was not a part of any sort of plan I had. The story, as many are, is complicated, yet the everyday life that my daughter and I share is probably not very different from many families living in the United States. The rhythm of preschool, play dates, and bedtime stories shape our routine just as much as my work as an academic does. However, due to the geographic distance between us and our extended familial circle, my childhood memories of a close-knit family life greatly differ from the life that my daughter and I share. *Familia* (family), as I lived it, was always close, serving simultaneously as either a source of support or tension. Despite the inevitable contradictions that these relationships implied, my sense of forming part of a larger community remained intact.

As a Chicana single mother juggling parenting, work, life, and love, I find myself wondering how I will be able to provide my daughter with the sense of self and community that I had. In my reflections, I recognize that my mother used *cultura* (culture), (embodied in strength), to teach us about life and love, and as a strategy to overcome daily hardships. This essay of narrative and *cuentos* represents a sharing of my mother's life lessons—lessons steeped in both social politics and those of *familia*, that shape and guide my own journey through motherhood.

A central theme that shapes this piece is the intergenerational conflict that emerges between mothers and daughters; tensions are informed by the stories of separation, loss, migration, race, and discrimination. By invoking these stories, I hope to inspire new conceptions on mothering to the growing literature on Chicana/Latina mothering as it relates to education, pedagogy, and ethics.[1] This essay looks at the ways in which Chicanas, who have come to embody *mestizaje* (mestization) as described by Gloria Anzaldúa in *Borderlands/La Frontera: The New Mestiza* (1987), negotiate raising children in a society that continues to denigrate people of color. How does our "motherwork"[2] not only reflect the tensions that emerged during our own identity formation, but also show the ways in which we continue to negotiate our experiences and histories with society? By examining the subtle strategies used by my mother in my own upbringing, I've come to recognize that her motherwork became a form of resistance. In spite of the myriad of misfires between us, the notion of *familia*, community, and *cultura* instilled in me by my mother became the building blocks from which I understood myself and my place in this world.

MI MADRE, MI HIJA Y YO: EL CAMINO

Sofia Villenas and Melissa Moreno have argued in "To *Valerse por si Misma* Between Race, Capitalism, and Patriarchy: Latina Mother-Daughter Pedagogies in North Carolina" that "the teaching and learning that occurs between mothers and daughters through *consejos* (advice), *cuentos* (stories) and *la experiencia* (experience) are wrought with tensions and contradictions yet open with spaces of possibility" (672). It is from these spaces of possibility that I speak as I explore three generations of women in my family: my mother, my daughter, and myself.

On a recent long drive with my mother and daughter, I decided to put some Mexican music on the car stereo. Immediately my mother began to sing and although she no longer remembered the lyrics, she still sang loudly. "*Que bonita musica*" ("What pretty music"), she said. I sang loudly too. I was immediately filled with nostalgia for my childhood and memories came flooding back: memories of Saturday morning house cleanings with Mariachi records blasting from our wooden stereo, of the yearly summer trips to my mother's hometown in the state of Jalisco, Mexico, of learning to dance the *zapateado* with my cousins in my *abuelita's* (grandmother's) house—memories that invoke *familia*, *cultura*, and home. My mother was the one who inspired this in me, this love of our history, language, and understanding of our ties to a place we never lived in for longer than several weeks of the year.

I will always be grateful to my mother for giving us access and exposure to a world and culture that we found a place in. Interestingly, throughout my life I've been told I look like my mother and our life parallels are also revealing: we both lost our fathers at age twenty and had our first child at age thirty-two. We both left our hometowns and our immediate families behind. Yet, my mother and I have a difficult relationship. When my father died and I walked into our house and to my mother's arms, I vividly remember thinking, "I do not know this woman." I could talk to my father in ways that I've never been able to talk with her, and I had a closeness with him that I have never shared with my mother. In part this was due to the fact that my father was born and raised in Chicago, the son of an immigrant mother from Mexico and a father born in El Paso, Texas. He understood the contradictions of biculturalism and did not belittle my youthful angst growing up in the U.S. The image of the typical *machista* father did not apply in my family either, and in fact, it was my mother who embodied the authoritative figure in our household. It was this very strength that allowed my mother to survive her father's murder in her hometown, her brother's death at an early age, and the hardships of migration, including learning a new language and dealing with the oppression that racialized immigrants face in this country. Yet, it was also this very strength that became the barrier that kept her from getting too close to her daughters.

I do admire my mother's resiliency; this strength is similar to what Ruth Trinidad Galván describes as an ability to survive: "*la sobrevivencia* (survival) is what lies ahead and beneath plain victimy, our ability to *saciar* (satiate) our hopes and dreams in creative and joyful ways" (163). Even during the toughest times, my mother kept me entertained with stories of her youth, of days spent in *el campo* (countryside), riding horses on bareback, swimming in *el rio* (the river), and going to the *fiestas del pueblo* (town parties) that brought the entire town together. I have recreated these memories as my own and, as such, my mother's birthplace has come to signify a homeland for me as well. My mother created links not only across national boundaries through family ties and visits, but also through language by teaching us Spanish. When we return to her hometown, the time and distance is erased and immediately we blend into the everyday family life with our *tias* (aunts), *primas* (cousins), and community. Conversely, she created boundaries in our home; if my actions were deemed too Americanized, or "*agringada*" as she called it, she would pull me closer to the home sphere. It is these practices and lessons that have helped shape my journey through motherhood.

DISRUPTIONS: UNDERSTANDING THE LESSONS

Through the teaching and learning of the home, "Chicanas are able to draw upon their own cultures and sense of self to resist domination along the axes of race, class, gender and sexual orientation" (Bernal 624). It is in the activities and actions of daily life that Chicana/Latina feminists should "theorize the everyday pedagogies of the home and the tenet of *la familia* as sites of affirmation and intervention for women's negotiations of their multiple identities within systems of oppression" (Knight et al. 42). With this sense of self, knowledge of culture as resistance, and an awareness of the "everyday pedagogies of the home and *la familia*," I have come to recognize within my mother's life lessons the intimacy of the politics and their power. These memories, or what I'll call disruptions, are significant lessons and are particularly poignant to me as a mother.

The first disruption began during a walk home from school in the second grade. As my friends and I turned the corner to our street, one of the boys we were walking with turned to me and said, "You know when your mom speaks English, she sounds like a broken record." I remember falling to the ground and sobbing because of this boy's callousness. I don't remember if he apologized and I don't remember how I stopped crying, but I did. I walked the rest of the way home and as soon as I walked into my house, my mother quickly noticed something was wrong. How could I tell her what this boy had said? How could I hurt her the way he had hurt me? But after just a little nudging, I relented and told her what had happened. My mother responded, "Well it's true. I don't speak English well, but don't let them get to you." With those simple words and a hug, my mother lifted the burden of shame, ignorance, and pain.

I learned then the power of what Graciela Sánchez in "La Cultura, La Comunidad, La Familia, y La Libertad" calls *cultura*: why "knowing how to converse and think in the language of [my] ancestors was important; that knowing about [my] history, and culture, and traditions would help [me] develop a better sense of [myself]" (76). In my mother's lesson with this boy, I learned to not only embrace my bilingualism, but I also learned how important it is to keep your cool in the face of bigotry. Using these "subtle acts of resistance" have become essential for my survival and a lesson that I must pass on to my daughter (Bernal 625). She must know how to embrace her roots, understand her cultura and the origins of our family, despite parts of U.S. society's capacity to undermine these connections.

The second disruption occurred as I began my academic career. I started college at UCLA in the fall of 1991. That first memory of leaving home is still fresh in my mind. My father took the morning off from work and drove me to Los Angeles on a Thursday morning. As soon as we arrived to campus, he dropped me, my bags, and my heavy heart off on the corner in front of the dorms and quickly got on the road for the two-hour drive back to work. There were no goodbye family lunches or dorm room decorating parties. With a lump in my throat, I watched as he drove off, feeling scared and a bit overwhelmed. Fear had no time to invade my body, as I quickly realized I needed a job to earn money. By the next night, I was working at the cafeteria and I remember watching the families come and go as I mopped the floors; there was disappointment on my part, but I also realized that I wasn't the only one suffering. Years later, my mother told me that both she and my father cried for days during those first days after my departure.

To this day, my mother has never forgiven me for leaving, even though she also left home. The difference, she argues, is that I left home for myself, and she left home to work for her family in Mexico. This tension continued through graduate school and during one afternoon, I finally blurted out, "You're just not interested in the work I do!" My mother responded, "*Ay, hija tu madre es una idiota. Lo único que sé es que estudias mucho y siempre estás ocupada. No entiendo lo que estás haciendo*" ("Oh daughter, your mother is an idiot. The only thing that I know is that you study a lot and you're always busy. I don't understand what you are doing"). At that moment, I realized that we were focusing on what was keeping us apart as opposed to what held us together. My mother had left her country of origin and had learned a new language as an adult. In doing so, she had created the opportunity for me to leave home and pursue my own endeavors; it was because of her that I was able to find my way that first day at UCLA alone. The lesson that comes from our shared moment of resistance is to understand that while we both left home, our shared stories and our *familia* have kept us intact.

The final disruption occurred while I was pregnant. My sister and my *comadre* had thrown me an amazing baby shower at a restaurant that my family and I had been going to for years. I had many friends and family members present, and I was sitting next to my mother. At one point, my cousin, who was also pregnant but married, came up to the table to say hello to us. When my mother turned around and saw her, she became very animated and began to rub her teeming belly. In witnessing this gesture, it dawned on me that my mother had not once touched me during my pregnancy. Although the birth of my daughter signified much joy for my mother, the announcement of my pregnancy was everything but. It did not matter to my mother that I had completed a doctoral degree; she never once expressed tears of excitement or joy at that accomplishment. But my being pregnant and unmarried caused her tears of despair that would not stop. As Gloria Anzaldúa states, "If a woman remains a *virgen* until she marries, she is a good woman. For a woman of my culture there used to be only three directions she could turn: to the Church as a nun, to the streets as a prostitute, or to the home as a mother" (17). We barely spoke during my pregnancy, a painful memory that is deeply buried and is outweighed by the delight I get in observing the relationship that my daughter and mother now have. This example highlights similar tensions raised by other women of color feminists who speak about the conflicts they have with their mothers.[3] In my case, I have conflict not only because I left, but also because of what I have become. To be unmarried and pregnant, despite my ability to care for both myself and my daughter, temporarily overshadowed the joy that my daughter brings.

My mother though, was very independent; in fact, she repeatedly made it clear that I should never "depend on a man." As Sofia Villenas and Melissa Moreno argue, our mothers push us in the direction of feminism by pointing out their life experiences as women (675). Similarly, Uma Narayan in *Dislocating Cultures: Identities, Traditions and Third World Feminism* asserts that "In seeing us in this mode, they fail to see how much of what we are is precisely a response to the very things they have taught us, how much we have become the daughters they have shaped us into becoming" (8). I, in fact, had told my mother several times that

I found the institution of marriage to be highly problematic, but that these inhibitions did not negate my desire for children. What I hadn't planned for though was an absent partner. Thus, despite my desperate need for *familia* during a vulnerable time, I failed to receive it and was stifled instead by the Chicana cultural norms of respectability, shame, and femininity. The *machista* elements to my culture, embodied by both men and women, are the norms I am hoping to disrupt as a mother. Clearly, I have witnessed the contradictions both in my mother's willingness to break norms as much as in her willingness to uphold them. However, the lesson that I glean is that nurturance and not fear should fundamentally guide me as I seek to support my own daughter. I must acknowledge that this perspective comes with the privilege of my positionality within U.S. society both as an educated woman and as a second generation Chicana further removed from the culturally defined rigidity of morality and expectations.

CHICANA MOTHERWORK

These memories help me make sense of several political, social, and cultural contradictions. As Gloria Anzaldúa so aptly describes in her poem "To Live In the Borderlands," in *Borderlands/La Frontera*, Chicanas continuously move in and out of cultural practices in ways that become normalized (194); we recreate and retain practices in ways that come to exemplify our "subtle acts of resistance" that allow us to mark our place in society as Chicanas. In my life with my daughter, this becomes evident in the kinds of experiences that she has with me. While I will expose my daughter to Mexican cultural icons, she will also know U.S. based artists, Sufi poetry, *indigenismo,* and have "Trader Joe's"-inspired chicken tikka masala for dinner. Our homeland will always be directly connected to my mother's small town in Mexico; but because of the larger Chicana community in which we are surrounded, she will also have access to the diversity that is Mexico, manifested in different music genres, foods, and ancestry. The kind of exposure to language that I give to my daughter is also very different from my own as a child. While I only spoke to her in Spanish for the first two years of her life, we now converse primarily in English. My mother fought to remove me from ESL classes because I was bilingual, but I look forward to putting my daughter in a dual-immersion Spanish language program to retain her bilingualism. Language codifies the ways in which we make meaning of the world and if I am not committed to this goal, the ways in which my daughter hears and feels the world will be entirely different. By using *cultura* as a tool to persevere, Chicana motherwork becomes a representation of praxis and resistance in contemporary U.S. society.

Moreover, while Chicana motherwork requires an adaptation of cultural practices tools and exposure, it also means reinterpreting motherhood. My mother was taught to sacrifice herself for her *familia*, a role she readily took on as she gave everything to her family of origin and to the one she created. I think her commitment has been admirable, her strength invincible; yet now that I find myself at a point in my life where my care work is extended to not only my three-year-old daughter, but to my seventy-three-year-old mother as well, I must consider at what costs this selflessness comes. Because my mother's memory is so affected by dementia and depression, everyday tasks have become practically impossible. At times, I'm also struck by the numerous similarities between my daughter and mother: their helplessness, their limited attention span, their inability to think beyond their own worldview. Being at this crossroads makes me realize that my mother has receded into her mind because it became easier to do that. While she embodied strength and perseverance throughout her life, she did little to care for her own emotional well-being. The reality is that in the process of giving it all to the *familia*, she never gave enough to herself. As a Chicana single mother I embrace many aspects of what my *cultura* has to offer, but I refuse to believe that motherhood implies a relinquishment of self. Instead, I choose to argue that motherhood implies the creation of a greater self that is in constant regeneration.

CONCLUSION

During the Christmas of 2008, my sister, my nieces, my daughter, my mother, and I all returned to my mother's *pueblo* for a long overdue visit. It was a first for my daughter and it was beautiful to see her taking in and adapting to the familiar sounds, smells, and rhythms of my own childhood. It was also the first time in months that my mother seemed stronger, happier, and alive. It dawned on me that for those few days she was almost complete again. Her children, grandchildren, siblings, and extended family were not only all together in one place, an experience that she has seldom lived throughout her adult life, but she too was also home. A big part of me felt at home as well. For a moment I actually considered what it would mean for us to stay and be filled physically and emotionally with this homeland; immediately, I'm reminded of the other part of us that remained on *el otro lado* (the other side)—the duality of our experience.

In order to *sobrevivir* (survive), the labor of mothering involves constant negotiations between and among mothers and daughters. For Chicana/Latina mothers, it also requires maneuvering and mothering across cultural and political borders by creating contradictions that meet at the intersections of race and patriarchy. It is a process that can be painful and joyous; the truth remains that I hope to give to my daughter as much of me as my mother gave to us; but, in embracing my multiple identities, I also hope that a part of me remains committed to myself, a lesson that I hope my daughter Milagro (miracle) will embrace.[4]

[1]For discussions on current concepts related to the intersection of Chicana/Latina mothering and education, pedagogy, and ethics, see Andrade and Gonzales Le Denmat; Bernal et. al.; Sandoval; Villenas and Moreno.
[2]See Collins for an explanation of her concept of "motherwork."
[3]For discussions by women of color feminists regarding conflicts with maternal figures see Narayan; Villenas; Woo.
[4]My daughter Milagro was born on the twelfth anniversary of my father's death. This date used to bring memories of terrific pain, but it now signifies the celebration of Milagro's new life, a new life that will be shaped by our family stories, geographies, and our journey together.

WORKS CITED

Andrade, Rosi and Hilda Gonzales Le Denmat. "The Formation of a Code of Ethics for Latina/Chicana Scholars: The Experience of Melding Personal Lessons into Professional Ethics." *Frontiers: A Journal of Women Studies* 20.1 (1999): 151-60. Print.

Anzaldúa, Gloria. *Borderlands/La Frontera: The New Mestiza.* San Francisco: Spinsters/Aunt Lute, 1987. Print.

Bernal, Dolores Delgado, C. Alejandra Elenes, Francisca E. Godinez and Sofia Villenas, eds. *Chicana/Latina Education in Everyday Life: Feminista Perspectives on Pedagogy and Epistimology.* New York: State University of New York Press, 2006. Print.

Collins, Patricia Hill. "Shifting the Center: Race, Class, and Feminist Theorizing About Motherhood." *Representations of Motherhood.* Ed. Donna Basin, Margaret Honey, and Meryle Kaplan. New Haven: Yale University Press, 1994. 56-74. Print.

Delgado Bernal, Dolores. "Learning and Living Pedagogies of the Home: The Mestiza Consciousness of Chicana Students." *Qualitative Studies in Education* 14.5 (2001): 623-39. Print.

Galván, Ruth Trinidad. "*Campesina* Epistemolgies and Pedagogies of the Spirit: Examining Women's *Sobrevivencia.*" *Chicana/Latina Education in Everyday Life: Feminista Perspectives on Pedagogy and Epistimology.* Ed. Dolores Delgado Bernal, C. Alejandra Elenes, Francisca E. Godinez and Sofia Villenas. New York: State University of New York Press, 2006. 161-80. Print.

Knight, Michelle G., Iris R. Dixon, Nadjwa E. L. Norton and Courtney C. Bentley. "Critical Literacies as Feminists Affirmations and Interventions: Contextualizing Latina Youth's Construction of their College-Bound Identities." *Chicana/Latina Education in Everyday Life: Feminista Perspectives on Pedagogy and Epistemology.* Ed. Dolores Delgado Bernal, C. Alejandra Elenes, Francisca E. Godinez and Sofia Villenas. New York: State University of New York Press, 2006. 39-58. Print.

Narayan, Uma. *Dislocating Cultures: Identities, Traditions, and Third World Feminism.* New York: Routledge, 1997. Print.

Sánchez, Graciela I. "La Cultura, La Comunidad, La Familia, y La Libertad." *Gender on the Borderlands: The Frontiers Reader.* Ed. Antonia Castañeda et al. Lincoln: University of Nebraska Press, 2007. 75-86. Print.

Sandoval, Anna. "Building up Our Resistance: Chicanas in Academia." *Frontiers: A Journal of Women Studies* 20.1 (1999): 86-92. Print.

Villenas, Sofia. "Pedagogical Moments in the Borderlands: Latina Mothers Teaching and Learning." *Chicana/Latina Education in Everyday Life: Feminista Perspectives on Pedagogy and Epistemology.* Ed.

Dolores Delgado Bernal, C. Alejandra Elenes, Francisca E. Godinez and Sofia Villenas. New York: State University of New York Press, 2006. 147-60. Print.

Villenas, Sofia, and Melissa Moreno. "To *Valerse por si Misma* between Race, Capitalism, and Patriarchy: Latina Mother-Daughter Pedagogies in North Carolina." *Qualitative Studies in Education* 14.5 (2001): 671-87. Print.

Woo, Merle. "Letter to Ma." *This Bridge Called My Back: Writings by Radical Women of Color.* Ed. Cherrie Moraga and Gloria Anzaldúa. Latham, NY: Kitchen Table, Women of Color, 1983. 140-47. Print.

II.
Counting the Ways to Mother:
Communities and Resources

Life, Death and Second Mothering

Mexican American Mothers, Gang Violence, and *La Virgen de Guadalupe*

RICHARD MORA

SINCE THE EARLY 1980S, LOS ANGELES HAS EXPERIENCED HIGH rates of gang-related homicides.[1] From 1979 to 1994, for example, the Los Angeles Police Department and the Los Angeles County Sheriff's Department reported a total of 7,288 gang-related homicides (Hutson et al. 1031). The high homicide rate has spurred a number of qualitative studies that examine the rise and activities of Los Angeles street gangs, especially Black and Latino gangs and cliques.[2]

Gang violence has a tremendous impact on the victims' families. Yet, the voices of the victims' mothers, and their points of view, are missing from studies that focus on street gangs and gang violence. In order to account for this shortcoming in the literature, this interview study focuses on the emic perspective of the mothers of children killed by gang-related violence.[3] However, this chapter is neither about the dynamics of gang violence, nor about the pathologizing of families with gang-involved children; it is about how ten Mexican American women altered their roles as mothers, independently of one another, by taking their mothering practices beyond the confines of their homes after having their children murdered. Despite their initial feelings of pain and anger, they transformed their children's deaths into affirmations of life. Inspired by *La Virgen de Guadalupe*, the mothers managed their grief and redefined their view of motherhood, extending their mothering practices to the children in their barrios.[4]

This chapter is divided into five sections. The first section is a review of the major literature on the community involvement of mothers, particularly working class women of color. In the second section, I introduce each mother by way of a brief biographical sketch. The third section examines how their children's deaths led the mothers to reflect on their fears of residing in their barrios. Then, I discuss how the mothers drew on their faith in *Guadalupe* to contend with loss, help others, and instruct other mothers about gang violence. The fifth and last section documents how, like *La Virgen*, the women mothered other people's children after the death of their own, and how they worked to improve the lives of the children in their barrios.

"OTHER MOTHERS" OF COLOR

For various reasons, familial and otherwise, women of color in the United States have extended their mothering beyond the confines of their nuclear family. For example, African American feminist Patricia Hill Collins in *Black Feminist Thought: Knowledge, Consciousness, and the Politics of Empowerment* (1991) details how women in African American communities take part in "other mothering," that is, caring for the well-being of children outside of their immediate family. Similarly, in "Chicana/o Family Structure Gender Personality," Denise A. Segura and Jennifer L. Pierce document that women in Chicana/o families tend not only to their own children, but also nurture their nieces, nephews, and godchildren, a practice the authors refer to as "nonexclusive mothering" (64).

For generations, mothers of color have participated in their communities, assisting others and fighting against social inequities, while also caring for their families. Mary Pardo, author of "Mexican American Women Grassroots Community Activists," finds for instance, that the Mexican American women who established the Mothers of East Los Angeles have extended their mothering practices beyond the confines of the home by organizing and lobbying on behalf of their neighborhoods (1-7). Likewise, in "Activist Mothering," a study on the civic participation of low-income Latina and African American women living in Philadelphia and New York, Nancy A. Naples documents that these women's mothering practices, which she denotes as "activist mothering," includes the nurturing of individuals outside their families (245). Additionally, in "Negotiating Power, Identity, and Community," a study comparing the community participation of Anglo women and Latinas from both working class and middle class backgrounds, Naomi Abrahams finds that unlike Anglo women who center their community participation around their own children, Latinas work on behalf of all Latino youth (768-96). Abrahams observes that while middle class Anglo women and middle class Latinas work through established civic organizations, the working class Latinas, whose "activist style ... included a great deal of direct intervention on a one-on-one basis," participated in informal community work (787). As a later section will show, the activist participation described here is echoed by the mothers interviewed. While working to curtail gang violence and improve the lives of children and young people in their communities, they too relied on their identities as mothers.

THE MOTHERS

Ten Mexican American mothers participated in this interview study.[5] All of the women had resided in the barrios of Northeast Los Angeles for at least fifteen years, and each of them had lost at least one child in a gang-related homicide in the previous decade. The interviews were held in either English or Spanish, whichever language each mother chose to express her feelings and experiences surrounding the loss of her child.[6] Initially, I invited each mother to speak freely without much interruption. As the conversation went on, I probed and asked follow-up questions. On average, each face-to-face conversational interview lasted ninety minutes.

In the following few pages, I provide profiles of the mothers. Common to each woman's experience was the blurring of economic/public and domestic/private spheres. That is, at some point during their motherhood, the women were employed outside of the home. Moreover, most of the mothers were married when they lost their child(ren). One major difference in the women's lived experience is that some of the mothers had children who were gang members.

Olga, a woman in her early sixties, was divorced and lived in her own house.[7] Olga's son who was shot to death years earlier was a gang member. While he was alive, the police raided her house on numerous occasions, and rival gang members shot at her house regularly. She had five surviving adult children and described her two daughters as "happily married." However, all three of her surviving sons were single, and two of them were gang members who had been in and out of prison. Her youngest son was in prison, and the other two lived with her. Olga was saddened that her oldest son, the only non-gang member, had refused to take her to the hospital when her son was shot, and refused to associate with his younger brothers because of their gang involvement.

Marta was an articulate woman in her late forties. She lived in a small apartment with her husband and their teenage daughter. It was Marta's second eldest child, a gang member, who was murdered while in his teens. She vividly remembered that she and her deceased son "ate out of the same plate" just hours before he was shot and killed by someone her son considered a friend. She visited her son's grave every week, taking flowers for him from a plant she had growing outside her apartment.

Alicia was in her late fifties. She lived in a house with her husband and her youngest daughter. Her other surviving children were all married and had families of their own. Alicia recalls the morning detectives knocked on her door to tell her that her son had been murdered. She had hoped that they were there to tell her he had been arrested for violating his parole, and that he would have to return to prison. While her son's death was "a big shock," it was "not … a real big shock" to Alicia because her son, who had been a gang member for many years, "was wild." Before his death, Alicia's son had been shot and wounded on multiple occasions. Unlike Marta, Alicia preferred not to visit her son's grave.

Natalia was in her early fifties, had two surviving sons, and lived alone with her cat, which she said watched the apartment when she was not home. Natalia's oldest son, who had been a gang member since he was a young man, was shot to death. Natalia said that what she remembered most was that he would come over to her apartment every Monday morning to take out her trash. She was considering exhuming her son's body and cremating his remains in order to spread his ashes throughout her barrio because she believed that her son, who volunteered with children in the area, belonged in the barrio.

Belen was a thin, fragile looking woman in her sixties. She lived with her husband and their three children, young men in their twenties. Belen lost her two oldest children, a son and a daughter, in two separate incidents. Belen's son was killed in a drive-by shooting. After the loss of her son, Belen's health declined and she became afflicted with diabetes. Some years after the death of her son, Belen's daughter was the victim of similar circumstances. When her daughter was killed, Belen's health worsened. She hardly visited her children's graves, which are side by side, in part because she became very ill after each visit.

Patricia was a single mother in her early fifties. She separated from her husband sometime before her son was killed in a drive-by shooting and subsequently lived in an apartment with her six surviving children, ranging in age from sixteen to thirty. Patricia had her teenage son buried in Mexico, and made a point of visiting his grave every year because visiting her son's grave gave her strength. When she was unable to make the trip, she sent her oldest son.

Josefina was a petite woman in her late forties.[8] She lived in a rented house with her husband and their three surviving children, two sons and a daughter, all in their early twenties. Josefina's youngest son was shot and killed because he refused to join the neighborhood gang. She had her son buried in Mexico because she wanted his grandparents to see that, contrary to the accounts they received, his body had not been disfigured. Soon after her son's murder, she moved a few blocks away to another house because her old house held too many memories of her deceased son. Being in the same neighborhood, she still saw the young men whom residents suspected of murdering her son. Josefina was troubled by the fact that she was unsure which of her son's "friends" were involved in his murder. To make matters worse, Josefina had to care for her two surviving sons, who turned to drugs following their brother's murder.

Beatriz was in her mid-fifties and lived in a house with her mother. When Beatriz's two sons were growing up, she "was [a] mother and father for them." Beatriz's oldest son was murdered by members of his own gang when he tried to defend a fellow gang member whom they were assaulting. Due to the brutal manner in which Beatriz's son was murdered, she was not allowed to view his body. Unlike many of the other mothers, Beatriz did not need or seek out economic assistance from barrio residents to bury her son. Being a single mother, she purchased a family funeral plan when her sons were young to ensure that she and her children would be buried side by side, and so that her family would not have to "wash cars" as others in her neighborhood sometimes did in order to cover funeral expenses.

Sofia was a woman in her mid-fifties. She lived in an apartment with her husband, her daughter, and her grandchild. Sofia's other three surviving children were all grown men living in Mexico. Her deceased son, who was not a gang member, was shot and killed as an adult. Still, she did not like to think about her son's death. "I would like to forget this like a dream," Sofia said. Even when her husband began to talk about how much he missed their son, she would not talk about her deceased child.

Adriana was a soft-spoken woman in her mid-forties. She lived in a rented house with her husband and five children. Adriana's oldest son died after being shot multiple times. He had been involved in a gang since the age of twelve, and was a teenager when he was killed. Adriana wanted to have her son buried in Mexico, but could not afford the expense. Instead, she buried her son in a Los Angeles area cemetery. Adriana had an album full of pictures of her son's burial, including a few of her son in his coffin, which she liked to look at even though doing so caused her to cry.

SAME BARRIOS, NEW FEARS

Preceding their children's deaths, the mothers had good cause to be concerned that their children could become victims of violence. As Father Martín, who has spent over twenty-five years at a parish frequented by many of the women, attested: "The funerals that have been held here, at the parish—there has been a much greater percentage of young people than of elderly people ... And the majority of the young people died in a violent manner." Nonetheless, some of the mothers did not want to accept that gang violence could ever touch their lives.

Regardless of what the mothers may have thought previously, their children's deaths introduced fear of gang violence into their lives. According to Alicia, the fear was persistent:

You just pray when your other children go out. There's always a fear, there is always a fear when your other children go out.... And, you are afraid. And, I think that fear will never go away. You are afraid for them after that.... So that has done something ... you don't feel safe anymore.

Other parents of murdered children have also experienced the fear that Alicia spoke of and often remained afraid until the murderer was incarcerated (Knapp 95-96). However, for the mothers in this study, the situation was somewhat different. Since gang violence was a daily reality in their barrios, the prospect of imprisoning those who murdered their children did not abate their fear. Thus, each mother's fear was rooted in her awareness that her children lived everyday under the same threat that claimed her deceased child(ren).

Why didn't the mothers move out of the barrios? One significant reason is that their limited income did not offer them much choice. As Alicia asserted, "You live where you *can*. You buy a house where you can. You rent where there is an apartment." The only neighborhoods where the women and their families could afford to reside were gang-ridden. Given their options, the mothers stayed in their barrios, concluding that their children were safer where they were known.[9]

"OH, HOLY MOTHER, YOU THAT KNOWS THE HEARTS OF THE MOTHERS."

Each of the women in this study acquired her veneration of *La Virgen de Guadalupe* while growing up in a Mexican Catholic home. The mothers saw *Guadalupe* as a safeguard, as a mother who provided divine intervention. As Sofia explained, "[W]e, as Mexicans, have a very special love for The Holy Virgin. My parents taught me to have that love for Her, that veneration for *La Virgen* because She is the mother of God. And, well, one trusts in Her and thinks that one can obtain everything from Her." According to Father Martín, the portrayal of *Guadalupe* as a maternal figure is based on Her first appearance:

> La Virgen, *Her role when She appeared was to demonstrate Her loving care and Her love to the children of this land…. She, more than anything else, came to be a mother…. [And, when She came She said to those who were suffering] "Am I not here, I that am your mother?"… [T]he role of* La Virgen, *more than anything else, is maternal…. The role that* La Virgen *now has is of a mother.*

Father Martín concludes that, "*La Virgen* had her son and now she has all of us as children."

As *Catolicas de crianza*, the mothers prayed regularly to *La Virgen*.[10] Before their children were killed, they asked Her for assistance with many problems, including marital and financial difficulties as well as protection for family members. Most of all, the mothers prayed to *La Virgen* for their children's safety, particularly in light of the gang violence in their barrios. The women whose children were gang members were especially distressed about their children's well-being. Alicia, for example, "prayed that [police detectives] would pick [her son] up and put him in jail [because] at least he would be alive."

While the women felt they could rely on all or most of their relatives and friends, they preferred to commune with *La Virgen* through prayer and meditation because She offered a level of comfort and support that others could not readily provide. Each of the mothers believed that *Guadalupe* could understand her grief and suffering because She too had lost her son. Olga, who attended mass almost every day and recited rosaries both on her own and with other women in her barrio, stated: "I used to always say [following the death of my son], 'Oh, Holy Mother, unite my sorrow with Yours.' I think that by saying that so much ... that my pain became less. Less each day." Similarly, Marta said, "*La Virgen* was all my moral support. Because ... I already believed in *La Virgen*. I have a very big faith in Her." Even Natalia, who no longer considered herself Catholic, continued to confide in *La Virgen*:

> *I pray to Her because She's a mother and I am a mother. And, we share the same hurt or that same hurting because She can understand where I'm coming from and a man can't.... If I ask Her for my kids or my family, She can understand me because She is a mother. She is a nurturer.... You talk to Her just like the mother in you. You ask Her for the help of a mother.*

Like Natalia, all the other mothers also turned to Guadalupe because above all else She was one of them—a mother whose child was murdered.

Guadalupe not only helped the mothers contend with their grief, but She also became an even greater model of motherhood for them. *La Virgen* provided these women with a sense of motherly determination and they, therefore, gave the social identity of mother even greater primacy in their lives. Moreover, like *Guadalupe*, the mothers volunteered their emotional support to other mothers who had lost children to gang violence.

The mothers' commitment to helping other women in their barrios was based on their understanding that nothing was more life altering for a mother than to outlive her child(ren). According to Patricia, a mother's loss of her child is devastating: "I, as a mother who has already lost mine, would not want to see that another mother lose her child, because you do not wish that on anybody. On the contrary, I wish that what happened to me no [other] mother suffers." Similarly, Natalia said, "When someone's son is killed, I pray to God because I know what [the mother] is going through. And, I just hope that she can deal with it because you always have that void. You always miss that person."

When advising other mothers on dealing with their loss, they offered their own experiences and suggested praying to *La Virgen*. Seeing *Guadalupe* as a source of their own relief, the mothers felt that the Holy Mother would aid others as well. Beatriz said that she "tell[s] all the mothers that go through [the loss of a child] to 'Ask *La Virgen* [for what you need to cope], because who more than She has suffered the same pain?'" In Josefina's case, she was even able to empathize with the mother of one of the young men suspected of murdering her son:

> *When they killed my son, the mother fell to her knees and told me, "[D]on't put my son in jail! Don't put him there!" I answered her: "Did you see your son kill my son? No? Well, neither did I. Only the people say it was him, but we don't know who it was." And, the mother cried and cried for her son. And, I cried for mine, as well. She was hurting for her son. I was hurting for mine.*

For Josefina, the potential loss of this other mother's son to incarceration was comparable to her loss. By connecting in this manner with other mothers, the women in this study emulated *Guadalupe*, who provided them with an example of how to nurture others.

ON BEING "A SECOND MOTHER": COMMUNITY INVOLVEMENT AND HOPE

The loss of their children gave each of these women a newfound purpose. With the hope of a better future for the children and parents in their communities, these mothers proactively worked to curtail gang violence by addressing the underlying causes of gang participation, such as the lack of employment, education, and guidance for the children in their communities. Like *Guadalupe*, they too sought to be of service to others in their capacity as mothers.

Of the mothers, six of them engaged in community level interventions.

As civically engaged residents of their communities, these women relied on their role as mothers while participating in community meetings, lobbying politicians on behalf of young people, and publicly attempting to influence policies that could impact their communities. By carrying out these actions, the mothers followed in the footsteps of not only *La Virgen*, but also of other women who have connected their civic participation with their motherhood, such as Las Madres de La Plaza de Mayo in Argentina (Navarro 241-43), some feminist politicos in Mexico (Escandón 199-206), and the women who influenced welfare states when these states were establishing their administrative structures (Koven and Michel 1076-98; Ladd-Taylor 1-11).

Natalia, for example, was involved in community planning meetings for the proposed construction of a new building intended to house a public library and a child care center. She attended the meetings because she believed that the project would be beneficial to young, working mothers in her community who were in need of child care. Similarly, she believed that the new library might attract young people who would otherwise be out on the streets. Natalia's inspiration for doing community work came from her deceased son, who regularly attended community meetings and coached little league baseball before he was murdered. Natalia reflected on losing her son and stated: "It made me more aware of my community. That's how it changed my life.... When he died, he made me more aware of what I needed to go out and do. That I needed to get involved. That I needed to talk with the kids. That I needed to be a second mother to them. That's how it changed my life. Doing community work."

Although some of the people in the mothers' barrios had given up on young men involved in gangs and believed they did not have any potential, the mothers I interviewed believed that these young men could and had to be reached. Marta eloquently added to the mothers' sentiment: "If those young men [in gangs] were given birth to by a woman, [then] those young men are human beings." The problem from their standpoint was that the young gang members were children in need of additional guidance from a mother as well as opportunities in society. Like a few of the other mothers, Marta tried to convince local politicians to create jobs for young people in her neighborhood. She believed that if they were employed, young men would not join gangs or participate in illicit gang activities, such as selling drugs.

Natalia, who worked at a neighborhood school, also reached out to young people, including gang members. She spoke to the young people that she interacted with at school about the problems they had at home and in school, and also tried to get them to think seriously about their futures by stressing the importance of an education. Natalia informed the teenagers in her community about college preparation programs, such as Upward Bound, and helped some gang members get part-time jobs. She said, "We all have to be there for the kids. If they have a problem, if they need a job, stuff like that. That's what I try to do now." Natalia believed that having young people work during their vacation would help them and their families financially. Additionally, she too felt that employment would keep teenagers off the streets and out of gangs.

For most of these mothers, being "a second mother" in their barrios also involved sharing their experiences with young people, no matter how painful, in the hopes that it would positively impact their lives.[11] These women, in fact, took every chance they had to intervene in the lives of adolescents with life stories, parables that held forewarning of the dangers in their barrios. By exposing themselves in this way, they drew upon their compassion to care for other people's children in much the same way they saw *Guadalupe* intervening in the lives of human beings.

For example, Josefina, who passed the spot where her son was murdered on her way to work each day, warned the young men she saw there about the dangers of drugs and that dressing like a gang member in her barrio could be as dangerous as actually being one:

> *When I run into [young men] I speak with them. Or, if I see them sitting in the place where my son died I tell them, "Remove yourself from there because cars pass by and they shoot bullets." Or, I see someone who is going wrong and I tell him: "Don't dress like that because you are not gang members, but [gang members] may mistake you [for one]. And, I am telling you all from experience because my son died." And, when I see that they are into drugs and all that, I tell them, "That is not right because that is drying your brain ... you forget things being into drugs and all that."*

Josefina's counsel was rooted in her lived experiences. Having had a child murdered because he refused to join the neighborhood gang, she warned the young men against wearing gang attire like that worn by her deceased son. Moreover, Josefina made a point of talking with young drug users she saw on the streets about the harmful effects drugs had on her surviving sons and how she had suffered as a result.

Likewise, Adriana talked with young men about the dangers that came with wearing gang attire and advised them against participating in gang activities. She mentioned her warnings:

> *I tell them that if they are not gang members they should not wear that [type of] clothing because they can be mistaken for them. I tell them that they should study. Here [in the U.S.] there are a lot of opportunities. That they should not get into gangs and that they not get others into [gangs].*
> [Researcher: And what do they respond?]
> *That they are not [gang members]. That they only like dressing that way. And, I tell them that they are not gang members, but they may be mistaken for them. There are many who have been killed because of that.*

The young men also received the same advice from Adriana about getting an education. Having come from Mexico with little education herself, she pointed out that in the United States there are more opportunities to get a good education than in Mexico, and advised them to take advantage of them.

Beatriz, whose son was murdered by "friends," advised the young men she ran across about the true nature of friendship: While she did not want them to distrust others, Beatriz believed that at their age they considered almost anyone they knew a friend.

> *I talk with them sometimes. When [the opportunity] offers itself. I talk with them and I tell them what I have seen and of the experiences that I have had…. I advise them not to believe everything their friends tell them. A real friend will not induce them to get into problems nor cause them harm. That is a real friend. But, the one that tells them, "Look, let's do this, let's do that, bad things that will harm [them], that is not [their] friend."*

To reinforce her point, Beatriz explained to young men that her son was killed by fellow gang members he had considered "friends." Beatriz was not sure whether young men took her advice, but since they listened attentively she felt that she was at least conveying her message.

Moreover, to dissuade young men in their barrios from joining gangs, jeopardizing their lives, and harming others, both Josefina and Adriana described for them the anguish that comes with being a mother. Josefina explained to them: "If you kill ... it hurts [a mother] the same.... If they shoot [a mother's] son it hurts [her] because as a mother everything hurts you. Everything hurts you. Because what your children do hurts you." Likewise, Adriana asked the young men "if they [had] want[ed] to see their mothers cry like they [saw her crying]."

The women possessed a great deal of moral authority, which they used effectively when interacting with young men and adolescents in their barrios. According to the mothers, the root of their moral authority was twofold. One, people empathized with their loss. Two, like *Guadalupe*, they were mothers, a social role valued within their culture and barrios.[12]

The mothers' second mothering was an extension of "nonexclusive mothering," which many Chicana/o families practice, "in contrast to the exclusive approach identified in European-American families" (Segura and Pierce 64). Reflecting on the role of Mexican women in their families, the Chicana writer Ana Castillo states in "Extraordinary Women": "We [women] do what we must to protect and provide for our young, our families, our tribes" (78). That such "a collectivist orientation" is part of the mothers' cultural traditions helps to explain why they felt comfortable extending their mothering practices beyond their extended homes (Segura and Pierce 70).

CONCLUSION

After the death of their children, the mothers in my study redefined their role of mothering. Inspired by *La Virgen de Guadalupe*, who they saw not as a passive deity, but as a mother engaged in the world—in the here and now—the mothers opted to turn their grief into action. They attended community meetings, and sought out jobs for, and spoke to, the young people in their barrios, all in the hopes of ensuring a better future for these children. By carrying out such community work, the women, like so many other women of color, defied "the dominant definition of motherhood ... [that emphasizes] work performed within the private sphere of the family or in face-to-face interaction with" the individuals who actually benefit from a mother's work (Naples 230).

[1]Law enforcement agencies throughout the country use different criteria to determine whether a homicide is gang-related. In this work, I use the criteria adopted by the Los Angeles Police Department (LAPD), since the geographical area under study falls within its jurisdiction. For details of the criteria, see Maxson and Klein 76.
[2]For a detailed discussion of how Mexican American street gangs formed in Los Angeles, see Moore (1991, 1978); Moore and Vigil; Vigil, *A Rainbow of Gangs*; Vigil, *Barrio Gangs*.
[3]An emic perspective refers to the perspective of insiders, or those under study. It stands in contrast to the etic perspective, which refers to the outsider perspective, or that of an observer.
[4]*La Virgen de Guadalupe* is a brown skinned manifestation of the Virgin Mary said to have appeared on Tepeyac Hill near Mexico City in 1531. For more details, see Burkhart 198-200. Throughout this study, barrio is used to refer to Latino-populated, low-income/working class neighborhoods in which established gangs exist.
[5]"Mexican American" is used in this study to refer to both U.S. citizens of Mexican heritage and Mexican citizens who reside in the United States.
[6]Two of the mothers, Alicia and Natalia, opted to speak in English. All other respondents conversed in Spanish. I provide the translations in this paper.
[7]All the names in this study have been changed. In order to ensure anonymity, the information in the sketches is intentionally vague. The timeframes mentioned are based on the 1998 period when the interviews were conducted.
[8]Josefina has since passed away.
[9]For research that examines the relationship between the social ties of community residents and issues of safety, see Wilson; Sampson et al.
[10]This phrase refers to individuals raised as Catholics. See Rodríguez for a discussion of the relationship between Mexican-American women who are *Catolicas de crianza* and *Guadalupe*.
[11]The mothers spoke primarily with young men because in their neighborhoods there were few female gang members.

¹²See Baca Zinn for a discussion of Mexican American families and the place of mothers within them.

WORKS CITED

Abrahams, Naomi. "Negotiating Power, Identity, and Community: Women's Community Participation." *Gender and Society* 10.7 (1996): 768-96. Print.

Burkhart, Louise M. "The Cult of the Virgin of Guadalupe in Mexico." *South and Meso-American Native Spirituality: From the Cult of the Feathered Serpent to the Theology of Liberation.* Ed. Gary Gossen and Miguel León- Portilla. New York: Crossroad, 1993. 198-223. Print.

Castillo, Ana. "Extraordinarily Woman." *Goddess of the Americas: Writings on the Virgin of Guadalupe.* Ed. Castillo. New York: Riverhead, 1997. 72-78. Print.

Collins, Patricia Hill. *Black Feminist Thought: Knowledge, Consciousness, and the Politics of Empowerment.* New York: Routledge. 1991. Print.

Escandón, Carmen Ramos. "Women's Movements, Feminism, and Mexican Politics." *The Women's Movement in Latin America: Participation and Democracy.* 2nd ed. Ed. Jane S. Jaquette. Boulder, C0: Westview, 1994. 199-221. Print.

Hutson, H. Range, Deidere Anglin, Demetrios N. Kyriacou, Joel Hart, and Kevin Spears. "The Epidemic of Gang-Related Homicides in Los Angeles County from 1979 through 1994." *JAMA* 274.13 (1995): 1031-36. Print.

Knapp, Ronald J. *Beyond Endurance: When A Child Dies.* New York: Schocken, 1986. Print.

Koven, Seth, and Sonya Michel. "Womanly Duties: Maternalist Politics and the Origins of the Welfare States in France, Germany, Great Britain, and the United States, 1880-1920." *American Historical Review* 95 (1990): 1076-108. Print.

Ladd-Taylor, Molly. *Mother-Work: Women, Child Welfare, and the State, 1890-1930.* Chicago: University of Illinois Press, 1994. Print.

Maxson, Cheryl L., and Malcolm W. Klein. "Street Gang Violence: Twice as Great, or Half as Great?" *Gangs in America.* Ed. C. Ronald Huff. Newbury Park, CA: Sage, 1990. 71-100. Print.

Moore, Joan W. *Going Down to the Barrio: Homeboys and Homegirls in Change.* Philadelphia: Temple University Press, 1991. Print.

Moore, Joan W. *Homeboys: Gangs, Drugs and Prisons in the Barrios of Los Angeles*. Philadelphia: Temple University Press, 1978. Print.

Moore, Joan W., and James Diego Vigil. "Chicano Gangs: Group Norms and Individual Factors Related to Adult Criminality." *Aztlán* 18 (1987): 27-44. Print.

Naples, Nancy A. "Activist Mothering: Cross-Generational Continuity in the Community Work of Women From Low-Income Urban Neighborhoods." *Race, Class, and Gender: Common Bonds, Different Voices*. Ed. Esther Ngan-ling Chow, Doris Wilkinson, and Maxine Baca Zinn. Thousand Oaks, CA: Sage, 1996. 223-45. Print.

Navarro, Marysa. "The Personal is Political: Las Madres de Plaza de Mayo." *Power and Popular Protest: Latin American Social Movements*. Ed. Susan Eckstein. Berkeley, CA: University of California Press, 1989. 241-58. Print.

Pardo, Mary. "Mexican American Women Grassroots Community Activists (Mothers of East Los Angeles)." *Frontiers: A Journal of Women's Studies* 11.10 (1990): 1-7. Print.

Rodríguez, Jeanette. *Our Lady of Guadalupe: Empowerment Among Mexican American Women*. Austin: University of Texas Press, 1994. Print.

Sampson, Robert J., Stephen Raudenbush, and Felton Earls. "Neighborhoods and Violent Crime: A Multilevel Study of Collective Efficacy." *Science* 277 (1997): 918-24. Print.

Segura, Denise A., and Jennifer L. Pierce. "Chicana/o Family Structure Gender Personality: Chodorow, Familism, and Psychoanalytic Sociology Revisited." *Signs* 19.1 (1993): 62-91. Print.

Vigil, James Diego. *Barrio Gangs: Street Life and Identity in Southern California*. Austin: University of Texas Press, 1988. Print.

Vigil, James Diego. *A Rainbow of Gangs: Street Cultures in the Mega-City*. Austin: University Texas Press, 2002. Print.

Wilson, William Julius. *When Work Disappears: The World of the New Urban Poor*. New York: Knopf, 1997. Print.

Zinn, Maxine Baca. "Familism Among Chicanos: A Theoretical Review." *Humboldt Journal of Social Relations* 10 (1982-3): 224-38. Print.

"No hay nada tan mala..."
(There Is Nothing So Bad)

Latina Mothering Across Generations

LAURA RUTH JOHNSON

A PUERTO RICAN WOMAN IN HER TWENTIES TAKES THE STAGE TO read a piece of her poetry at an International Women's Day conference. She wears a black pantsuit and her hair is neatly pulled and slicked back into an attractive bun. She begins a bit nervously, her cheeks a little flushed, and becomes emotional during her first poem, which addresses her experience of childhood sexual abuse. She regains her composure and confidently proceeds, raising her fist at times for emphasis. She exudes a confidence that contrasts with the tentativeness of some of her initial poetic performances, and after a few years of sharing her poetry publicly, she has obviously found her "voice." Her performance receives thunderous applause and she beams brightly at the attention. Afterwards, she tells me about the recent events in her life. She has started a new job at a hospital which pays over $10 an hour plus benefits, and provides tuition remission for medical classes she is taking at a local college. She tells me that her husband, an Ecuadorian immigrant, is also beginning a new job as a train operator for the local transportation authority, where he will be starting at a salary of close to $20 an hour.

The above woman, named Rosa,[1] had recently graduated from The Family Learning Center (FLC), a family literacy program serving Latina mothers on the Near Northwest Side of Chicago. In addition to offering classes towards a high school diploma, the program provided on-site child care and parenting workshops. The FLC was part of the Puerto Rican Cultural Center (PRCC), a community-based organization that has been offering educational and cultural services to the community for thirty-five years. Many of the women attending the FLC were single heads of households and all had given birth to their children while adolescents. They all had also left high school before graduating for a variety of reasons and were returning to the FLC to achieve their high school diploma. Many of the women's mothers were also heads of households; a number of their mothers had grown up in Puerto Rico or Mexico and had migrated to Chicago, often under perilous conditions. Unfortunately, in Chicago, their lives were often not much improved than the situation in their homeland: women remembered their mothers as suffering abuse at the hands of their fathers and having to work two jobs to support the family. Yet, despite some of these memories of the obstacles their mothers faced, FLC participants also described their mothers as finding time to celebrate birthdays, or providing life lessons that they have used in their own roles as mothers. While their mothers had certainly struggled throughout their lives, the women were determined to have a better life, or at least—to borrow the words of one participant—"not a worser thing" than what their mothers had experienced.

The women's experiences, as children *and* mothers, are compelling in the way that they speak to some of the current discourses about poverty and mothering, especially the ways in which poor young mothers have often been negatively portrayed within the media: irresponsible, un-educated, and promiscuous, and above all as underprepared and unfit to raise a child. Under this deficit-oriented stereotypical view, such mothers are portrayed as caught up in a "cycle of stigma" (Kelly 445), and often viewed as "girls from flawed backgrounds making tragic mistakes" (429). While more recently there have been more positive and complex popular media images of teen childbearing, such as in the film *Juno* (2007) and the television show *The Secret Life of the American Teenager* (2008), these portrayals have mostly focused on white middle to upper class young mothers. Young Latina mothers, on the other hand, have largely been absent as the subject of more upbeat or nuanced images of teen mothers.

Much of the rhetoric utilized within public policy debates has referred to negative traits associated with mothering in poverty that are trans-mitted from generation to generation. For example, ad campaigns for literacy programs refer to the need to break intergenerational cycles of poverty, illiteracy, adolescent childbearing, and bad mothering (Lewis; Moynihan). In her historical work examining issues related to Puerto Rican women and reproduction, Laura Briggs has discussed how such deficit-oriented notions have promoted the stereotype of the Puerto Rican "welfare queen," who abuses public assistance for her own benefit, and have forwarded negative images of Puerto Rican women as sexualized and immoral. Briggs asserts that the "narratives of bad mothering" about Puerto Rican mothers were employed to explain the causes of Puerto Rican poverty, as well as to support policies aimed at controlling the growth of the Puerto Rican population (76-77).

While there are certainly harmful behaviors and practices that are repeated by successive generations, the problem with the aforementioned view is that it ignores the benefits and strengths that are often passed down from parent to child, or the ways that painful experiences could be transformed into lessons that help women chart a more positive course for the future, for themselves, and their children. Moreover, such perspectives often promote a unitary view of parenting and mothering—positing a particular parenting style as most optimal—and in the process ignore the myriad other ways that parents rear and socialize their children.

Given some of the above issues and perspectives, this chapter aims to provide an alternate window on Latina motherhood, by exploring the resources that Latina mothers at the FLC drew on in their mothering role, which often included the stories and experiences of their own mothers. While many theorists and researchers have examined the ways in which familial knowledge frameworks serve as resources for children (Delgado-Gaitán; González, Moll, and Amanti; Zentella), these "funds of knowledge" theories have usually focused on specific skills or expertise rather than on the role that sharing experiences of struggle can play in imparting life lessons and developing resilience in children (González, Moll, and Amanti). Some researchers have focused on strategies that mothers use to help impart lessons of resistance in their daughters, lessons that are particularly important for low-income women of color. More specifically, Janie V. Ward examined the ways that African American women helped "raise resisters," through the sharing of stories and valuable lessons about racism (89-93). Similarly, Nancy López's research with young second-generation working class Caribbean women in *Hopeful Girls, Troubled Boys: Race and Gender Disparity in Urban Education* (2003) demonstrated how they built upon the struggles and experiences of their mothers, and in the process "articulated a homegrown feminist discourse rooted in their mothers' actions" (127). In a similar vein, research conducted with Latina women and mothers by Michelle Fine and Lois Weis in *The Unknown City: The Lives of Poor and Working-Class Young Adults* (1998) revealed how the Latinas they interviewed for their study were "refusing the betrayal of a life they were promised and denied," by challenging traditional gender roles, embodying a spirit of resistance, and attempting to provide a better life for their children (207). These studies provide substantiation regarding the importance of stories and life lessons as a survival and child-rearing strategy for women of color, in general, and Latina mothers, in particular.

The data shared here is drawn from a larger dissertation study, conducted from 2002-2004, at the FLC and within the surrounding community. It is hoped that such information can contribute to more informed and enriched perspectives on low-income Latina mothers and add to existing research that has sought to better understand and portray low-income motherhood (Fine and Weis; Kelly) and, more particularly, describe specific mothering strategies used by Latina mothers and families. My aim is to demonstrate how challenges, such as the difficult situation incurred by Rosa and described at the beginning of this chapter, can serve as sources of strength and sites of transformation, rather than as missteps to be replicated intergenerationally. Within the research literature and the public discourse, adolescent childbearing has usually been viewed as a ruinous situation for mother and child, and the cause of societal ills such as increasing high school dropout rates and poverty. However, researchers, such as Amira Proweller and Lee SmithBattle, have spotlighted the ways that, for some women, especially those engaging in destructive practices, motherhood can function as a site of transformation, a possibility that helps them chart new goals and develop more positive life purposes (Proweller 107-8; SmithBattle 124). Another take on teen motherhood is offered in Nilda Flores-González's study of Latino students' identity development, which found that when deciding to drop out of high school to care for a child—what she refers to as experimenting with a "family identity"—many young Latina women had already "adopted a pattern of increased disengagement from school that made the choice an easy one" (131). Such research findings underscore the need to rethink the "consequences" of adolescent childbearing and offer more nuanced portrayals of the experience of teen motherhood that include descriptions of its challenges *and* successes.

STUDY DETAILS

I first became acquainted with the Puerto Rican Cultural Center (PRCC) and its programs as the director of the Family Learning Center (FLC). Hired off the initial grant, I was responsible for designing family literacy activities and developing curriculum, and served in the director role for five years (1993-1998). In 2002, I returned to the FLC to conduct my dissertation research. One specific area I explored involved the ways that women obtained knowledge about child rearing and the different ways that they enacted this knowledge (Johnson, "Challenging Best Practices"; Johnson, "History in Our Hands"). I also instructed an oral history course that provided me with information regarding how stories and experiences were transmitted intergenerationally.

As stated earlier, the FLC was a project of the PRCC, a community-based organization with programs that included an alternative high school, a bilingual childcare, a youth-run cultural space, and a health initiative. All of the programs focused on Puerto Rican culture and encouraged participants to engage in community events and activities. The PRCC was founded in the 1970s to provide an educational and cultural alternative to mainstream institutions that were focused on assimilation and provided little in the way of culturally relevant services. This emphasis reflects other efforts within the Puerto Rican diaspora to reclaim and preserve their history, culture, and traditions (Flores). Within the FLC, this cultural focus meant that participants' familial experiences were viewed as resources; the program often incorporated oral history projects into classes and parenting workshops included discussions of cultural child-rearing practices, Spanish children's songs, and traditions alongside some of the more standard parent education fare, such as child development.

The FLC has been providing family literacy and educational services to families since 1994. Initially funded through an Even Start family literacy grant, the program offered adult education and early childhood services, along with family activities and parenting workshops. During my study, women attending the program ranged in age from 17-29. They had enrolled in the FLC to pursue their high school diploma and attended classes and workshops five days a week. The majority of women enrolled in the FLC were Puerto Rican, but there were also Mexican, Dominican, and African American students attending. This chapter focuses primarily on the experiences of the Puerto Rican students who attended the program. The women who participated in my study mostly spoke English as their first language, but also spoke Spanish, and often mixed Spanish and English together. Most all of the women were born in the mainland United States, although one young woman was born in Puerto Rico and another in Mexico.

This particular study utilized an ethnographic approach to gather data and gain insight into particular Puerto Rican and Latina child-rearing strategies and knowledge. I conducted in-depth interviews with 15 enrolled women, (12 Puerto Rican, 1 Mexican, 2 Puerto Rican/Anglo) as well as observed program classes and activities, and participated in community events. The women enrolled in the program—about 40 during the period of my study—also conducted life history interviews with their mothers, aunts, and grandmothers, which provided another source of data. Data was analyzed inductively and theories about Latina motherhood in this setting were generated from a close reading of the data. Although it is hoped that this study can offer useful information regarding Latina motherhood, in accordance with a qualitative approach, the findings included herein are certainly not meant to be generalized to all Latina mothers.

"*NO HAY NADA TAN MALA*" OR "THERE IS NOTHING SO BAD THAT GOOD CANNOT COME FROM IT": LESSONS IN RESILIENCY AND SURVIVAL

Within parenting classes and oral history workshops, women at the FLC often discussed particular child-rearing strategies utilized by their own mothers. These included common disciplinary practices, folk remedies for curing the hiccups, beliefs about how to ward off *el mal de ojo* (the evil eye), and proverbs utilized to inculcate behavior or dole out advice. Many of these proverbs, referred to as *refranes*, also contained important values and moral teachings. Other researchers have documented the salience of proverbs in Latino communities and their role in child rearing, such as the use of *consejos* (advice) or *dichos* (sayings) within Mexican immigrant families (Delgado-Gaitán; Espinoza-Herold; and Valdés). These proverbs also represent "a reservoir of culturally based resilience strategies" that Latino families deploy to teach lessons of survival and resistance to adverse and marginal circumstances (Espinoza-Herold 262).

In an interview, Rosa described her memories of her mother employing proverbs as a way of reinforcing respectful behavior in herself and her sister: "When I used to make fun of her she used to be like, 'How you see me, you will be.'"

The *refranes* that I heard utilized within the community addressed a multitude of concepts, such as independence, respect, reciprocity, optimism, and patience. Some tackled these values or behaviors directly, while others were more nebulous. For example, "children talk when roosters piss" refers to children being quiet and well-behaved. The particularly prevalent *refrán* "*no hay mal que por bien que venga,*" ("There is nothing bad that good cannot come from it") refers to being optimistic in the face of adversity and trying to draw benefits from especially painful situations (Rivera). The sentiment of this proverb is useful in that it provides an alternative to the "breaking cycles" discourse often used to describe low-income Latino mothers. In the sections that follow, I will deploy this *refrán* to examine how Latina women in the FLC navigated their roles as mothers.

THE IMPORTANCE OF SHARING STORIES

During interviews and within classes, the Latina women enrolled in the FLC often discussed the experiences of their mothers and grandmothers and especially spoke about the struggles and obstacles incurred by the females in their family. Other researchers have described how, among Latinas, the telling and sharing of stories of survival and resistance is part of a pedagogy of "*convivencia,*" or communalism, and thus provides "communal spaces for teaching and learning" (Villenas, "Convivencia" 274). The struggles discussed at the FLC included abuse at the hands of husbands, working multiple jobs to support the family, and being exploited at work. For example, 19-year-old Raquel described her father as having "that everything problem," and detailed how he expended familial resources on his drug and alcohol addiction:

> *He would be home every day after work, eating, you know whatever, and when he gets that check, he would never come home, until he wastes every [bit of] money, you know.... They used to cut our lights off. We used to be a month without lights. For a month without hot water. Or gas.... So [my mom] was always out, trying to look for a job or cleaning houses and [doing] stuff for money.*

Raquel's experience illustrates how Latina women have often had to marshal together resources to provide for their children, by piecing together temporary work or working in the domestic sphere (Toro-Morn). Raquel's reflection on the challenges faced by her mother also illustrates the important life lessons that young Latinas glean from their observation of their mothers.

The oral history interviews FLC women conducted with women in their family provided an opportunity to learn about the struggles of their female forebears in their own words. For example, when Inés, a nineteen-year-old mother of three children, was recounting her interview with her mother to classmates, she shared how as a child her mother regularly witnessed her own mother being abused by her father, who she described as a "king" who "got to eat everything good at the table and they were eating *avena* (oatmeal) made out of water." Eventually, Inés' grandmother was forced to live under Chicago's viaducts with her eight children. After her interview, Rosa summed up her mother's life with the following statement: "The life of my mom is just like struggles." In addition, Marta's mother provided a similar description of her own life when she referred to it as "*una vida bien sufrida*" (a life of suffering) and described in detail the many hardships she incurred, which included having to drop out of school as a young girl to work and being forced to marry a man thirty years her senior as part of an arranged marriage.

The sharing of stories between generations of women taught the young mothers valuable life lessons about struggle, particularly as related to the situation of Latinas. Other researchers (Benmayor et al.; Olmedo) have documented the importance of sharing stories across generations of Puerto Rican women and the role such an interaction can play in promoting both intergenerational "continuity and change" (Benmayor et al. 1-13). That is, although the women often maintained certain traditions and had experiences in common with previous generations of Latinas in their family, they also sought to break away from some of these experiences. While women at the FLC were often shocked and angered at the adversity experienced by their mothers and grandmothers, for some these stories of struggle also fostered an awareness and appreciation of the sacrifices their mothers made to provide for them. Learning about these experiences also taught them powerful lessons of resilience, and many of the women described how they hoped to transform some of these negative experiences into a more positive life course for themselves and their children.

"NOT A WORSER THING": INTERRUPTING AND TRANSFORMING "CYCLES"

Within the context of interviews and classroom activities, enrolled women often articulated aspirations for the future of themselves and their children. In many cases, these were discussed in relation to the experiences of their mothers and other women in their family. While there were certainly practices and values that they wanted to emulate, they often used these experiences as exemplars of a life that they wanted to avoid. For example, when she was asked what she envisioned her life would be like in three to five years, Raquel referenced the struggles incurred by her mother as something she wanted to sidestep. She utilized the term "good mother and father life" as the type of life she aspired to, and defined this phrase as follows:

> I don't know what it means, but I know it's not what my mother went through. You know, and I know it's not what my aunt's going through. Or what my grandma went through. Or what some of my friends are going through right now…. Or always getting whooped. Having that mother and father life…. I don't know what it is, but I know it's gotta be different than what my family did. It's not going to be a worser thing, but a better thing…. I'll get there. I'll make sure I do everything right. I'll have my diploma.

In the process of delineating her idealized life goals, Raquel also narrated the difficult history of other women in her family and community. While she admitted that her vision of her future life was still indeterminate, she possessed a well-defined idea of the type of life she wanted to steer clear of, or more specifically, what her mother, aunt, and grandmother "went through," which included regularly "getting whooped" by their spouses.

In order to have a "better life," FLC women often had to make conscious choices regarding their relationships with men, which involved actively resisting the limitations of traditional gender roles and expectations. For example, Wanda, a 19-year-old mother of a male toddler, recounted why she did not want to remain with her son's father:

*He wanted a woman type that was always in the house. He didn't
want me to go to school. He wanted me at home, [to] wash dishes,
take care of his house, take care of his kids, and that's it. .... And I
didn't want that type of life.*

Wanda's description of the "woman type" desired by her boyfriend
suggests the traditional homemaker whose life is confined to the domestic sphere, who is "always in the house." Interestingly, although she
regularly, and at times vehemently, complained about these expectations
and cited these as why she would not go back to her son's father (and
even wrote a poem about the topic), Wanda reconciled with him a
few times during the course of this study. She actually pointed to her
mother as partly responsible for her willingness to reunite with him,
as her mother tried to convince her that he had changed and would be
more supportive of her.

Wanda's situation illustrates the difficulty of straddling values and
discourses about women and family that are strongly entrenched in
Latino culture, and that often confine the opportunities available to
women, while at the same time asserting one's independence and
trying to better one's self through schooling. Such discourses value
women who are confined to the domestic sphere, or *una muchacha de
la casa*, rather than *de la calle*, or as some of the FLC women described,
"always on the street" (Pérez 116). Because many Latino families often
privilege the needs of the familial unit over the desires and aspirations
of the individual, it is at times difficult for Latina mothers to pursue
educational and personal goals on their own terms. The societal push
to try to maintain the family unit, even in the face of physical abuse or
emotional confinement, continues to be pervasive across communities
and cultures, and Wanda was obviously grappling with such pressures
from her family that at times conflicted with her notions of being an
independent woman—of forging her own brand of "woman type"—on
one hand, while also striving to provide a family life for her son. In
contrast to Wanda's quest for independence, Raquel's description of her
idealized future relationship mirrors that of the traditional breadwinner
and homemaker, the "good mother and father life"; yet, her image also
included her obtaining her diploma and working in a bank—markers
of her desire to be economically independent. Thus, while these Latina
women embraced many of the positive aspects of their culture, and

certainly also endorsed somewhat traditional notions of family and women, they also sought to challenge some of the more restrictive and destructive elements of their cultural milieu, most notably *machismo*, and in this way, attempt to "stretch the borders of gender *within Latino culture*" rather than wage a struggle *against* their culture around gender issues (Fine and Weis 206).

For many of the Latina women, the act of going to school—seemingly simple when viewed on a surface level—represented an act of a resistance, for it often posed a threat to the authority and dominance of the Latino male, many of whom themselves did not have their high school diploma; such findings have been replicated in other studies of Latina women attending literacy programs, where incidences of domestic abuse increased due to the fact that they were attending school (Rockhill). The fact that these women were receiving their high school diploma also set them apart from previous generations of Latinas in their families. By achieving their high school education, the young Latinas attending the FLC were already forging a different path from their mothers as well as one that diverged from many other adolescent Latina women across the country, who have the highest dropout rates among females across all ethnic groups (Ginorio and Huston). In many ways, the lessons of resilience and strength imparted by their own mothers provided the motivation for attaining educational goals; a number stated that they wanted to make their own mothers proud and that gaining their diploma would also help them challenge negative stereotypes about Latinas as uneducated, a goal which has been supported in other research with Latina youth and young Latina mothers (Cammarota 62).

However, while many of these Latinas clearly outlined what they saw as the shortcomings of their parents' and their own relationships and family life, and identified ways they hoped to dodge these in their own lives, they also expressed a certain amount of fatalism regarding the plight of women in their community and the men available to them as boyfriends and spouses. When she imagined her life in the future, Wanda provided a pessimistic outlook on the possibility for a good relationship with a man and a strong role model for her son:

> *I see myself living by myself. Because I think it's better off that way. You know, I don't want to end up meeting a guy and then fall in love with him and then … what happens if all of a sudden that*

guy starts hitting me and abusing me. I don't want my son living in that environment because then he's gonna learn ... it's cool, it's right to hit a woman.

When I asked her about options for meeting other types of men, she answered: "Like [not] abusive and stuff? I really don't. Those are the types of guys they are." She seemed to view relationships with men as a hindrance to the actualization of her goals: "I'm trying to fix up my life and I'm not trying to make it even more screwed up." Wanda's predicament demonstrates the challenges Latina mothers face in confronting the realities of *machismo* and patriarchy in their families and communities while at the same time providing positive role models and a safe environment for their children. For many Latina mothers, the only "choice" is to go it alone.

Despite a certain sense of hopelessness regarding men and relationships, there were instances of women being able to overcome and escape abusive and constrictive situations and develop supportive relationships with men. For example, Rosa was able to marshal together her resources so as to leave her first husband, who she described as "fatal," was active in a gang, and regularly, and sometimes violently, abused her. She described how she started to "hustle" so as to be more independent:

I started hustling to go to work and learning how to take the eł and looking for a job myself.... I knew that I was going to give him the boot.... I started putting money on the side. Working and putting money on the side.... And hopefully by the end of the year I was going to ... push him to the curb.

In order to achieve her goal of leaving her husband, Rosa had to acquire new skills and knowledge, such as familiarizing herself with public transportation and conducting a job search, and she described the process as a "new experience" for her. She also detailed how her mother was a great source of support to her in this regard by taking care of her son while she worked. Rosa suggested that her mother was so helpful because she had been through the same experience, or as Rosa put it: "Knew what I had." This support exemplifies the ways in which generations of Latina women proffer support to one another and how mothers' painful experiences can provide the impetus for ensuring that such experiences are not repeated by successive generations.

As this group of Latinas identified what they viewed as the deficiencies of their parents' lifestyle, as well as discussed some of the problematic areas in their own intimate relationships, they elaborated ways they hoped to forge a different pattern of life for themselves and their children. Rosa was explicit regarding the type of life she wanted for her family: "I knew if I made a difference in my kid's lives, they wouldn't have the life that I had gone through." And, as mentioned in the introduction, Rosa was able to improve her life circumstances considerably, leaving her husband and marrying a man she described as supportive and a good father. After graduating from the FLC, she also obtained full-time employment and bought a house with her husband. In discussing some of her aspirations for her son, Marilyn, a nineteen-year-old mother of a toddler boy, spoke of her plans of being a different type of parent than her mother and father: "I'm not gonna do like my mom and dad did me, they hit me all the time. I'm gonna talk to him more, make sure to tell him, you know, 'Tell me whatever's going on with you.'" Marilyn's desire to take a different, more communicative approach with her son than the abuse deployed by her parents demonstrates the possibility for intergenerational change and how certain child-rearing practices can be "reinvented and ruptured" (Villenas, "Diaspora" 423). It also illustrates how young women's experiences with less than optimal child rearing can generate reflection on their own parenting strategies.

Despite the women's aspirations to fashion a more stable life for themselves and children, their efforts were not always successful. Unlike Rosa's triumph over adversity, Raquel's desire for the idealized "good mother and father life" was not realized. In a follow-up interview conducted four years after graduation, her situation was less than optimal. While she was working at a local gym, she only had part-time hours, and her plans to attend school had been stymied because of lack of childcare. Her relationship with her boyfriend was also strained and they were in the process of separating, although at that time they were still living together because of finances. The case of Raquel underscores the great obstacles that face many young Latina low-income mothers, of attempting to advance their educational and professional goals, while providing for their family with limited material support. Although obtaining their high school diploma was a first step towards a more positive life trajectory, it was often not enough to attain more than a modicum of financial stability in their lives. Regardless of their high hopes and good intentions, there are a host of societal and economic factors that often constrain their attempts to overcome personal, professional, and financial circumstances and challenges.

CONCLUSION

The experiences of Latina women in the FLC, along with those of their female forebears, provide testimony to the struggles incurred across generations of Latina women. By focusing on the more downbeat experiences in their lives, I do not mean to imply that their lives were devoid of positive experiences and resources. Rather, my aim is to refute the notion that certain harmful behaviors are inevitably repeated by successive generations, as well as provide a more nuanced view of the realities faced by Latina mothers. The Latina women at the FLC illustrate how young mothers not only have to confront "the bad with the good," but also the ways that they can overcome and transform the challenges and obstacles in their lives and achieve success. Their experiences also speak to the significance of sharing stories and life lessons across generations of Latina women, and how this storytelling comprises an important element of Latina mothering.

That they were all mothers at a young age meant that they were already following in the footsteps of their mothers, who were themselves teen mothers. Some would assert that this fact alone had already positioned the women, and their children, at a disadvantage in terms of life consequences. While young Latina mothers are often blamed for their inability to "break the cycle" of all sorts of social ills, even prominent researchers who once emphasized the negative consequences of adolescent childbearing have more recently acknowledged that "ill effects of early childbearing had been overstated, because contributing factors, like poverty and school failure, had been confused with consequences" (Bernstein 52, 781; see also, Kelly; SmithBattle). In addition, as noted earlier, other researchers have called attention to some of the ways that the adverse educational and social conditions that Latinas are often faced with cause them to choose a "family identity," rather than one as a student (Flores-González 131; Luker 120). However, the pathways of the Latinas at the Family Learning Center hopefully offer an alternative choice, where familial, educational, and professional identities can coexist; and wherein motherhood does not have to stand in the way of or detract from achieving personal and professional success, but can instead serve as a resource for the attainment of these goals.

[1]The names of individuals referred to in this chapter have been changed to protect identities of participants.
[2]The "el" refers to the elevated train in Chicago.

WORKS CITED

Benmayor, Rina, Ana Juarbe, Celia Alvarez, and Blanca Vazquez. *Stories to Live by: Continuity and Change in Three Generations of Puerto Rican Women*. New York: Centro de Estudios Puertorriquenos, 1987. Print.

Bernstein, Nina. "Behind Fall in Pregnancy, a New Teenage Culture of Restraint." *New York Times* 7 Mar. 2004: 52, 781. Print.

Briggs, Laura. "La Vida, Moynihan, and Other Libels: Migration, Social Science, and the Making of the Puerto Rican Welfare Queen." *CENTRO: Journal of Center for Puerto Rican Studies* 14.1 (2002): 75-101. Print.

Cammarota, Julio. "The Gendered and Racialized Pathways of Latina and Latino Youth: Different Struggles, Different Resistances in the Urban Context." *Anthropology & Education Quarterly* 35.1 (2004): 53-74. Print.

Delgado-Gaitán, Concha. "Consejos: The Power of Cultural Narratives." *Anthropology & Education Quarterly* 25:3 (1994): 298-316. Print.

Espinoza-Herold, Marielle. "Stepping Beyond *Si Se Puede*: Dichos as a Cultural Resource in Mother-Daughter Interaction in a Latino Family." *Anthropology & Education Quarterly* 38.3 (2007): 260-77. Print.

Fine, Michelle, and Lois Weis. *The Unknown City: The Lives of Poor and Working-class Young Adults*. Boston: Beacon, 1998. Print.

Flores, Juan. *From Bomba to Hip-hop: Puerto Rican Culture and Latino Identity*. New York: Columbia University Press, 2000. Print.

Flores-González, Nilda. *School Kids/Street Kids: Identity Development in Latino Students*. New York: Teachers College, 2002. Print.

Ginorio, Angela B., and Michelle Huston. *Si, Se Puede! Yes We Can: Latinas in School*. Washington, DC: American Association of University

Women, 2001. Print.

González, Norma, Luis Moll, and Cathy Amanti, eds. *Funds of Knowledge: Theorizing Practices in Households and Classrooms*. Mahwah, NJ: Erlbaum, 2005. Print.

Johnson, Laura Ruth. "Challenging Best Practices in Family Literacy and Parent Education Programs: The Development and Enactment of Mothering Knowledge Among Puerto Rican and Latina Mothers in Chicago." *Anthropology & Education Quarterly* 40.3 (2009): 257-76. Print.

Johnson, Laura Ruth. *History in Our Hands: Identity Development, Cultural Ideologies of Motherhood, and the Critical Practice of Family Literacy in Puerto Rican Chicago*. Diss. University of California, Berkeley, 2005. Berkeley: UMI, 2006. AAT 3187063. Print.

Juno. Dir. Jason Reitman. Fox Searchlight, 2007. Film.

Kelly, Deirdre M. "Stigma Stories: Four Discourses About Teen Mothers, Welfare, and Poverty." *Youth & Society* 27.4 (1996): 421-49. Print.

Lewis, Oscar. *La Vida: A Puerto Rican Family in the Culture of Poverty—San Juan and New York*. New York: Random, 1961. Print.

López, Nancy. *Hopeful Girls, Troubled Boys: Race and Gender Disparity in Urban Education*. New York: Routledge, 2003. Print.

Luker, Kristen. *Dubious Conceptions: The Politics of Teenage Pregnancy*. Cambridge, MA: Harvard University Press, 1996. Print.

Moynihan, Daniel Patrick. *The Negro Family: The Case for National Action*. Washington, DC: U.S. GPO, 1965. Print.

Olmedo, Irma. "Puerto Rican Mothers Share and Relive Their *Memorias*." *CENTRO: Journal of Center for Puerto Rican Studies* 13.2 (2001): 99-115. Print.

Pérez, Gina. *The Near Northwest Side Story: Migration, Displacement, and Puerto Rican Families*. Berkeley: University of California Press, 2004. Print.

Proweller, Amira. "Re-writing/-righting Lives: Voices of Pregnant and Parenting Teenagers in an Alternative School." *Construction Sites: Excavating Race, Class, and Gender among Urban Youth*. Ed. Lois Weis and Michelle Fine. New York: Teachers College, 2000. 100-20. Print.

Rivera, Maria Elisa Diaz. *Refranes Mas Usados en Puerto Rico*. San Juan, Puerto Rico: Editorial de la Universidad de Puerto Rico, 1984. Print.

Rockhill, Kathleen. "Literacy as Threat/desire: Longing to be Somebody."

Women and Education: A Canadian Perspective. Ed. Jane Gaskell and Arlene McLaren. Calgary, Alberta: Detselig, 1987. 315-31. Print.

Secret Life and American Teenager, The. ABC Family, 2008. Television.

SmithBattle, Lee. "Reframing the Risks and Losses of Teen Mothering." *MCN: The American Journal of Maternal Child Nursing* 34.2 (2009): 122-28. Print.

Toro-Morn, Maura I. "*Yo era Muy Arriesgada*: A Historical Overview of the Work Experiences of Puerto Rican Women in Chicago." *CENTRO: Journal of Center for Puerto Rican Studies* 13.2 (2001): 25-43. Print.

Valdés, Guadalupe. *Con Respeto: Bridging the Distance Between Culturally Diverse Families and Schools.* New York: Teachers College, 1996. Print.

Villenas, Sofia A. "Diaspora and the Anthropology of Latino Education: Challenges, Affinities, and Intersections." *Anthropology & Education Quarterly* 38.4 (2007): 419-25. Print.

Villenas, Sofia A. "Latina Literacies in *Convivencia*: Communal Spaces of Teaching and Learning." *Anthropology & Education Quarterly* 36.3 (2005): 273-77. Print.

Ward, Janie V. "Raising Resisters: The Role of Truth Telling in the Psychological Development of African American Girls." *Urban Girls: Resisting Stereotypes, Creating Identities.* Ed. Bonnie J. Ross Leadbeater and Niobe Way. New York: New York University Press, 1996. 85-99. Print.

Zentella, Ana Celia. *Building on Strength: Language and Literacy in Latino Families and Communities.* New York: Teachers College, 2005. Print.

Transformational Caring

Mexican American Women Redefining Mothering and Education

GILDA L. OCHOA

We want everyone to feel good about themselves, maybe that's part of being Latino. I want—we want—children to be successful in everything they do. I want each kid to blossom to his [or her] fullest, and let's help them do that.
—Denise Villarreal, Mexican American Elementary School Administrator

DESPITE A LEGACY OF COMMITMENT BY PEOPLE SUCH AS Denise Villarreal, there is a long history of exclusionary ideologies and programs aimed at Mexican Americans, especially mothers, under the pretense that Mexican American families are to blame for the educational outcomes of their children and that mothers need to learn how to speak English, prepare nutritious meals, and instill the value of education. Such cultural deficiency perspectives and the Americanization or integrationist programs that have accompanied them misrepresent Mexican American families and women. Within the context of schooling, they maintain hegemonic school policies such as English-only classrooms that may actually divest students of family and cultural resources. In the end, programs and dominant images based on cultural deficiency frameworks exacerbate the structural and institutional inequalities within U.S. schools and society. When families are blamed, larger processes and systems of inequality are easier to ignore.

Focusing specifically on the experiences of a group of middle and working-class Mexican American women in the Los Angeles area, this chapter uses in-depth interviews and participant observations to capture some of the everyday and collective strategies that they are employing to enhance educational opportunities for their children and for the community's children. In their homes, communities, and schools, they contest hierarchical and assimilationist schooling practices, and they demonstrate broad conceptions of mothering that are not rooted in stereotypical, biological, or individualistic ideologies. Instead, their everyday actions and philosophies reveal the nuanced ways that they are engaged in what I refer to as transformational caring—activities that are undertaken within or beyond the home space for the good of individuals and communities in order to challenge or change traditional ideologies or practices.

Key to the narratives included in this chapter are the ways that mothering and education are socio-political-economic constructs that are shaped by macro factors and dominant ideologies and are enacted individually and collectively through activities involving teaching, nurturing, and protecting others regardless of biological ties. Combined, the Mexican American women's narratives reveal a range of often unacknowledged and politicized caring and demonstrate the complex and situationally specific ways that some are redefining and resisting narrow conceptions of Mexican American women, mothering, and education. They also capture how, for Mexican American women, mothering and education may be mutually constitutive such that mothering transcends the familial space and education extends beyond the school gates. For working-class women and women of color whose positions and experiences are often contested, devalued, and marked by barriers, mothering and education can also involve additional labor including countering injustices and raising children who resist the status quo (Tatum 47). By focusing on the experiences of a group of Mexican American women, this chapter offers an important standpoint on a neglected topic and community, and it captures some of the overlooked labor undertaken by Mexican American women as they try to counter patterns of injustice in schools.

At a time when top-down market-based educational policies drive schools, Mexican American families are blamed, and students continue to be short-changed, examples of transformational caring should be examined, rather than undermined. If those forming educational policies listened to the individuals often most engaged in teaching students—mothers, community residents, and teachers—blame might then be shifted from families and appropriately attributed to unequal social structures and educational practices. In particular, with Mexican American youth representing a growing percentage of U.S. students, much is to be learned by listening to Mexican American women who offer a unique angle of vision that is informed by a history of exclusion, lived realities, and aspirations of greater opportunities for future generations. Their perspectives demonstrate some of the limits of traditional conceptualizations of mothering and the inadequacies in today's schools.

DOMINANT CONSTRUCTIONS OF
MEXICAN AMERICAN FAMILIES, WOMEN, AND MOTHERING

In the rare cases when Mexican and Mexican American mothers are visible in popular discourse, they have alternatively been cast as either problems or romanticized as ideal. As analyzed by sociologist Gloria González-López in *Erotic Journeys* (2005), this binary conceptualization is apparent in academic scholarship and media representations that use the madonna/whore paradigm to cast Mexican American women as either morally "good" or sexually "bad and loose" (77). Equally as harmful as this misrepresentation are the ways that various school officials, politicians, and academics have reinforced such good/bad binaries by either representing Mexican American women as traditional, self-sacrificing women who passively accept others' dictates or as obstacles to their children's educational advancement and depleters of social services. Such negative sentiments have been rampant in public debates over immigration and education where Mexican women have often been the targets of so-called Americanization programs. For example, in *Fit to Be Citizens?* (2006), historian Natalia Molina explains how in the 1920s Mexican women were often seen as "culturally backward," "bad parents," and "obstacle[s] to progress" (10). In the current period, such sentiment persists and has been apparent in various legal cases, including in the 1990s when a district judge in Texas threatened a Mexican American mother with losing custody of her child if she did not speak to her in English (González 206). Such binary and exclusionary conceptions of Mexican American women have been used to camouflage systematic inequality and justify discriminatory policies thereby reproducing class, racial/ethnic, and gender hierarchies.

Until the 1970s and 1980s, academic scholarship on Mexican American families and women did little to rectify these gross assumptions (Ortiz 19-20; Zinn 178-79). During this period, it was common for scholars to adopt cultural deficiency and assimilationist perspectives that blamed Mexican American women and families for their socio-economic positions in society (Hurtado 41). Such approaches justified Americanization Programs in schools and homes and reinforced hierarchies and discriminatory practices by positioning White middle class heterosexual and nuclear families as normative and in opposition to Mexican American families who were critiqued as traditional, overly patriarchal, too present-time oriented, and "clannish."[1] Within such cultural deficiency perspectives, it is believed that the Spanish-language and Catholicism, not a history of conquest, colonization, and discrimination, hinder socio-political-economic progress (see Huntington 40).

Beginning in the 1970s, early work in Women's Studies and Chicana/o Studies was instrumental in contesting supposed ideal family types and deficiency perspectives. However, much of this scholarship either focused on the experiences of middle-class White women as though their experiences were universal, or this scholarship adopted a Chicano nationalist framework and celebrated Chicano families from a masculinist standpoint (Glenn 3; Hurtado 55). In both cases, the experiences and perspectives of Mexican American women were largely ignored or misrepresented, and the salience of race, class, and gender were overlooked.

DISRUPTING DOMINANT CONSTRUCTIONS OF MOTHERING AND EDUCATION

Despite a scholarly tradition of overlooking race, class, and gender, these interlocking factors have shaped dominant conceptions of both "good mothering" and "quality education." Within the U.S., dominant patriarchal constructions typically cast White, heterosexual, married, and middle class women who are part of nuclear families as "good mothers" (O'Reilly 10-11). In contrast, as sociologist Elena Gutiérrez details in *Fertile Matters* (2008), Mexican American women are often deemed "hyper-fertile baby machines," "teen-age mothers," or barriers to children's educational success (xi). Likewise, women who work outside of the home or engage in "maternal activism" are typically excluded from idealized conceptualizations (O'Reilly 10). In *Up Against White-ness* (2005), sociologist Stacey Lee describes how similar hierarchical constructions are apparent in conceptions of quality education and "good students" where "whiteness defines what is normal, desirable, and good at the school" (23). Not only are schools with high percentages of White and middle-class students typically deemed "good schools," but the school culture, course curriculum, teachers' actions, and overall organization typically privilege White middle-class students and parents and often marginalize working-class, English-language learners, and students or parents of color (24-26). The criteria used to determine "good students" includes high grades, top performance on standardized tests, friendliness to teachers, and participation in prestigious school activities such as band, varsity sports, and leadership. In contrast, students with family responsibilities, enrolled in non-college preparatory tracks, or engaged in ethnic-specific organizations are typically excluded from this categorization (30).

Since the 1980s and 1990s as Women's Studies and Chicana/o Studies have grown and increasing numbers of working class and women of color have entered academia, a burgeoning body of scholarship has developed that addresses previous gaps and complicates facile representations of Mexican American women, mothering, families, and education.[2] This research has been important for contextualizing women's lives, center-ing the voices and experiences of Chicanas/Latinas, and documenting multiple and intersecting forms of exclusion and resistance. In particular, *Mexican American Women Activists* (1998) by Chicana/o Studies scholar Mary Pardo was foundational for capturing the ways that Mexican American women may engage in grassroots activism for their families and communities by strategically drawing upon their gendered posi-tions and obligations. This newer scholarship shifted the focus from middle-class White women and expanded the definition of mothering beyond the activities undertaken within the family-unit by biologically or legally-defined mothers. Furthermore, research by sociologists Nancy Naples on "activist mothering" in *Grassroots Warriors: Activist Mothering, Community Work, and the War on Poverty* (1998) and Patricia Hill Collins on "community othermothers" in *Black Feminist Thought: Knowledge, Consciousness and the Politics of Empowerment* (1990) also incorporated the nurturing work done inside and *outside* of one's kinship group *and* within the context of racism and economic struggles. These authors emphasized the mothering work that is done beyond the confines of the family and as a part of "group survival" and "institutional transformation" in multiple arenas (Collins 146-56).

Building on this recent scholarship, I employ broad and intersecting conceptualizations of mothering and education. In comparison to authors such as Andrea O'Reilly and Nancy Naples who have used concepts such as feminist mothering, empowered mothers, or activist mothering, I use the term transformational caring because it is removed from essentialist conceptions of mothering that assume that mothering is natural, apolitical, undertaken by all women, confined to the private arena, not the purview of men, and based on biological relationships. Also since much of the scholarship and theorizing on mothering is still largely based on the experiences of middle-class White women, "transformational caring" allows for a distancing of the racialized constructions of mothering and its traditional positive associations with White middle class-ness. Finally, the work involved in mothering—nurturing, caring, and protecting—is typically obscured, especially when it is performed by women, because such labor is often expected and seen as an essence of womanhood. Thus, the concept transformational caring works to name the labor and power behind such activities and to link them to broad forms of education that occur within and across multiple spaces, including homes, schools, and communities. This broader conceptualization is especially salient for capturing the range of activities undertaken by Mexican American women on behalf of their families and communities and in situations where the labor of caring has been compounded by a history of inequality and exclusion.

RESEARCH METHODOLOGY AND COMMUNITY BACKGROUND

This chapter draws on fifteen years of qualitative research that I have completed on communities, immigration, and education in the Los Angeles-area. In particular, I base this work on my participation in school and community activities and forty-four in-depth interviews with Mexican American and Mexican immigrant women. At the time of these interviews, the women's ages ranged from 23 to 77. On average, they were 44 years old, had two children, and were second generation—the adult children of Mexican immigrants.

These open-ended, semi-structured, and tape-recorded interviews averaged one to two hours in length, and while they typically began as interviews, many of them became dialogues where we shared our experiences and perspectives. In homes, offices, classrooms, and restaurants, women discussed their family backgrounds, schooling histories, work experiences, and reflections on contemporary issues such as race/ethnicity, immigration, and public education. All of the interviews were fully transcribed, and the quotes appearing in this chapter are verbatim from the transcripts. While some of the women hoped that I would use their names, others preferred to remain anonymous. Thus, to ensure the confidentiality of all, I have changed all of their names. To best capture some of the critical themes from the interviews and to not lose the essence of individual experiences, I have organized this chapter around the narratives of the following five women. They are listed below in the order in which they appear in the chapter.

Name	Age	Generation in U.S.	Number of Children
Denise Villarreal	46	2nd	0
Iris Zuñiga	58	2nd	2
Mari Ramírez	40	2nd	4
Irene Renteria-Salazar	35	2nd	2
Raquel Heinrich	40	1st	2

The following qualitative snapshots are of Mexican American women engaged in transformational caring. Each has adopted philosophies or behaviors that broaden traditional constructions of mothering that are rooted in biological origins and individual interests. By working for the good of children, the community, Latinas/os, and the future, they are also contesting school practices and carving out broad and inclusive conceptions of mothering and quality education.

WORKING FOR OUR CHILDREN, OUR FUTURE

Forty-six-year-old Denise Villarreal remembers being shocked when a school official in her La Puente community reprimanded her, "If you don't have children, you can't participate." As a recent homeowner, Villarreal had just offered to assist her neighborhood school. Having attended several bilingual advisory committee meetings where "a school district employee was yelling at parents," she thought, "Man, those people need help ... those poor parents." Feeling compelled to help, she approached the school official and generously said, "Hi, I live in your attendance area, and I was wondering if you could let me know when your school council meetings are so I can come to participate because I live in the community." When the school official inquired into why Denise wanted to participate, Denise explained, "I'm going to have children who are going to end up going to your school. I can sell tacos at a fundraiser or something." However, before she could finish, Denise was abruptly denied and deemed unqualified because she did not have any children of her own. Rather than be silenced, Denise corrected, "Excuse me! I'm a taxpayer in this community. I live in your attendance area. If I want to run for your PTA [Parent Teacher Association], I'm entitled to it."

Undeterred and committed to working with her area schools, Denise eventually applied for and was hired as a school administrator at a local school. Given her experience with the policing of participation and dismissing of parents, Denise implemented an open door policy at the school that welcomes the working class Latina/o community onto campus, even though some teachers oppose this approach. Seeing the community as an asset, she tells teachers, "Please don't mistreat [members of the community]. They employ us.... Remember, it takes a village to raise a child, and we're the village. If you don't want to participate in the village, please go somewhere else."

As part of her collaborative and community-based framework, Denise Villarreal is working on behalf of today's youth and tomorrow's future:

> I'm here for the kids, and I want them to have the best instructional
> program I can offer them, and that's always my focus. Let's make
> it great for the kids because they're our hope for the future.... We're
> not going to see the changes in our lifetime, okay. Maybe it's for your

*children's lifetime, maybe it's for your grandchildren's lifetime. Not
me, I'm not going to have any children.*

By working as part of a broad and inclusive struggle for the community
and children in general, Denise Villarreal challenges constructions of
motherhood that focus on individualism, one's own biological or legal
children, and activities that occur primarily in the home. Likewise, her
community-centered approach is unique within schools where working
class and Latina/o families often encounter a double bind. They are either
accused of not participating in the education of their youth, labeled as
"troublemakers" or "irrational" when they question school practices or
school officials (Shannon 83), or as was the case with Denise Villarreal
they are excluded from participating in meaningful ways. In essence,
they are expected to "assume the role of audience" by being passive
consumers or uncritical supporters of the formal educational process,
an expectation that is racist and classist because the participation of
middle-class White parents is often more encouraged and favored in
schools by teachers and administrators who are also likely to be middle
class and White (Shannon 72; Ochoa 197).

With her framework of a village, Denise Villarreal is blurring the
traditional boundaries between schools and communities in the U.S. As
a resident of her primarily working class Latina/o community and as
a school principal in the same community, she deconstructs normative
forms of mothering and schooling that assume that mothering is premised
on biological ties and that education happens only by trained professionals in institutional settings. By challenging such narrow frameworks,
Denise Villarreal's actions capture the types of transformational caring
undertaken by many of the Mexican American teachers and principals I
have interviewed who are also trying to remove the exclusionary barriers
and ideologies they have encountered for future generations. Having
had to navigate unjust schools when they were students, as adults, they
are now drawing on their lived realities to advocate for and construct
open and affirming schools for students and community members.
Their experiences, commitments, and actions have the possibility of
transforming historically unequal and distant relationships between U.S.
schools and Latina/o communities. Such schools value the contributions
and forms of education offered by all community members—including
Latina/o mothers and families.

BELIEVING IN OUR COMMUNITY

Denise Villarreal's emphasis on working for the community and youth was repeated by many Mexican American women who describe their actions as part of a larger struggle. For fifty-eight-year-old Iris Zuñiga, an elementary school teacher, this larger struggle included not abandoning her community by sending her two sons to a more highly regarded middle school outside of her neighborhood:

> *A lot of people would say, "Oh, don't go to Maple Grove. Go to La Montaña." I always said, "No, they need to go where—I know these groups of kids that have grown up with [my sons], and they are good kids.... This is where they have to stay. I am not going to send them to another [school]. No, we've got to stay—believe in our community."*

As with Denise Villarreal, Iris Zuñiga's commitment to community is fueled by her awareness of the disparities encountered by Mexican Americans. This disparity was evident at her sons' high school where students from the two area middle schools eventually became schoolmates, but overall few Mexican American students were being prepared for college. Iris reflects on how she would like to change this aspect of the high school: "I really want to see more emphasis on their college. I want to see more [Mexican American students] in college. I just don't see it as much. I think that [my son]—quite a few of his friends did continue, but I know that there are a lot that didn't."

Iris Zuñiga's decision to not leave the community for her own self-interest can be seen as a political statement and a form of transformational caring that is also reflected in how she raised her sons. As an elementary school teacher, Iris Zuñiga has greater economic resources and options than her more working class Mexican American neighbors. However, by aligning with her neighbors, she contests individualistic actions rooted in capitalist constructions that expect her to place the advancement of her own children above the interests and at the expense of other children and families. Her actions also challenge assimilationist frameworks regarding education that are premised on the belief that socio-economic advancement is the preeminent goal and that it is only achieved by forgoing one's racial/ethnic and class origins. Likewise, she rebukes negative assumptions about the primarily working-class Mexican American students who attend Maple Grove, in comparison to the more favorable opinion of the predominately middle- and upper middle-class Asian American/Pacific Islanders at La Montaña. Finally, she implicitly questions dominant beliefs that standardized test scores and student racial/ethnic-class backgrounds are determinants of a good school. By arguing "I know these groups of kids that have grown up with [my sons], and they are good kids," Iris explicitly critiques the racist, classist, and sexist constructions of whom are "good kids." In particular, she contests dominant images that cast Mexican American males as troublemakers or uninterested in education. Aware of the history of racial/ethnic and class subordination faced by Mexican Americans, Iris enacts a form of love, care, and belief in Mexican American males and in her Mexican American community. Her actions of love and consideration are important forms of transformational caring that strengthen Mexican American families and communities.

SUPPLEMENTING OUR SCHOOLS

An awareness of a history of exclusion and contemporary forms of prejudice and discrimination has fostered a shared sense of identity, community, and commitment for change among many Mexican Americans, including forty-year-old Mari Ramírez. As an administrative assistant at her sons' high school—the same school attended by Iris Zuñiga's children—Ramírez connects the neglect that her two sons have experienced to larger patterns of exclusion of Mexican American students by teachers and counselors. In particular, she has observed a racial/ethnic hierarchy where Mexican Americas, who are primarily working class at the school, are largely absent in the school's high status activities, even though they constitute about half of the student population:

> You see the list of students that are always going on a field trip to superior court on a mock trial. You rarely see a Mexican or Hispanic name on that list.... You see the list for playing tennis and going to a tennis game, [but] you don't see Hispanics in sports other than soccer or maybe football.

Not only are Latina/o students underserved at her school, but Mari

Ramirez also finds that school officials may disregard Latina/o parents. As a staff member in the disciplinary office, she regularly receives phone calls from Latina/o parents who have left multiple unanswered messages for teachers. Mari mentioned that she "feel[s] badly, and as a parent would want to know what is going on." Despite dominant misperceptions that Latina/o parents do not care about their children's schooling, Mari observes the reverse—that her school does not care about Latinas/os. By blaming the school for ignoring the phone calls of Latina/o parents, Mari calls attention to ironic and disparate perceptions and actions that detrimentally hinder Latinas/os.

As a Mexican American mother who is conscious of the inequalities encountered by Latinas/os, Mari Ramírez possesses an important perspective about the school disparities. This has led her to become an advocate for Latinas/os. Identifying with the larger Latina/o community and concluding that the high school does not "really cater to Mexican or Hispanic students," Mari has informally expanded her position as an assistant to the administrator of discipline to also provide the advice and support that she sees missing for such students and their parents: "They are part of my race, and I want the students to do better. Hispanics are so down low, and I want them to get up there. That is why I talk to them, and that is why [another assistant and I] council them, and we talk to them and talk to them and talk to them." With "nobody there to really talk to the students and help the parents," Mari provides as much assistance as she can. Thus, rather than align with the school practices that perpetuate the dismissal of Latina/o students and parents, she enacts a form of care and education that she believes is lacking at the school—one that involves listening, encouraging, and just "talk[ing] to [students] about life, about what you want to do." This form of caring is transformational because it contests the traditional running of schools, and it helps to offset some of the distant and negative interactions to which Mexican American parents and students are commonly subjected.

As with other Mexican American women working in schools, Mari Ramírez expands her role at work, and she does not confine her responsibilities as a mother to only the care and concern of her own children. As such, she provides critical supplementary and uncompensated support to Latinas/os in an attempt to offset the school-based deficiencies. That Latinas/os and other women of color are often the ones who perform such unrecognized and uncompensated labor suggests the crucial role that they play in trying to rectify institutional and individual forms of discrimination.

BRINGING THE WHOLE COMMUNITY
TOGETHER FOR BILINGUAL EDUCATION

While the everyday actions undertaken by Mexican American women such as Denise Villarreal, Iris Zuñiga, and Mari Ramírez strike at the exclusionary practices, philosophies, and interactions occurring in schools, transformative caring also happens collectively; it is done in a community and by men as well as by women. The barriers and exclusionary practices encountered by many Mexican Americans require multiple forms of labor by a wide range of community members, and caring or mothering activities are neither the purview of all women nor only enacted by women. In particular, the organizing activities of a group of Mexican American and Mexican immigrant women through "Parents for Quality Education" typify this inclusionary ethos and expanded focus on transformational caring. Among the lessons learned from this group are the power of community organizing, the significance of gendered responsibilities, and the socio-political-economic constructions of "good" mothering.

In 1996 as the debate surrounding the elimination of bilingual education soared in California, a group of primarily Mexican American and Mexican immigrant women in the La Puente area formed Parents for Quality Education to ensure that the bilingual education program in their school district would not be lost. Since they believe that the entire community benefits when its children are bilingual, the group's organizers Irene Renteria-Salazar and Raquel Heinrich adopted a philosophy and practice of community inclusion (Ochoa 206-07). Hoping to have the largest impact and with an awareness of the gender division of labor within society where women are typically responsible for the work undertaken at home and in schools, the organizers strategically included the participation of men in their events. They accomplished this by working around families' schedules, providing food and drinks at meetings, and advising men on how they could provide support. Raquel Heinrich reflects on the group's success in bringing the whole community together for a bilingual education march at the school district office—even though women were the ones doing much of the initial planning:

> *It was the first time that I saw the magnitude on the part of the men on the picket line, and that was what I was very proud of. So, regardless of who[m] takes part in the event planning, as long as the men are there to support what we are doing, I am happy with it.*

She also remembers a Latina/o family who worked together to collect signatures in support of bilingual education during masses at a local Catholic church:

> *They showed up, not only husband and wife. They were carrying a baby, and they had a stroller with a two-year-old, and their ten-year-old was passing out flyers with them. So they took turns signing people up, passing the flyers out, inviting them to the meetings, and signing the petition.*

While Mexican American and Mexican immigrant women were the majority of Parents for Quality Education, and they were primarily responsible for the group's everyday activities—including galvanizing the transformational caring activities of men—the involvement of men and children in the group's events was critical for rallying and conveying a broad range of community support for bilingual education. Thus, while this example of Parents for Quality Education reflects transformational caring, it also reveals a fundamental gap in mothering literature that focuses on the activities of women and overlooks the additional labor of working to include the entire community in their organizing. In particular, biological determinist frameworks fail to capture the intersections of race, class, and gender in influencing gendered participation and community collaboration in caring activities. As such, they overlook the supportive and caring roles that men—especially, as in this example, Mexican American men—may also undertake for the enhancement of their communities, families, and children—even if they are done at the urging of Mexican American women.

Just as the philosophies and activities of Parents for Quality Education complicate gendered constructions of mothering, they also contest dominant modes of education and reconceptualize exclusionary constructions of "good mothering" that privilege White, heterosexual, married, and middle-class women and families. In the historical context where Mexican American mothers have been deemed unfit for speaking Spanish to their children and where families have been blamed for hindering educational advancement, by fighting for bilingual education, Parents for Quality Education confronted assimilationist perspectives, emphasized the value of bilingualism, and illustrated how parents, school officials, and institutional practices that do not teach children a language other than English—not Spanish-speaking women—were actually the ones who were limiting children's opportunities. Thus, in the context of English-only policies, their transformational caring involved inverting the pervasive equating of Mexican Americanness with poor parenting and speaking Spanish as a deficit. Instead, they characterized the group's activists and others who supported bilingual education as good mothers precisely because they were fighting to sustain opportunities that foster bilingualism.

CONCLUSION

By listening to the narratives of Mexican American women, we see the everyday and collective forms of transformational caring that some are engaged in within their schools and communities. The Mexican American women profiled in this chapter are contesting biological, individualistic, and assimilationist practices and expectations by working on behalf of children outside of their kinship relationships, demonstrating a commitment to community schools, infusing authentic caring in work places, and organizing for bilingual education. As such, their philosophies and actions reveal the broadly defined and inclusive paradigms to mothering and education that was also illustrated by Denise Villarreal at the beginning of this chapter—approaches that help "everyone to feel good about themselves" and "to blossom" to their fullest, especially in the context of exclusionary practices and ideologies that work against marginalized individuals and communities like Latinas/Chicanas.

These expanded approaches to mothering and education challenge academic scholarship, dominant discourses, and institutional practices. Despite the power behind the individual and collective caring provided by the Mexican American women profiled in this chapter, schools and society cannot rely on their labor to augment, buffer, or contest the deficiency of institutions. The emotional labor involved in constantly trying to redress the wrongs of institutional practices and policies takes a toll on the individual health and collective wellbeing of Mexican American women and communities. Transformational caring is typically unrecognized and devalued labor that is performed by groups with limited institutional power. Thus, a radical rethinking and restructuring of schools, communities, homes, and societies are needed to ensure that those individuals and communities who are already the most taxed by historical and institutional injustices are not expected to continue to pick up the slack of the very institutions and everyday practices that continue to subjugate their less powerful communities. Without such a change, racial/ethnic, class, and gender hierarchies will persist as excluded groups are forced to engage in more unrecognized and uncompensated labor for youth, families, and communities. Meanwhile, those privileged under the current system may have little impetus to affect change or even to see how their benefits may come at the expense of marginalized individuals and families, in this case Mexican American women.

[1]For examples of such work, see Madsen and Heller.
[2]For examples, see Moraga; Collins; Glenn, Chang, and Forcey; Zinn; Pardo; Naples; and Valenzuela.

WORKS CITED

Collins, Patricia Hill. *Black Feminist Thought: Knowledge, Consciousness and the Politics of Empowerment*. Boston: Unwin Hyman, 1990. Print.

Glenn, Eveyln Nakano. "Social Constructions of Mothering: A Thematic Overview." *Mothering: Ideology, Experience, and Agency*. Ed. Evelyn Nakano Glenn, Grace Chang, and Linda Rennie Forcey. New York: Routledge, 1994. 1-29. Print.

Glenn, Evelyn Nakano, Grace Chang, and Linda Rennie Forcey, eds. *Mothering: Ideology, Experience, and Agency*. New York: Routledge, 1994. Print.

González, Juan. *Harvest of Empire: A History of Latinos in America*. New York: Viking, 2000. Print.

González-López, Gloria. *Erotic Journeys: Mexican Immigrants and their*

Sex Lives. Berkeley: University of California Press, 2005. Print.

Gutiérrez, Elena R. *Fertile Matters: The Politics of Mexican-Origin Women's Reproduction*. Austin: University of Texas Press, 2008. Print.

Heller, Ceila S. *Mexican American Youth: Forgotten Youth at the Crossroads*. New York: Random, 1966. Print.

Huntington, Samuel P. "The Hispanic Challenge." *Foreign Policy* (2004): 30-37. Print.

Hurtado, Áida. "Variations, Combinations, and Evolutions: Latino Families in the United States." *Understanding Latino Families: Scholarship, Policy, and Practice*. Ed. Ruth E. Zambrana. Thousand Oaks, CA: Sage, 1995. 40-61. Print.

Lee, Stacey L. *Up Against Whiteness: Race, School, and Immigrant Youth*. New York: Teachers College, 2005. Print.

Madsen, William. *Mexican-Americans of South Texas*. New York: Holt, 1964. Print.

Molina, Natalia. *Fit to Be Citizens? Public Health and Race in Los Angeles, 1879-1939*. Berkeley: University of California Press, 2006. Print.

Moraga, Cherrie. *Loving in the War Years*. Boston: South End, 1983. Print.

Naples, Nancy. *Grassroots Warriors: Activist Mothering, Community Work, and the War on Poverty*. New York: Routledge, 1998. Print.

Ochoa, Gilda L. *Becoming Neighbors in a Mexican American Community: Power, Conflict, and Solidarity*. Austin: University of Texas Press, 2004. Print.

O'Reilly, Andrea, ed. "Introduction." *Feminist Mothering*. New York: State University of New York Press, 2008. 1-22. Print.

Ortiz, Vilma. "The Diversity of Latino Families." *Understanding Latino Families: Scholarship, Policy, and Practice*. Ed. Ruth E. Zambrana. Thousand Oaks, CA: Sage, 1995. 18-39. Print.

Pardo, Mary. *Mexican American Women Activists: Identity and Resistance in Two Los Angeles Communities*. Philadelphia: Temple University Press, 1998. Print.

Shannon, Sheila M. "Minority Parental Involvement: A Mexican Mother's Experience and a Teacher's Interpretation." *Education and Urban Society* 29.1 (1996): 71-84. Print.

Tatum, Beverly Daniel. *"Why Are All the Black Kids Sitting Together in the Cafeteria?" and Other Conversations About Race*. New York: Basic, 1997. Print.

Valenzuela, Angela. *Subtractive Schooling: U.S.-Mexican Youth and the Politics of Caring*. Albany: State University of New York Press, 1999. Print.

Zinn, Maxine Baca. "Social Science Theorizing for Latino Families in the Age of Diversity. *Understanding Latino Families: Scholarship, Policy, and Practice*. Ed. Ruth E. Zambrana. Thousand Oaks, CA: Sage, 1995. 177-89. Print.

III.
Scenes of *La Familia*:
Facing Challenges

Latina Teenage Mothering

Meanings, Challenges and Successes

ELIZABETH TREJOS-CASTILLO AND HELYNE FREDERICK

THOUGH OFF-TIMED MOTHERHOOD IS NOT A NEW SOCIETAL phenomenon, for teenagers it brings a different set of challenges that places teen mothers and their children not only at a higher risk for health problems and complications (pre-partum and post-partum), but also creates personal, academic, and social negative consequences. For instance, national statistics show that only 40 percent of mothers younger than 18 years old finish high school, 75 percent of teen mothers are financially dependent on their families or on welfare, and approximately 64 percent of children born to teens live in poverty and are more likely to experience neglect and/or abuse (Martin et al. 1-3; Whitman et al. 11). The National Campaign to Prevent Pregnancy reports that since 1995, Latina teens have had the highest rates of teen pregnancy (53 percent get pregnant before age 20) and they are more likely to drop out of school than pregnant teens from other ethnicities (1). Thus, with the rising teen pregnancy rates reported by national and empirical data particularly among Hispanic and Latina descendant adolescents, the prognosis for Latina teen mothers' future and their children is not surprisingly catastrophic (Martin et al. 1-3). Unfortunately, most of what is known about Latina teen mothers is based on national data and empirical scholarship that, for the most part, have failed to present a more comprehensive view of motherhood in the Latino culture.

The current chapter aims to shed light on the understanding of motherhood among Latina adolescents. While exploring the dynamics of becoming a "teen mother" among Latinas, we draw attention to core cultural factors that contribute to positive outcomes for these young mothers and their children. Unfortunately, current literature is plagued by stigmatized categorizations of Latinas' reproductive behaviors and life choices. Furthermore, among existing studies, limited scholarship has been guided by a theoretical framework as suggested by a literature review across disciplines recently conducted by Gloria González-López and Salvador Vidal-Ortiz (315-17). Thus, we believe it is imperative to start first by disentangling the meaning of motherhood in the Latino culture from a theoretical perspective and then discuss the challenges and successes that are particular to Latina teen mothers.

From a theoretical perspective, symbolic interactionists argue that sexual scripts defining culturally normative affective and sexual inter-actions are deeply rooted on patterns of gender socialization, which at the same time, also define the nature and length of such relationships (Longmore 50; O'Sullivan and Meyer-Bahlburg 225). Among Latina adolescents, cultural norms such as the need to prove their womanhood and fertility, lower educational and labor expectations (as compared to men), and traditional feminine roles have been described as key factors for understanding the significance of motherhood in this population (Pantelides 13-14; Stern 144). Paradoxically, whereas empirical evidence suggests that cultural norms may place Latina adolescents at a higher risk for off-time motherhood, traditional views of the Latino culture (e.g., familismo, religiosity) as well as strong kin relationships have been described to function as a supportive network that provides multiple resources for teen mothers during and after pregnancy (Escobar, Nervi and Gara 70; Kahn and Berkowitz 2). In a similar way, current scholar-ship on this area of study is not only scarce, but it lacks analytical depth mostly due to the use of inappropriate methodological approaches that impede thorough comparisons across ethnic/racial groups. As a result, Latina adolescent mothers continue to be an underserved population because their needs and concerns are not adequately addressed by policy-makers and multidisciplinary professionals, as well as by current intervention and prevention efforts. This chapter also discusses some of the often overlooked pieces of the Latina adolescent motherhood puzzle when seen from an etic perspective (compared to other cultures) as opposed to using an emic perspective (within a specific culture; for more on etic and emic, see Ofori-Dankwa and Ricks 175).

At last, motherhood (as much as fatherhood) represents the heart and foundation of society and as such, it deserves a more comprehensive understanding of its meaning deeply rooted in the palpable culture of our day-to-day life—a meaning that transcends society, history, and human existence.

UNDERSTANDING LATINA TEEN MOTHERHOOD: WHAT DOES PREGNANCY MEAN?

In general, being an adolescent means mastering certain developmental tasks. Erik Erikson's theory of psychosocial development across the lifespan describes eight stages of development. Each stage focuses on a conflict that should be solved before the individual moves success-fully into the next stage. For adolescents, Erik Erikson described this stage as identity vs. role confusion (261-62). Across any ethnic group, becoming pregnant and having a baby add to the challenges that young pregnant adolescents face. During the pregnancy and after childbirth, adolescents must cope with typical physiological, social, and psycho-logical developmental challenges of adolescence as well as dealing with parenting issues (Adams and Kocik 89; Stevenson, Maton and Teti 109). In discussing teen pregnancy among Latinas, it is imperative that we consider not only the developmental aspects of teen pregnancy, but also how the processes involved in Latina mothering might be understood as a function of the cultural values and meanings that Latinas attach to pregnancy and child-rearing practices, as well as future aspirations of Latina mothers. Having this in mind, we discuss in the following sections: first, empirical research on Latina teen mothers organized in two main areas, namely challenges and successes; second, we discuss methodological shortcomings of current research on Latina teen moth-ers; and finally, we draw attention to current programs and resources available for Latina teen mothers.

CHALLENGES

According to reports from national data, Latinas had the smallest decrease in teen birth rates compared to other ethnic groups (National Campaign to Prevent Pregnancy 1). Overall, for U.S. teens, between 1991 and 2000, there was only a 12 percent decrease in the birth rate among Latina teens, in comparison to over 30 percent among African American teens, and 24 percent among White teens (Ventura et al. 2-5). There have also been reports that over two-thirds of Latina teen moms drop out of high school, compared to 58 percent of teen moms overall. Although teen pregnancy is a problem across all ethnicities, teenage Latina mothers are more likely to face unique circumstances than adolescents of other ethnic and racial backgrounds. Some scholars have indicated that teen moms from minority groups not only have lower educational attainment, but they also are more likely to live and raise their children in high poverty neighborhoods (Averett, Rees, and Argys 1774; Villarruel 78).

Although such reports paint a bleak picture for teenage mothers, it is not fair to assume that all teen mothers experience these problems. Support systems for teen mothers, especially for Latinas, often help lessen the likelihood of living in marginal conditions indefinitely. In particular, for Latina teen mothers whose cultural norms tend to be more family-oriented, favor strong family ties, and have higher levels of fertility, becoming pregnant and giving birth may have different meanings for Latinas than teenage moms from other cultural and ethnic backgrounds (Population Resource Center 3). Therefore, compared to other ethnicities, Latinas' positive view of childbirth and extended family allows for more understanding and support of teens when they become pregnant. Furthermore, support provided by immediate family members and extended relatives as commonly happens in Latino families (e.g., grandparents) represents additional resources for babysitting, models for positive parenting behaviors, and close monitoring of teenagers' child-rearing practices.

Teenage mothers are often expected to drop out of school, be on welfare, and remain in poverty (SmithBattle 409). Studies have even indicated that due to poverty, limited access to health care, racism and discrimination, and acculturative stress, Latinas generally are at a social and economic disadvantage (Gloria, Castellanos and Orozco 176; Villaruel 75). Empirical evidence shows that among Latina teen mothers, approximately 80 percent receive welfare assistance during the first ten years after giving birth to their first child whereas 44 percent receive welfare during five years or more after they have their first child (Population Research Center 3). Other negative consequences of early childbearing can include dropping out of school because of parenting responsibilities, limited vocational skills, additional pregnancies, and homelessness as a result of poverty (Jones et al. 402; Scott-Jones and Turner 41-42).

Elaine Esbaugh and Gayle Luze compare how resources and needs differ for adolescent and adult low-income mothers in their article "Adolescent and Adult Low-Income Mothers: How Do Needs and Resources Differ?" In particular, they question whether teen parenthood is solely responsible for all of these negative consequences and argue that poverty and socioeconomic class could be a cause for both teen childbearing and negative life events (1039-40). In addition, they cast doubt on the notion that teen mothers have negative outcomes because of their early childbearing; perhaps the same young women would have similar outcomes if they delayed child rearing. Such an approach takes on a deficit model in which teen mothers are expected to only have more negative outcomes and incompetent child-rearing practices. An example of this is the available empirical evidence which suggests that social stress due to migration and adjustment to a new culture as well as strict traditional child-rearing practices and values may be important factors in understanding child maltreatment among Latino families (Warner-Rogers, Hansen, and Hecht 141; Zayas 291-293). This, of course, needs to be further explored also in terms of existing misconceptions and stereotyped assumptions regarding child-rearing practices inherent to the Latino culture and how those might defer from the Anglo culture without necessarily implying negative practices or outcomes.

SUCCESSES

Although studies have reported such trends, not all teen mothers end up in economic and socially disadvantaged conditions. Some studies have put forward that positive behavioral changes are possible after teen pregnancy. In particular, for Latina teen mothers, a growing body of research supports this claim. For example, in an article published in the Journal of Qualitative Health Research, Daniel Sciarra and Joseph Ponterotto interviewed Latina teen mothers (ages 14-16 years) and their mothers about teen pregnancy. This study found that positive interaction with their mothers helped these Latina teen moms through their pregnancy and child rearing (753). The study also found that the mothers' reactions to their daughters' pregnancies varied with whether they had been teen mothers themselves (755-58). The mothers of the teenagers who had been pregnant as adolescents understood what their daughters were experiencing, though they wished it did not occur. Most teens were more dependent on and accepting of their mothers' supervision after their pregnancy than before. In general, the mothers were against aborting the babies. They saw the baby as a way for the adolescent to assume a responsible role, even though they were quite upset about their daughters' pregnancy. This study indicates that the meanings that Latina teenagers attach to a pregnancy and childbirth are important. For the teens and their mothers viewing pregnancy as a way to become more responsible takes away from the negative perceptions. It is also important to note that the Latina mothers supported their teenage daughters during pregnancy and in raising their baby. Therefore, with support from their families, Latina teen mothers can defy the norm of being impoverished and unfit mothers.

Recently, Erum Nadeem and Laura Romo examined the expectations of Latina mothers for their teen pregnant daughters. The authors found that the emphasis mothers put on the family unit and interdependence along with conversations about teenagers' feelings regarding their pregnancies, self-sufficiency, child care needs, and future educational goals provided a secure environment for pregnant teens (234-38). In addition, teenagers reported experiencing positive feeling about their pregnancies, perceived higher social support, and were more optimistic towards their future. Similarly, Stephen Russell and Faye Lee conducted a qualitative study on Latina teen perspective on pregnancy. Twenty-seven women in California were interviewed; the interviews focused on the adolescents' stories about inspiration and sources of strength as teen mothers. Findings from the study indicated that the Latina teen mothers said that motherhood increased their aspirations for the future—mostly, due to their desire to rise from their situation; some planned to get high school diplomas and even advanced degrees (212, 217-19). For most Latina teens, the motivation was the need to care for and support their child/children and being pregnant made them more aware of the responsibilities of supporting themselves and their babies. The Latina teens who were mothers also indicated that their relationship with the fathers of their babies improved since they became parents. Relationships with their parents also improved; adolescents reported feeling closer to their parents, especially their mothers. One adolescent said that her relationship with her mother improved because now that she was a mother herself, she better understood her mother. Some Latinas also reported improved relationships with their fathers, particularly due to the advice that their fathers gave them about raising children. The results also indicated that Latina teen mothers, whose relationships with their fathers improved, were more likely to report improvements in their schooling. Most importantly, this study revealed strengths in the lives of Latina teen moms. In particular, some of these mothers had a new commitment toward educational attainment and improved relationships with their family. Teenage mothering does not necessarily have to be negative by default; with family and social support, an adolescent can successfully navigate the challenges of being a teen mother. The above-mentioned studies shed light on an area of research that has been widely neglected and underscore the need for further exploring the factors that might turn teenage pregnancy into a constructive experience with positive outcomes for Latino teen mothers and their children.

Discussing successes of teen motherhood for Latinos must be also considered in the context of the extended family. As Felipe Gonzales-Castro and colleagues indicate, family bonds run deep in Latino culture, and Latino family members often feel a strong, mutual responsibility to support and care for one another (154). In the Latino culture, families also represent a significant source of guidance and social support. Additionally, family traditions emphasize cooperation and collective needs over individual needs. The cultural importance of social connections and family ties also means that family members often play an important role in influencing the well-being of Latina teens. Furthermore, the meanings and interactions with Latina teen mothers, their babies, and their own parents are often influenced by immigration and cultural values and traditions held by Latinas from various backgrounds. We do know that family relations across generations bear particular significance for Latino families in general. However, less has been reviewed about how immigration and generation status affect this value transmission.

Previous findings have shown that with acculturation and adaptation to a different culture (Warner-Rogers, Hansen, and Hecht 141; Zayas 291), some Latinos may experience stressors in having to assimilate into mainstream American culture. As Anne Driscoll and colleagues further discussed, when compared to more acculturated teens less acculturated teens displayed more positive attitudes about their pregnancy and similar or better birth outcomes ("Adolescent Latino Reproductive Health" 315). To date, literature on the potential effects of acculturation on Latina teen mothers is mostly inconclusive and scarce, and thus, it represents an area of scholarship that needs to be further explored.

ELIZABETH TREJOS-CASTILLO AND HELYNE FREDERICK

METHODOLOGICAL SHORTCOMINGS OF
CURRENT EMPIRICAL RESEARCH

Despite a recent increase in rates of teen pregnancy experienced during 2005-2007 (five percent increase), in general, rates of teen pregnancy in the U.S. have steadily declined since 1991 across all ethnic groups with a greater drop among younger teens (ages 10-14 years). Indeed, teen pregnancy rates fell from 61.8 percent per 1,000 in 1991 to 40.5 percent in 2004 (Centers for Disease Control 1). Among Latina adolescents, however, national statistics report the highest rate of teen pregnancy when compared to other ethnic/racial youth; approximately 53 percent of Latina teens get pregnant at least once before turning 20 years old (Centers for Disease Control 3). Official data shows that rates of fertility and live births were considerably higher for Hispanic/Latina adolescents as a whole group than for non-Hispanic teens for all age groups during 2005-2007 (V2). It is also reported by national data that Latina youth abortion rates during 2004-2006 were 31 percent compared to 43 percent among African American and 65 percent among Caucasian adolescents; in addition, Latina teens reported the smallest decline in birth rates between 1991 and 2005 (22 percent per 1,000) when compared to African American (48 percent per 1,000) and Caucasian teenagers (40 percent per 1,000; Centers for Disease Control 2). The slower decline in Latina teen birth rates compared to other ethnic groups needs to be understood in the context that Latina adolescents are generally more likely to have their babies than have an abortion. This argument is supported by the lower rate of abortion reported by Latina teen mothers compared to other ethnic groups as well as the support provided by Latino families to pregnant teens to have their babies and follow traditional values and expectations (Driscoll et al. "Adolescent Latino Reproductive Health" 256).

Though scarce, a few studies have documented that teenage mothers might see their children as a source of motivation to change their lives by performing better in school, increasing their attendance rates, and making healthier decisions about future romantic relationships (McGaha-Garnett 19). Unfortunately, not only are studies on the aftermath of childbirth among teenagers limited, but they are mostly focused on Caucasian youth or lack an appropriate methodological approach to draw conclusions about potential differences in outcomes

132

across multi-ethnic adolescent mothers. In addition, most studies are based on epidemiological quantitative data that fail to assess the dynamics of motherhood among this greatly heterogeneous population (O'Sullivan and Meyer-Bahlburg 226; Unger, Molina and Teran 210). Thus, even though previous studies have documented the importance that values such as marianismo (spiritual virtue related to motherhood), familismo, machismo, and perceived educational and labor opportunities versus domestic work play on Latina teenagers' decision towards motherhood (Laureano and McVicker, 2; Villarruel 74), little is known about the role those values play after childbirth and during the childbearing period.

Of particular interest is the need for further understanding the potential effects that generational status and nationality might have on Latina adolescent motherhood. For instance, Margaret Kelaher and Dorothy J. Jessop in their article "Differences in Low-Birth Weight among Documented and Undocumented Foreign-Born and U.S. Born Latinas" argue that first-generation immigrant Latina teenagers are less likely to have healthier babies and experience less post-partum problems as compared to their second and subsequent generation counterparts (2173). They point out that first-generation Latina adolescents experience more problems during pregnancy due to limited health care resources and lack of knowledge about their own bodies. Similarly, decisions made regarding sexual intercourse and dating an older or similar age boyfriend as well as contraceptive negotiation skills seem to differ across generations of Latina adolescents and thus, might have a different effect on motherhood among Latina adolescents. Other scholars also argue that less acculturated Latina teenagers are more likely to stay virgins until they marry and are less likely to engage in risky sexual behaviors due to family values and norms (Afable-Munsuz and Brindis 210).

Finally, assimilation and adaptation into the mainstream culture in addition to language barriers, limited financial resources, and lack of access to community resources have also been identified as potential factors related to variations in pregnancy rates among generations of Latina adolescents (Escobar et al. 70; Minnis and Padian 627). In general, generational effects on Latina teen pregnancy as well as the role that family plays throughout generations in the transmission of values regarding pregnancy among Latina adolescents remain unanswered pressing questions that could provide important insights for the understanding of the Latina teen pregnancy phenomenon. In summary, perhaps one of the most important barriers that needs to be conquered in current research on Latina youth motherhood is the development of statistically sound and competent methodologies to better understand this phenomenon and to enhance prevention/intervention programs and other community services targeting this particular population.

SUPPORTING LATINA TEEN MOTHERS: TAKING ASSISTANCE TO THE NEXT LEVEL

Several programs such as the National Campaign to Prevent Teen Pregnancy and Advocates for Youth have been designed to prevent teen pregnancy, sexually transmitted infections/diseases, and risky sexual behaviors across the country; however, fewer programs are in place to help adolescents after they have given birth. Given that meanings and experiences may be unique across ethnic backgrounds, programs to help Latina teen mothers are likely to be more effective when cultural factors as well as factors unique to the adolescent mother are addressed. Thus, we suggest that policy targeting Latina teen mothers should consider the following issues:

1. Immigrant or generation status of the Latina. Given that many Latino youth may be first generation or foreign born, programs and services should be sensitive to cultural backgrounds as well as language barriers. When possible, programs should be in Spanish and English. Having the services available in the adolescents' language will make them more comfortable when accessing pre-pregnancy and post-pregnancy services. For example, Anne Driscoll and several other scholars interviewed Latina teen mothers between the ages of 15 and 19 with one child on their perspectives of prevention programs and services provided for them. Latina teen mothers identified the lack of Spanish-speaking staff and more importantly, the lack of culturally sensible staff and professionals as main gaps in services provided for them ("In Their Own Words" 122).

2. Increasing Latino family involvement to maximize the effectiveness of pregnancy prevention programs. Involving the family extends beyond parents to include the extended family network of siblings,

grandparents, aunts, and uncles. As indicated in the aforementioned studies, having the support from this wider family network will help the adolescent; family members can baby-sit and provide nurturance for the adolescent and her baby. It is important to clarify here that whether scholars suggest that extended family members should be involved in the prevention/intervention programs as a "culturally appropriate strategy" (Russell and Lee 148), independence and autonomy should also be emphasized for Latina teen mothers. Furthermore, the involvement of extended family members should not challenge the goals of the services intended for the expecting mothers (Driscoll et al. "In Their Own Words" 123; Russell and Lee 148).

3. Promoting community involvement in program planning and implementation to increase effectiveness and more resources for Latina teen moms to rely on. Engaging the community in advocating and volunteering to work with Latina adolescent mothers to help and provide social support for them as they transition into the role of parenthood is highly encouraged. Several scholars have discussed the important role that the community plays in the prevention of pregnancy among Latina teenagers as well as minority teen girls in general (Denner, Kirby, Coyle and Brindis 19; Donoso 224; Johns, Moncloa and Gong 178). One salient factor identified by most researchers is the importance of developing a community consensus regarding pregnancy prevention efforts to maximize the resources for the improvement of sexual education programs and to better serve the youth and their families.

4. Increasing Latino male involvement in preventing teen pregnancy. This is an area that has often been overlooked, and little is known on the subject of how to shape programming to address the needs of Latino teen males. In recent years, however, knowledge has been accruing about how to develop pregnancy prevention programs that involve males. For example, Latina pregnant teenagers identified the importance of involving their children's fathers in child care and receiving support from them (Driscoll et al. "In Their Own Words" 124).

5. Expanding educational and career opportunities for Latina teen mothers and improving health care services. Programs should instill a belief in Latina teen moms that despite their pregnancy a successful life is possible. In addition, there is no doubt that health care services are expensive and many Latina teen mothers are uninsured (Population Research Center 3). Thus, providing cost effective health care may help

ease the burdens of child rearing. In addition, access to reproductive health services is important for sexually active Latino teenagers since they need support and encouragement to use contraception effectively and consistently. Particularly among Latina teenagers, professionals and practitioners should be sensitive to the role that family values (e.g., respect), beliefs (e.g., religiosity), and expectations (e.g., gender roles) might play in decision making regarding contraception (Abma, Driscoll and Moore 18; Russell and Lee 148).

6. Revising current pregnancy and STD prevention programs. Comprehensive sexual education as well as information on AIDS is very important for providing Latina teens with the knowledge and skills necessary to make safe and healthy choices about sexual relationships. Therefore, if unwanted teen pregnancy can be prevented then there will be fewer adolescents who navigate to early motherhood.

CONCLUSION

Scholarship on teen pregnancy particularly for Latina adolescents is quite robust. Across studies, research has consistently discussed multiple correlates of Latina teen pregnancy such as low use of family planning services, poverty, acculturative stress, and lack of contraceptive use. Though, in general, several researchers have made key recommendations for reducing and preventing pregnancy, less attention has been paid to the experiences of these adolescents after their baby is born (Denner, Kirby, Coyle, and Brindis 19; Donoso 224; Johns, Moncloa, and Gong 178; Russell and Lee 148). In addition, there is an imperative need for more evaluation of current programs that cater to Latina teenage mothers, and thus, identifying what works and what does not work are important steps for improving the lives of Latina teen mothers and their children.

The significance of further exploration on the factors underlying Latina teen pregnancy is greatly needed. It is our hope that professionals and scholars across multiple disciplines would join efforts to examine this phenomenon using "multiple lenses" to generate insights on the factors that can improve current prevention and intervention programs. Such knowledge would inform practitioners, policy makers, and all individuals providing services to Latino families and teenagers about the needs of this particular population and how to better serve them.

WORKS CITED

Abma, Joyce, Anne Driscoll, and Kristin Moore. "Young Women's Degree of Control over First Intercourse: An Exploratory Analysis." *Family Planning Perspectives* 30.1 (1998): 12-18. Print.

Adams, Diane and Susan M. Kocik. "Perinatal Social Work with Childbearing Adolescents." *Social Work Health Care* 24.3 (1997): 85-97. Print.

Afable-Munsuz, Aimee and Claire D. Brindis. "Acculturation and the Sexual and Reproductive Health of Latino Youth in the United States: A Literature Review." *Perspectives on Sexual and Reproductive Health* 38.4 (2006): 208-19. Print.

Averett, Susan L., Daniel I. Rees, and Laura M. Argys. "The Impact of Government Policies and Neighborhood Characteristics on Teenage Sexual Activity and Contraceptive Use." *American Journal of Public Health* 92.11 (2002): 1773-78. Print.

Centers for Disease Control and Prevention's National Center for Health Statistics (NCHS). "NCHS Data on Teenage Pregnancy." 2008. Web. 20 March 2009.

Denner, Jill, Douglas Kirby, Karin Coyle, and Claire Brindis. "The Protective Role of Social Capital and Cultural Norms in Latino Communities: A Study of Adolescent Births." *Hispanic Journal of Behavioral Sciences* 23 (2001): 3-21. Print.

Donoso, Raquel. "Coalition-based Strategies for Improving Health Access and Outcomes for Underserved Women." *Berkeley Women's Law Journal* 37.1 (2001): 224-28. Print.

Driscoll, Anne K., Anthonia M. Biggs, Claire D. Brindis, and Ekua Yankah. "Adolescent Latino Reproductive Health: A Review of the Literature." *Hispanic Journal of Behavioral Science* 23.3 (2001): 255-326. Print.

Driscoll, Anne K., Michael S. Brockman, Peggy Gregory, Melina M. Bersamin, Marilyn Johns, Faye Lee, Darlene Liesch, Fe Moncloa, Carla Sousa, Stephen T. Russell, and Denise Alvarado. "In Their Own Words: Pregnancy Prevention Needs of Latino Teen Mothers." *California Journal of Health Promotion* 1.2 (2003): 118-29. Print.

Erikson, Erik. *Childhood and Society.* 2nd ed. New York: Norton, 1963. Print.

Esbaugh, Elaine M. and Gayle J. Luze. "Adolescent and Adult Low-

Income Mothers: How Do Needs and Resources Differ?" *Journal of Community Psychology* 35.8 (2007): 1037-52. Print.

Escobar, Javier I., Constanza H. Nervi, and Michael A Gara. "Immigration and Mental Health: Mexican Americans in the United States." *Harvard Review of Psychiatry* 8.2 (2000): 64-72. Print.

Gloria, Alberta M., Jeanette Castellanos, and Veronica V. Orozco. "Perceived Educational Barriers, Cultural Fit, Coping Responses, and Psychological Well-being of Latina Undergraduates." *Hispanic Journal of Behavioral Sciences* 27.2 (2005): 161-83. Print.

Gonzales-Castro, Felipe, Gina R. Boyer, and Hector G. Balcazar. "Healthy Adjustment in Mexican American and Other Hispanic Adolescents." *Adolescent Diversity in Ethnic, Economic, and Cultural Contexts*. Ed. Raymond Montemayor, Gerald Adams, and Thomas Gullota. Thousand Oaks, CA: Sage, 2000. 141-78. Print.

González-López, Gloria and Salvador Vidal-Ortiz. "Latinas and Latinos, Sexuality, and Society: A Critical Sociological Perspective." *Latinos/as in the United States: Changing*. Ed. Havidán Rodríguez, Rogelio Sáenz, and Cecilia Menjívar. New York: Springer, 2008. 308-22. Print.

Johns, Marilyn J., Fe Moncloa and Elizabeth J. Gong. "Teen Pregnancy Prevention Programs: Linking Research and Practice." *Journal of Extension* 38.4 (2000): 151-78. Print.

Jones, Allison S., Nan M. Astone, Penelope M. Keyl, Young J. Kim, and Cheryl S. Alexander. "Teen Childbearing and Educational Attainment: A Comparison of Methods." *Journal of Family & Economic Issues* 20.4. (1999): 387–418. Print.

Kahn, Joan R., and Rosalind E. Berkowitz . "Sources of Support for Young Latina Mothers." The Urban Institute. 1995. Web. 25 February 2009.

Kelaher, Margaret and Dorothy J. Jessop. "Differences in Low-Birthweight among Documented and Undocumented Foreign-Born and U.S. Born Latinas." *Social Science and Medicine* 55.12 (2002): 2171-75. Print.

Laureano, Bianca and Carrie McVicker. "Preventing Latino Teen Pregnancy: Research to Practice." 2003. Web. 20 March 2009.

Longmore, Monica A. "Symbolic Interactionism and the Study of Sexuality." *Journal of Sex Research* 35.1 (1998): 44-57. Print.

Martin, Joyce A., Brady E. Hamilton, Paul D. Sutton, Stephanie J. Ventura, Fay Menacker, Sharon Kirmeyer, and Martha L. Munson, eds.

Births: Final Data for 2005. United States Department of Health and Human Services, National Vital Statistics Report (Vol. 56). Atlanta: Centers for Disease Control, 2007. Print.

McGaha-Garnett, Valerie. "Needs Assessment For Adolescent Mothers: Building Resiliency and Student Success Towards High School Completion." *Compelling Counseling Interventions. Celebrating VISTAS' Fifth Anniversary.* Ed. Garry R. Walz, Jeanne C. Bleuer, and Richard K. Yep. Ann Arbor, MI: Counseling Outfitters, 2008. 11-20. Print.

Minnis, Alexandra M. and Nancy S. Padian. "Reproductive Health Differences among Latin American- and U.S.-Born Young Women." *Journal of Urban Health* 78.4 (2001): 627-37. Print.

Nadeem, Erum and Laura F. Romo. "Low-Income Latina Mothers' Expectations for Their Pregnant Daughters' Autonomy and Interdependence." *Journal of Research on Adolescence* 18.2 (2008): 215-38. Print.

National Campaign to Prevent Pregnancy. "An Overview of Latina Teen Pregnancy and Birth Rates." 2008. Web. 23 March 2009.

Ofori-Dankwa, Joseph C. and David A. Ricks. "Research Emphasis on Cultural Differences and or Similarities: Are We Asking the Right Questions?" *Journal of International Management* 6 (2000): 173-86. Print.

O'Sullivan, Lucia F. and Heino F. L. Meyer-Bahlburg. "Sexual Development African-American and Latina Inner-City Girls." *Journal of Social and Personal Relationship* 20.2 (2003): 221-38. Print.

Pantelides, Edith A. "Aspectos Sociales Del Embarazo Y La Fecundidad Adolescente En América Latina." 78, 7-33. Centro Latinoamericano y Caribeño De Demografía/ Comisión Económica Para América Latina y El Caribe (CELADE/CEPAL). 2004. Web. 15 March 2009.

Population Research Center. "Teen Pregnancy and Welfare Reform: Solutions to the Puzzle of Poverty." 2002. Web. 12 July 2009a.

Population Resource Center. "Latina Teen Pregnancy: Problems and Prevention." 2004. Web. 10 March 2009b.

Russell, Stephen T. and Faye C. H. Lee. "Practitioners' Perspectives on Effective Practices for Hispanic Teenage Pregnancy Prevention." *Perspectives on Sexual and Reproductive Health* 36.4 (2004): 142-49. Print.

Sciarra, Daniel T. and Joseph G. Ponterotto. "Adolescent Motherhood Among Low-Income Urban Hispanics: Familial Considerations of Mother-Daughter Dyads." *Qualitative Health Research* 8.6 (1998): 751-63. Print.

Scott-Jones, Diane and Sherry L. Turner. "The Impact of Adolescent Childbearing on Educational Attainment and Income of Black Females." *Youth & Society* 22.1 (1990): 35–53. Print.

SmithBattle, Lee. "Legacies of Advantage and Disadvantage: The Case of Teen Mothers." *Public Health Nursing* 24.5 (2007): 409-20. Print.

Stern, Claudio. "Vulnerabilidad Social Y Embarazo Adolescente En México." *Papeles De Población* 39 (2004): 129-58. Web. 20 March 2009.

Stevenson, Wendy, Kenneth I. Maton, and Douglas M. Teti. "Social Support: Relationship Quality and Well-Being Among Pregnant Adolescents." *Journal of Adolescence* 22.1 (1999): 109-21. Print.

Unger, Jennifer B., Gregory B. Molina, and Lorena Teran. "Perceived Consequences of Teenage Childbearing among Adolescent Girls in an Urban Sample." *Journal of Adolescent Health* 26.3 (2000): 205-12. Print.

Ventura, Stephanie J., Joyce C. Abma, William D. Mosher, and Stanley K. Henshaw. "Estimated Pregnancy Rates by Outcome For The United States, 1990–2004." *National Vital Statistics Reports; Vol. 56 No. 15*. Hyattsville, MD: National Center For Health Statistics. 2008. Web. 11 July 2009.

Villarruel, Antonia M. "Cultural Influences on the Sexual Attitudes, Beliefs and Norms of Young Latina Adolescents." *Journal for Specialists of Pediatric Nurses* 3.2 (1998): 69-81. Print.

Warner-Rogers, Jody E., David J. Hansen, and Debra B. Hecht. "Child Physical Abuse and Neglect." *Assessment of Family Violence: A Clinical and Legal Sourcebook*. Ed. Robert T. Ammerman and Michael Hersen. New York: Wiley, 1999. 127-56. Print.

Whitman, Thomas L., John G. Borkowski, Deborah A. Keogh, and Keri Weed. *Interwoven Lives: Adolescent Mothers and Their Children*. Mahwah, NJ: Erlbaum, 2001. Print.

Zayas, Luis H. "Hispanic Family Ecology and Early Childhood Socialization: Health Implications." *Family Systems Medicine* 12 (1994): 315-25. Print.

Motherhood Unbound

Homeless Chicanas in San Francisco

ANNE R. ROSCHELLE

THERE IS A LONG HISTORY IN THE SOCIAL SCIENCES FIELD OF arguing that women of color share a common disdain for marriage and traditional family values. This body of literature dates back to the late 1800s and early 1900s when scholars began to characterize poor African Americans as inherently pathological.[1] High rates of poverty, unemployment, and low educational attainment were blamed on out-of-wedlock births and the rejection of marriage, rather than on structural inequality (Frazier 47). During the 1960s proponents of this pathological approach (Moynihan 7-9) applied their analysis to Latina/o families as well (Lewis 18; Madsen 36). These theorists argued that low-income Latinas/os have distinctive values, aspirations, and psychological characteristics that inhibit their achievement and produce behavioral "deficiencies" that keep them impoverished. Moreover, they contend that these "deficiencies" result in a perpetual cycle of poverty (Zinn 858) and a fundamental rejection of marriage (Andrade 99; Mirandé 146-64; Ybarra 94).

After two decades of scholarly work refuting this fallacious perspective, the Culture of Poverty approach, which argues that poor families of color are responsible for their own poverty as a result of pathological values, made a searing comeback in the 1980s and 1990s (Mead 21; Murray 53). Much of the research during this resurgence focused on teenage and nonmarital pregnancy, welfare dependency, and a lack of normative family values. Poor Latina/o families were once again vilified as pathological, welfare reliant, and most importantly as opposed to the sacred institution of marriage. Conservative policy analysts such as Charles Murray and Lawrence Mead pointed to the decline in marriage among impoverished women and the concomitant increase in nonmarital childbearing to promote their racialized anti-welfare agenda. These analysts argue that the increase in female-headed families and out-of-wedlock births over the last thirty years reflects an endemic disregard for normative family values. Although poor women do have higher rates of nonmarital births and single parenthood—characteristics that are often associated with poverty and welfare recipiency (Aasve 105),[2] this reflects structural inequality, not deviant family values. Subsequently, having children outside of marriage has now become the norm for economically disenfranchised families (Ventura and Bachrach 2).

Culture of Poverty theorists seized upon this datum to argue that poor women of color devalue marriage, depend on welfare, and reject middle-class values (Mead 78; Murray 54). While these datum do represent significant changes in family formation that cannot be ignored, they do not reflect pathological family values. Having children without being married is a consequence of poverty in which race, class, and gender oppression conspire to prevent couples from realizing their familial aspirations. In fact, having children outside of marriage reflects structural inequality, particularly for poor women and women of color, who overwhelmingly indicate that they want to get married.

Most women and men, regardless of their social location, want to get married. There is strong support for marriage across racial ethnic and class boundaries and most people say they intend to marry (Lichter, Batson, and Brown 2; Mauldon et al. 615). Among welfare recipients an overwhelming majority (70 percent) indicated that they expected to get married (Mauldon et al. 615) and they shared the same values about marriage as non-welfare recipients (Ciabattari 66). Similarly, there are very few racial ethnic differences in marriage norms (South 357), although Latinas, African Americans, and low–income women actually express the most traditional views on marriage (Bulcroft and Bulcroft 345; Ciabattari 66; Kaplan 79; Mauldon et al. 616; Oropesa, 49).

This research provides overwhelming evidence that poor women and women of color do value the institution of marriage and would prefer to be married before they have children. Fallacious arguments about the lack of family values among poor women and women of color reflect racist and classicist ideologies that are deeply embedded in American culture and are not supported by the empirical evidence. Low marriage rates among poor mothers reflect social structural obstacles to successful relationships, not pathological values. Unfortunately, the discourse of pathology remains pervasive among scholars and policy analysts who ignore the realities of social structural inequality.

There are a variety of economic and social barriers to marriage that help explain why poor women of color do not marry before giving birth. In their groundbreaking ethnographic book *Promises I Can Keep: Why Poor Women Put Motherhood Before Marriage* (2005), Kathryn Edin and Maria Kefalas provide insight into the specific socio-economic barriers that prevent low-income women from marrying the fathers of their children and the complicated reasons why they put motherhood before marriage. Other sociologists such as Andrew Cherlin, Sara McLanahan, and Joanna M. Reed have built upon this work and there is now a rich body of qualitative and quantitative research that provides compelling evidence that social and economic barriers are responsible for the increase in nonmarital births among impoverished women not aberrant family values (Cherlin et al. 925; Edin, Kefalas, and Reed 1011; Gibson-Davis, Edin, and McLanahan 1307; Smock, Manning, and Porter 687; Waller 474).

This research has identified the specific relational and financial obstacles that discourage poor couples from marrying. A lack of financial resources, the importance of economic stability, gender mistrust, domestic violence, high expectations about marriage, and fear of divorce all contribute to declining marriage rates among the poor (Coley 101; Edin 117-22; Gibson-Davis, Edin, and McLanahan 1307). In addition, men's income is an important consideration in the willingness of women to get married. In particular, women frequently articulated that they would only marry men with steady incomes and that those incomes could not come from illicit or illegal work (Edin 117; Gibson-Davis, Edin, and McLanahan 1307; Smock, Manning, and Porter 687). Furthermore, most poor couples wanted to have some financial security, to establish good credit, and to pay off debt before marrying. Women also said they wanted to be able to pay their bills and to save enough money for a mortgage on a small house, some furniture, and maybe a car (Edin, Kefalas, and Reed 1012; Gibson-Davis, Edin, and McLanahan 1307).[3] Financial security, usually associated with middle-class life, is also of concern to impoverished women before they consider getting married. Poor women frequently articulated the importance of being financially secure to prevent marital stress that could ultimately lead to divorce (Edin, Kefalas, and Reed 1011; Gibson-Davis, Edin, and McLanahan 1309). Low-income respondents consistently cited the importance of economic factors in their marital decision making with only slight differences among racial ethnic groups (Smock, Manning, and Porter 687).[4] Respondents articulated that rushing into marriage as a result of a pregnancy was foolish and would increase the likelihood of divorce (Edin 120). Clearly, low-income women do not enter into marriage without considering how their financial status will impact that marriage. This finding suggests that rather than having non-normative family values, poor women actually share the same financial concerns about marriage as middle-class women.

In addition to financial considerations, relational concerns also impacted marital decision-making among poor women and men. Domestic violence, sexual jealousy, and fears about infidelity, referred to as gender mistrust, were common reasons given for not getting married. Men who initially denied their paternity, who were seen as potentially unfaithful, and who had high incidences of incarceration were not trustworthy enough to marry (Edin 124; Edin and Reed 123; Edin, Kefalas, and Reed 1012). Women who reported drug and alcohol abuse and criminal activity among their partners were also fairly pessimistic about marriage. In addition, women who were victims of domestic violence were highly skeptical of having successful marriages. Stories of domestic violence were common among poor mothers (Edin 126) and were frequently cited as reasons for not marrying the fathers of their children. Women who were abused, who reported high conflict relationships, and who did not trust their boyfriends to be faithful, had significantly reduced marital expectations (Waller 474).

A consistent finding in most of the research is that women from disenfranchised communities view marriage as a sacred institution. Women openly discussed the seriousness of marriage and the importance of making a life-long commitment. More importantly, poor women did not want to ridicule the institution of marriage by frivolously marrying and then divorcing, even if they got pregnant. An unintended pregnancy was not considered reason enough to marry among poor women who attributed tremendous symbolic importance to marriage and wanted to avoid divorce (Edin 120; Edin, Kefalas, and Reed 1013; Gibson-Davis, Edin, and McLanahan 1309).

The overwhelming evidence demonstrates that low-income African

American women and Latinas do not denigrate marriage and do not have values that conflict with mainstream society, despite their high rates of nonmarital births. Low rates of marriage among poor women of color are the result of structural inequality that creates barriers to successful marriages. Racial discrimination, economic disenfranchisement, and gender inequality all contribute to a lack of opportunities for low-income women in urban America. It is the lack of these opportunities, not pathological values, which contribute to low rates of marriage and high rates of nonmarital births among disenfranchised women. As a result, poor women of color have very little to lose by having a child outside of marriage and in fact motherhood might be their only chance for a rewarding and emotionally fulfilling life (Anderson 152; Bourgois 273; Edin and Kefalas 56; Hays 84).

Although previous research tells us a great deal about why welfare recipients and low-income couples have children outside of marriage it does not include the experiences of homeless families. My research extends this body of work by focusing specifically on homeless women and their marital decisions. This chapter is based on a four-year ethnographic study of homeless Chicanas in San Francisco, California.[5] By giving voice to these women and analyzing their stories from a race, class, and gender perspective, my research further confirms that homeless Chicana mothers in San Francisco actually have traditional attitudes about marriage and motherhood. Unfortunately, the exigencies of poverty force many of them to delay marriage indefinitely. Putting motherhood before marriage makes sense in a social context in which homeless women have no other means of achieving social status or recognition (Anderson 152; Bourgois 273; Edin and Kefalas 56; Hays 85). Like other poor women, most of the Chicanas in my research were very pro-marriage, and were extremely opposed to divorce. Many of the mothers were precariously housed when they had their first child, some were already homeless, but all were destitute. As a result many Chicanas preferred to delay marriage until they were sure their partners could help support them, would not cheat on them, would not engage in illegal behavior, and would not become physically and/or emotionally abusive. For homeless Chicanas in San Francisco their disenfranchised economic position prevented them from realizing their dream of marriage before motherhood and presented significant obstacles to creating stable families, pushing them further onto the margins of society.

A HOME AWAY FROM HOMELESSNESS

The research site where I conducted my study is an organization in San Francisco called A Home Away From Homelessness. Home Away serves homeless families living in shelters, residential motels, foster homes, halfway houses, transitional housing facilities, and low-income housing. The program operates a Beach House in Marin county, shelter support services, a crisis hotline, a family drop-in center (called the Club House), a mentorship program, and, in conjunction with the San Francisco Unified School District, an afterschool educational program (called the School House). Because of the lack of draconian and often arbitrary rules typically found at homeless service agencies and the fact that families sleep elsewhere, Home Away is neither a typical service agency nor is it a shelter.

The ethnographic component of my research included participant observation at the Beach House, the School House, and the Club House where I collected data and did volunteer work for four years (1995-1999). During this time I also attended meetings of relevant social service agencies, met with numerous case workers, and took copious notes. In addition, I conducted observational research at residential motels, transitional housing facilities, and homeless shelters throughout the San Francisco Bay Area. Moreover, I conducted thousands of hours of informal interviews, sometimes asking leading questions other times just listening (Gubrium and Holstein 5). Many of these informal interviews were taped[6] and transcribed, others were not. Lastly, I conducted and transcribed verbatim formal taped interviews with ninety-seven children and parents who were currently or previously homeless. I typically spoke my field notes and critical interpretations of the days' events into a tape recorder immediately after working with the families and transcribed and coded these tapes.

A significant challenge of studying homeless Chicanas is being attentive to their devalued social position. This awareness is particularly necessary because of the stigma associated with being homeless and having children outside of marriage. Because of the social structural location of the women in my sample, the issue of reflexivity was essential. I paid great attention to the intersections and reciprocity between myself as the researcher and those being researched. By attending to the political, material, and cultural context in which the study took place, and by recognizing how my race, class, and gender location influenced the research site, I consciously resisted reproducing hegemonic colonial relationships typically found between middle-class white researchers and impoverished Chicana study participants. To this end, I avoided academic jargon, developed questions around participants' discursive expressions, and respected the mothers' interpretations of social reality and the meanings they attributed to their social interactions.

Along with reflexivity, I was also attentive to the issue of representation that has been articulated by feminist ethnographers (Alcoff 289; Heyl 378; Mohanty 36). I tried to minimize the risk of reproducing white power relations and privilege through my presentations of Chicana homeless mother's narratives (Stacey 115), by giving voice to a variety of women's perspectives within the sample. These stories poignantly illustrate that homelessness is not a monolithic experience. Although individuals who are homeless share a similarly devalued social position, both the content and the process of their interpersonal relations may vary. As a result, I made a concerted effort to interview and present the voices of a wide array of Chicanas who are homeless. In addition, the extensive amount of time I spent in the field provided insight into the multiplicity of experiences faced by homeless Chicana mothers in San Francisco.

VOICES FROM THE FIELD

Chicanas in my sample were among the poorest residents in San Francisco. Although many of the women were not homeless at the time of their first pregnancy, they were precariously housed and on the verge of homelessness. Other women became homeless prior to becoming pregnant. Despite their grinding poverty, homeless Chicanas articulated traditional values about marriage including the importance of economic stability and of marrying a man who could contribute financially to the household. For example, Flora stated her opinions about marriage:[7]

When I got pregnant, my boyfriend José asked me to marry him—but I said no way. I did want to marry him, but we had no money and our future looked dark. José works from time to time, but he is not good at keeping a job. He worked at a car wash for a while, but he got fired for being late to work. I can't marry someone who can't help support me—that's crazy. If we get married and he has no job, I'll be stuck with him. We decided to live together first and wait until he had a steady paycheck before getting married. That never happened!

Similarly, Aixa gave her story of not getting married:

When I got pregnant I wasn't homeless. Horatio and I both lived with our parents. We knew we couldn't get married because we were broke. Horatio and I both worked, but we never made very much money and neither one of us was good at keeping a job for very long. We decided to wait to get married so we could save some money. We talked about having enough money to get a decent apartment, to buy some new furniture, and maybe even put some in the bank. We talked a lot about our future and how important it was for Horatio to have steady work and for us to start saving money. He seemed like he really wanted to take care of us. As you can see, that plan didn't work out too well. Horatio never found steady work. I was so angry and hurt because he promised he would take care of me and our baby. He broke his promise and then I was on my own.

Many of the women in my research were wary of marrying men who could not contribute financially to their household. Several of the women told me that their boyfriends were out of work or had low-paying jobs in the service economy. These women knew that marrying a man with little or no resources would lead to conflict and could potentially end in divorce. Elisa shared her precarious situation:

My boyfriend Eduardo asked me to marry him—but I said no way. He works sometimes—when he can find work, but he always seems to get in fights with his boss and get fired. When he is working, he hardly makes any money. He gets really angry when he has no money and I hate to be around him when he is like that. How can you be married to someone like that? Fighting all the time—that's too fucking stressful and I know that could split us up—If we are going to break up I don't want to be married and get divorced. I'd rather just break up and move on. Breaking up with a boyfriend is painful, but it is not the same thing as getting divorced. Marriage is serious, it is sacred. You can't just jump into marriage because you are pregnant. It is better to live with the person first to see if you get along. If things don't work out, you can always leave. But marriage is forever.

Marta also stated that marrying someone who had few economic resources was a recipe for disaster. She understood that a lack of financial security can create enormous stress in a relationship and could ultimately lead to divorce:

When I first found out I was pregnant, I was very excited and did think about getting married. I always dreamed about having a family and living in a house with a fenced in yard for a dog to run around in. Yeah, I know it is silly—the white picket fence thing, but isn't that what we all dream of? Well, I got over that pretty fast. I knew I couldn't really marry someone that never had any money. Julio had a steady job, but the pay was so low he could barely pay his bills. I knew we wouldn't be able to set up a decent place to live on his salary. I [had] always wanted to save money before I got married so I could get some furniture, new curtains, a new microwave oven for the kitchen—you know things like that.

When I asked her what other problems might arise from marrying someone who is economically unstable, she replied:

When you are poor, it creates a lot of stress. People get frustrated and sometimes feel like the weight of the world is crushing down on them. When Julio and I first lived together, we were very excited about the baby and our new lives together. But once the reality of being poor with a new baby hit us—things got really bad. Julio was angry all the time. He felt bad because he couldn't support his family. He hated his job, but couldn't quit because we needed the money. We were struggling so hard to survive that we forgot how to be nice to each other. We were always yelling at each other and saying mean things. All we could think about was how we were going to pay our bills. By the end of two years we could barely stand each other and that's when we split up. I guess we were right not to get married after all. You know, I grew up in a very Catholic family and divorce is considered a sin. I would feel like such a failure if I had married Julio and [had] then gotten divorced.

Ironically, having children outside of marriage only furthers their societal stigmatization.

In addition to economic barriers, Chicana mothers also faced a myriad of social and relational barriers to marriage. Throughout my research, I heard numerous stories of deceit, infidelity, criminality, domestic violence, and drug and alcohol abuse. Chicanas courageously recounted painful stories of failed relationships with the fathers of their children, many of whom betrayed their trust. Women spoke mournfully about men cheating on them and their unwillingness to be faithful. They also expressed concern about fathers who engaged in illegal behavior or were periodically incarcerated. Drug and alcohol abuse was rampant among the men in these women's lives. In addition, domestic violence was a significant problem for homeless Chicanas in San Francisco. Given the brutal conditions of poverty, it is not surprising to find romantic relationships fraught with so much conflict—conflict that contributed to women's decisions not to marry the fathers of their children. As she noted about relationships, Cecilia recalled tension with her partner:

You know how guys are, they sweet talk you—convince you they love you and want to be with you forever. Once they get you into bed, they stop talking about being together forever. How can I marry someone like that? I can't trust that he will really stick by me forever and that he won't cheat on me. That's what happened with Diego. When I first got pregnant, he was really pissed off. He said it wasn't his kid. He knew that was bullshit, but he didn't want the responsibility. After that, I didn't trust him for a while. Once he admitted that he was the father, I moved into his apartment. We didn't have any money and he didn't have a job. Diego started selling drugs to make money, even though I begged him not to. I was afraid he would get shot or end up in jail. At first he made pretty good money and we were able to buy diapers, a stroller, and some other stuff for the baby. Even though we were able to buy the stuff we needed, I didn't like him selling drugs. The guys he hung out with were nasty and I didn't like them coming around. After the baby was born, Diego started staying out all night selling and partying. I'm pretty sure he was cheating on me with some skanky bitch. He started coming home high all the time. I told him he was being disrespectful to me and that my family thought he was a loser. He kept saying that we should get married—that if we got married my family would respect him. I told him that my family would only respect him if he got a real job and stopped selling drugs. I mean, how is being married to a drug dealer respectable? We started fighting all the time and then he started hitting me. He beat on me pretty bad and even sent me to the hospital a couple of times. This went on for almost three years. Finally, it got so bad that I took Carlos and left. I went to a battered women's shelter first and then I ended up in Hamilton Family Shelter. I guess being homeless is better than being a punching bag!

When I asked Cecilia if she was disappointed that she never married Diego, she said, "Hell no." From the beginning of their relationship Cecilia was skeptical of Diego's ability to provide economic stability and emotional support to their family. Like other Chicanas in the study, Cecilia expressed deep gender mistrust about Diego and did not think he would make a reliable and emotionally supportive husband. Ultimately, her fears were realized as they are for so many impoverished women whose dreams of happy marriages rarely materialize.

Like Cecilia, many of the homeless women in my study were victims of domestic violence. I met several women who were ravaged physically and psychologically by years of poverty and violence. Although these women aspired to marry the fathers of their children, they were hesitant to make a legal commitment to untrustworthy and abusive men. The following impromptu conversation illustrates this point:

Laura: *When I first got pregnant, Miguel started hitting me. At first he slapped me around then after the baby was born he really beat the shit out of me. I figured I would stay with him, but I wasn't gonna marry him. Good thing I didn't—he never stopped beating me—I was young and stupid then. I thought he would change—but they never do.*

Anna: *Yeah, Candido beat me too. I know what you mean about not wanting to get married right away—you think if you hang in there long enough they'll stop beating you. I've always wanted to get married and I thought we would get married after he stopped hitting me. Of course, it only got worse over the years. I finally left after I couldn't take it anymore—that's how I became homeless—but at least I finally left the bastard.*

Sylvia: *Franky never hit me when we were going out; he was really sweet. When I got pregnant, I didn't want to marry him though because we didn't have any money. I figured we should save money first—that way we would get along better. Plus, I wanted to make sure he was serious about being with me forever. You know guys—they promise you they'll be faithful and take care of you forever, and then they dog you with other women. I wanted to be sure we were really compatible and that he would be a good husband. I didn't want to be married to someone who ran around behind my back or was doing sketchy illegal shit. Things were pretty good the first year and then things got real bad. Franky got fired from his job for mouthing off to his boss. He got real angry and started drinking and hanging out all day. When he came home he would start fights with me all the time—then he started hitting me. He was so angry about being poor, getting fired, and just feeling like he was trapped in a shitty life. I could understand that—it is fuckin' hard being poor—but he shouldn't have taken it out on me. I tried to leave a bunch of times, but I had no money and no place to go. Eventually, me and my daughter went to a battered women's shelter and then got a place at the Franciscan Hotel. At least, I was smart enough not to marry him.*

Over several years, Laura, Anna, and Sylvia expressed, in poignant detail, the painful relationship experiences they endured. Each of them hoped for happy marriages and fulfilling family lives. Unfortunately, because of their disenfranchised economic position, those hopes were never realized.

DISCUSSION

In order to understand the realities of marriage for extremely poor women, we must examine the interlocking nature of race, class, and gender oppression. Racial stratification influences family resources and subsequent patterns of family organization (Zinn 873). In addition, patriarchy is inextricably linked to class, race, and gender inequality. Cultural norms and social-structural conditions constrain poor women's choices about marriage and family life. Most of the Chicana mothers in my study valued marriage as an institution and aspired to traditional marital arrangements. Marriage is particularly important for Chicanas because it is the nexus of their extended social support networks and represents their commitment to familism. Unfortunately, as a result of economic disenfranchisement, many low-income minority families are unable to participate in their extended kinship networks (Menjivar 183; Roschelle 154). Despite their adherence to cultural norms valuing familism, the constraints of a hostile economic system prevent home-less Chicanas in San Francisco from marrying before having children and ultimately from participating in exchange networks. Consequently, Chicanas are oppressed both culturally and economically: they are un-able to live by the values essential to their cultural survival because they are economically disadvantaged.

Chicanas in my study often chose motherhood over marriage because of the exigencies of poverty. My findings provide additional support to existing research that illustrates that poor women of color not only aspire to be married, but in fact have very traditional family values. These findings also negate pejorative stereotypes that poor women of color have deviant family values. Refuting these stereotypes allows us to undermine the racialized discourse that demonizes the poor and to develop more humane social welfare policies. However, by continuing to represent traditional heterosexual marriage as the quintessential norm, we are ultimately reinforcing a highly patriarchal societal institution. In our desire to move poor women of color from the margins of public discourse into the center, we are unintentionally reproducing hegemonic notions of marriage and the role of women.

Of course, there are many ways that women undermine the constraints of patriarchal marriage and transgress conventional gender norms. Al-though Chicanas do aspire to traditional families, they also engage in creative strategies to obtain autonomy within marriage (Hurtado 96; Toro-Morn 280). The unrelenting historical depiction of Chicana/o families as beleaguered by power-crazy men who demand obedience has been deconstructed by Chicana/o feminists. While the notion of machismo is not unique to the pathological perspective, it has been uncritically accepted with no attempt at verifying its prevalence in Chicano culture. As a result there are many distortions in both the definition and the usage of "machismo," and in the subsequent conceptualization of family structure. Groundbreaking books, such as *The Mexican American Family: Tradition and Change* (1990) by Norma Williams, *La Chicana: The Mexican-American Woman* (1979) by Alfredo Mirandé and Evangelina Enríquez, *Women's Work & Chicano Families: Cannery Workers of the Santa Clara Valley* (1987) by Patricia Zavella, and *La Chicana and the Intersection of Race, Class, and Gender* (1992) by Irene I. Blea have undermined the monolithic depiction of Chicanas as subservient martyrs desperate to be dominated by their men. While Chicana feminists recognize that machismo has been overemphasized as the fundamental determinate of Chicana/o family structure, they do not argue that it is nonexistent. Rather male domination exists in all cultures in varying forms and in varying degrees (Ybarra 97). More recently, Latina feminists such as Gloria Anzaldúa, Aída Hurtado, and Maura Toro-Morn point to the ways in which Chicanas/Latinas resist subordination in their everyday lives.[8]

One way that Chicanas assert their autonomy is through control of their sexuality. By making decisions about their sexual and reproductive behavior Chicanas, as well as other Latinas, resist subordination by men. Chicanas refuse to passively accept rigid patriarchal norms about sexuality and do not simply bend to the will of their men. This resistance is vital, since a fundamental way of subordinating women is by controlling their sexuality (Hurtado 94). Several Chicanas in my research exerted their agency by having children before getting married. Because mothering is a central role for Chicanas, and women in my study had bleak marital prospects, their decisions to have children outside of marriage, reflected their resistance to patriarchal domination. Unfortunately, this resistance strategy sometimes had the unintended consequence of reinforcing Chicanas' disenfranchised economic position and miring them further in poverty.

By giving voice to homeless Chicanas in San Francisco, my work aims to refute depictions of Chicana/o family life as inherently pathological. Poor Chicanas have been demonized by social scientists and policy makers as being overly submissive, promiscuous, lazy, drug addicted, and welfare dependent. Single Chicana mothers continue to be depicted as rejecting the institution of marriage and of ultimately threatening the very fabric of American society. The racialized discourse that surrounds poor Chicanas does not include a comprehensive analysis of social structural inequality nor does it acknowledge the violence endemic to poverty. Homeless mothers live in a perpetual state of chaos as they try to navigate the complexities of being poor in San Francisco. Frequent moves, horrific living conditions, interpersonal violence, and relentless uncertainty pervade their lives. Despite these challenges, these Chicanas took pride in being good mothers and they made important life decisions based on what they believed to be best for their children. For example, several mothers in my study became homeless after fleeing physically and emotionally abusive men. They chose to become homeless to protect their children from family violence. Other women took pride in making sure their children were clean, well dressed, and on time for school. Most mothers took great pleasure in cooking meals for their children, even if those meals were cooked on a hot pot or in a microwave oven in a residential motel. In addition, Chicana mothers were vigilant about who they allowed to interact with their young children. These examples support the findings of Latina scholars such as Aída Hurtado, Maxine Baca Zinn, Irene I. Blea, Gloria Anzaldúa, Patricia Zavella, and Mary Romero and contribute to a growing body of literature that rejects one-dimensional depictions of Chicana/o family life.

[1]See for example Hoffman 209-249; Puckett 8-12; Tillinghast 60-79.
[2]Female-headed households with children had a poverty rate of 32.5% in 2000 which is six times higher than the 4.7 percent poverty rate for married couples with kids (U.S. Bureau of the Census 3).
[3]Cherlin et al. did not find any support for the fear of divorce thesis and reported that there was very little stigma associated with divorce in poor urban communities (928). Nonetheless, they argue that poor women will only marry if they are convinced that economic and socioemotional factors are in place and that women did not want to settle for an inadequate relationship. Perhaps these women don't "fear" divorce; however, they are clearly unwilling to marry if they think it won't last.
[4]Economic security was an essential component in the decision of whether

or not to marry among 82 percent of African American, 67 percent of Latina/o, and 71 percent of white cohabiting couples (Smock, Manning, and Porter 687).

⁵The four-year ethnography included African American, European American, and other Latina/o respondents. However, because of the focus of this book, I will only discuss the experiences of Chicanas in the sample.

⁶All interviews were conducted in English. Surprisingly, a majority of Latina/o respondents in my study spoke English. Perhaps their proficiency with the language is what enabled them to initially access Home Away programs.

⁷All names have been changed to ensure anonymity.

⁸These Chicana feminists have made important contributions to our understanding of the complexities of family life and how women transgress boundaries of marriage and motherhood.

WORKS CITED

Aasave, Arnstein. "The Impact of Economic Resources on Premarital Childbearing and Subsequent Marriage among Young American Women." *Demography* 40.1 (2003): 105-26. Print.

Alcoff, Linda. "The Problem of Speaking For Others." *Feminist Nightmares Women at Odds*. Ed. Susan Ostrov Weisser. New York: New York University Press, 1994. 285-309. Print.

Anderson, Elijah. *Code of the Streets: Decency, Violence, and the Moral Life of the Inner City*. London: Norton, 1990. Print.

Andrade, Sally J. "Family Roles of Hispanic Women: Stereotypes, Empirical Findings, and Implications for Research." *Work, Family, and Health: Latina Women in Transition*. Ed. Ruth E. Zambrana. New York: Hispanic Research Center, Fordham University, 1982. 95-106. Print.

Blea, Irene, I. *La Chicana and the Intersection of Race, Class, and Gender*. Westport, CT: Praeger, 1992. Print.

Bourgois, Phillipe. *In Search of Respect: Selling Crack in el Barrio*. Cambridge: Cambridge University Press, 1995. Print.

Bulcroft, Richard, and Kris A. Bulcroft. "Race Differences in Attitudinal and Motivational Factors in the Decision to Marry." *Journal of Marriage and the Family* 55 (1993): 338-55. Print.

Cherlin, Andrew, Caitlin Cross-Barnet, Linda M. Burton, and Raymond Garrett-Peters. "Promises They Can Keep: Low-Income Women's Attitudes Toward Motherhood, Marriage, and Divorce." *Journal of Marriage and the Family* 70 (2008): 919-33. Print.

Ciabattari, Teresa. "Single Mothers and Family Values: The Effects of Welfare, Race, and Marriage on Family Attitudes." *The Marriage & Family Review* 39.1-2 (2006): 53-73. Print.

Coley, Rebekah Levine. "What Mothers Teach, What Daughters Learn: Gender Mistrust and Self-Sufficiency Among Low-Income Women." *Just Living Together: Implications of Cohabitation on Families, Children, and Social Policy.* Ed. Alan Booth, Ann C. Crouter, and Nancy Landsdale. Mahwah, NJ: Erlbaum, 2002. 97-105. Print.

Edin, Kathryn. "What Do Low-Income Single Mothers Say about Marriage?" *Social Problems* 47.1 (2000): 112-33. Print.

Edin, Kathryn and Joanna M. Reed. "Why Don't They Just Get Married? Barriers to Marriage among the Disadvantaged." *Future of Children* 15.2 (2005): 117-37. Print.

Edin, Kathryn, and Maria Kefalas. *Promises I Can Keep: Why Poor Women Put Motherhood Before Marriage.* Berkeley: University of California Press, 2005. Print.

Edin, Kathryn, Maria J. Kefalas, and Joanna M. Reed. "A Peek Inside the Black Box: What Marriage Means for Poor Unmarried Women." *Journal of Marriage and the Family* 66 (2004): 1007-14. Print.

Frazier, E. Franklin. *The Negro Family in the United States.* Chicago: University of Chicago Press, 1939. Print.

Gibson-Davis, Christina, Kathryn Edin, and Sara McLanahan. "High Hopes But Even Higher Expectations: The Retreat From Marriage Among Low-Income Couples." *Journal of Marriage and the Family* 76 (2005): 1301-12. Print.

Gubrium, Jaber F., and James A. Holstein. *The New Language of Qualitative Method.* New York: Oxford University Press, 1997. Print.

Hays, Sharon. *Flat Broke With Children: Women in the Age of Welfare Reform.* New York: Oxford University Press, 2003. Print.

Heyl, Barbara Sherman. "Ethnographic Interviewing." *Handbook of Ethnography.* Ed. Paul Atkinson et al. Thousand Oaks, CA: Sage, 2001. 369-83. Print.

Hoffman, Frederick. *Race Traits and Tendencies of the American Negro.* New York: McMillan, 1986. Print.

Hurtado, Aida. *Voicing Chicana Feminisms: Young Women Speak Out on Sexuality and Identity*. New York: New York University Press, 2003. Print.

Kaplan, Elaine Bell. *Not Our Kind of Girl: Unraveling the Myths of Black Teenage Motherhood*. Berkeley: University of California Press, 1997. Print.

Lewis, Oscar. *Five Families: Mexican Case Studies in the Culture of Poverty*. New York: Basic, 1959. Print.

Lichter, Daniel T., Christie D. Baston and J. Brian Brown. "Marriage Promotion: The Marital Expectations and Desires of Single and Cohabitating Mothers." *Social Service Review* 78.1 (2004): 2-25. Print.

Madsen, William. *The Mexican-Americans of South Texas: Studies in Cultural Anthropology*. New York: Holt, 1964. Print.

Mauldon, Jane G. et al. "Attitudes of Welfare Recipients Toward Marriage and Childbearing." *Population Research and Policy Review* 23 (2004): 595-640. Print.

Mead, Lawrence. *The New Politics of Poverty: The Nonworking Poor in America*. New York: Basic, 1992. Print.

Menjivar, Cecilia. *Fragmented Ties: Salvadoran Immigrant Networks in America*. Berkeley: University of California Press, 2000. Print.

Mirandé, Alfredo. *The Chicano Experience: An Alternative Perspective*. Notre Dame: University of Notre Dame Press, 1985. Print.

Mirandé, Alfredo, and Evangelina Enríquez. *La Chicana: The Mexican-American Woman*. Chicago: University of Chicago Press, 1979. Print.

Mohanty, Chandra Talpade. "Cartographies of Struggle: Third World Women and the Politics of Feminism." *Third World Women and the Politics of Feminism*. Ed. Chandra Talpade Mohanty, Ann Russo, and Lourdes Torres. Bloomington: Indiana University Press, 1991. 1-47. Print.

Moynihan, Daniel Patrick. *The Negro Family: A Case For National Action*. Washington, DC: Government Printing Office, 1965. Print.

Murray, Charles. *Losing Ground: American Social Policy, 1950-1980*. New York: Basic, 1984. Print.

Oropesa, R. S. "Normative Beliefs about a Marriage and Cohabitation: A Comparison of Non-Latino Whites, Mexican Americans, and Puerto Ricans." *Journal of Marriage and the Family* 58 (1996): 49-62. Print.

Puckett, Newbell. *Folk Beliefs of the Southern Negro*. Chapel Hill, NC: University of North Carolina Press, 1926. Print.

Roschelle, Anne R. *No More Kin: Exploring Race, Class, and Gender in Family Networks*. Thousand Oaks, CA: Sage, 1997. Print.

Smock, Pamela J., Wendy D. Manning, and Meredith M. Porter. "'Everything's There Except the Money': How Money Shapes Decisions to Marry Among Cohabitators." *Journal of Marriage and the Family* 67 (2005): 680-96. Print.

South, Scott. J. "Racial and Ethnic Differences in the Desire to Marry." *Journal of Marriage and the Family* 55 (1993): 337-70. Print.

Stacey, Judith. "Can There be a Feminist Ethnography?" *Women's Words: The Feminist Practice of Oral History*. Ed. Sherna Berger Gluck and Daphne Patai. New York: Routledge, 1991. 111-20. Print.

Tillinghast, Joseph A. *The Negro in Africa and America*. Ithaca, NY: Press of Andrus & Church, 1902. Print.

Toro-Morn, Maura I. "Beyond Gender Dichotomies: Toward a New Century of Gendered Scholarship in the Latina/o experience." *Latinas/os in the United States: Changing the Face of América*. Ed. Havidán Rodríguez et al. New York: Springer, 2008. 277-93. Print.

U.S. Bureau of the Census. "Poverty Status of Families by Type of Family, Age of Householder, and Number of Children." Retrieved from <http://www.census.gov/hhes/poverty/histpov/hstpov4.html>. Table 16a, 2001. Date of access July 15 2008.

Ventura, Stephanie J., and Christine A. Bachrach. "Nonmarital Childbearing in the United States, 1940-1990." *National Vital Statistics Reports* 16, Hyattsville, MD: National Center for Health Statistics. 2000. Print.

Waller, Maureen. R. "High Hopes: Unwed Parents' Expectations about Marriage." *Children and Youth Services Review* 23.6-7 (2001): 457-84. Print.

Williams, Norma. *The Mexican American Family: Tradition and Change*. Dix Hills, NY: General Hall, 1990. Print.

Ybarra, Lea. "Empirical and Theoretical Developments in the Study of Chicano Families." *The State of Chicano Research on Family, Labor, and Migration*. Ed. Armando Valdez, Albert Camarillo, and Tomas Almaguer. Stanford, CA: Stanford Center for Chicano Research, 1983. 91-110. Print.

Zavella, Patricia. *Women's Work and Chicano Families: Cannery Workers of*

the Santa Clara Valley. Ithaca: Cornell University Press, 1987. Print.
Zinn, Maxine Baca. "Family, Race, and Poverty in the Eighties." *Signs: Journal of Women in Culture and Society* 14 (1989): 856-74. Print.

Surviving Political Warfare and Trauma

Consequences for Salvadorian
Mother-Daughter Relationships

MIRNA E. CARRANZA

THIS CHAPTER PRESENTS HOW EXPERIENCES OF LOSS, DUE TO migration and witnessing violent acts of war prior to migration, have impacted the relationships of Salvadorian mothers and their daughters in their settlement country. The research findings show how mothers and daughters search for ways to stay connected, while concurrently processing their own individual traumas. The chapter begins with a brief summary of the key concepts related to mothering, trauma, and loss, followed by a brief discussion of the participants' context of settlement. The results section begins with a presentation of the mothers' perceptions, or lack thereof, of their loss and trauma. The daughters' perceptions about their upbringing and the mother–daughter relationship are presented next, followed by a discussion of the implications.

CONTEXTS:
MOTHERING, TRAUMA, AND MIGRATION

Patrice DiQuinzio in *The Impossibility of Motherhood: Feminism, Individualism and the Problem of Mothering* (1999) argues that mothering is influenced by social, cultural, political, economic, psychological, and personal experiences (viii). While giving attention to context is important, the cultural background of the mothers that shape the motherhood experience is also significant (Yoda 867; Peeke and Fothergill 97). For example, Latina mothers' perceptions about mothering—including what it means to be a "good" or "bad" mother—have been shaped significantly by their history of colonization and oppression which is manifested in the present day through class, race, ethnicity, and religion (Carranza

194). Celia Falicov in *Latino Families in Therapy: A Guide to Multicultural Practice* (1998) even goes so far as to argue that Latina mothers have been socialized to emulate the Virgin Mary with regard to self-abnegation and the sacrifices they make for their children (199).

Mothering in a country different from one's own entails a completely new experience for Latina women. Migration across borders challenges mothers to go beyond their expected mothering roles (Rosenthal and Roer-Strier 28-29; Wang and Phinney 187). For example, immigrant mothers of Latin American heritage living in North America perceive their role as nurturers to be acutely heightened after they have migrated to another country. After migration, these mothers tend to become the gatekeepers of their country of origin's key values, such as virginity, respect, obedience (Carranza 197), and familism (Baron 237). Thus, mothering children in a context different than the mothers' own becomes even more taxing after migration.

LOSS AND TRAUMA

Refugees' multiple losses may hold emotional, social, practical, or spiritual significance (Falicov 55-59). For instance, they may have trauma related to having been unwilling witnesses to painful events. For the most part, traumatic experiences tend to destroy the taken-for-granted systems of care[1] that give people a sense of control over their everyday life and meaning and attachment to their community (Herman 51). According to Charles R. Figley in *Trauma and its Wake: The Study of Treatment of Post-traumatic Stress Disorder* (1985), the trauma experienced by one family member will impact the functioning of the entire family system (5). Thus, for those who left countries experiencing political violence, the horror of the war will likely continue to affect them and their families in their new homes.

SALVADORIAN MIGRATION TO CANADA
AND CONTEXT OF STUDY

Salvadorians began to massively arrive in Canada during the civil war in El Salvador (1980–1992), when they fled to North America in search of a safe haven (Kusnir 256). In 1982 and 1983, approximately 3,000 Salvadorian refuge seekers came directly to Canada (Statistics Canada). A second wave of approximately 7,000 arrived during the mid-1980s

(Carranza 67). In recent years, Salvadorian immigrants have arrived more gradually through Canada's family reunification program. The total number of Salvadorians in Canada is currently 59,140 and the majority of them have settled in Ontario and Quebec (Statistics Canada; *2006 Census of Canada*).

METHODS

The findings are based on the qualitative analysis of 38 in-depth interviews[2] with Salvadorian-born mothers and their daughters who during the study were living in a mid-sized city in Southwestern Ontario, Canada. Thirty-two interviews were conducted with mothers and daughters separately: eight mothers and their eight adolescent daughters (Set 1), and eight mothers and their eight adult daughters (Set 2). In addition, six conjoint interviews were conducted with mothers and their daughters: three mothers and their three adolescent daughters, and three mothers and their three adult daughters (Set 3). A grounded theory approach[3] was employed to explore emergent themes in the interviews.

SAMPLE RATIONALE

Participants were selected through English language programs, immigration and settlement organizations, and other community contacts. Phone calls and several conversations were then held with potential participants prior to setting up interviews. The purpose of such was to answer any questions they had about the legitimacy of the study. The interviews with Salvadorian adolescents and their mothers provided information concerning their current struggles and successes. To complement this data and to encompass the adult development process, interviews with Salvadorian mothers and their adult daughters provided a reflective retrospective view of struggles and successes in negotiating Salvadorian mother–daughter relationships in the Canadian context.

DATA COLLECTION

All interviews lasted approximately two-hours, were conducted in Spanish, and were audio taped with the participants' permission. In addition to the initial interviews in Sets 1 and 2, individual follow-up interviews were conducted with eight of the participants (two mothers and two daughters from each set). Follow-up interviews integrated the data by adding to the theme categories and providing more in-depth information. These interviews also clarified and confirmed information.

DATA ANALYSIS

The bottom-up analytical strategy of grounded theory was applied, using theme analysis (Strauss and Corbin 23). Margot Ely in her book *Doing Qualitative Research: Circles within Circles* (1991) defined a *theme* as a significant account that contains important meanings and that appears through all or most of the collected data or that carries heavy emotional and factual impact (104).

RESULTS

The findings highlight both the struggles as well as the resilience of Salvadorian mothers and daughters as they process their individual traumas and negotiate their relationship in a foreign context. The Salvadorian mothers' need for their daughters' safety is enhanced, because the mothers perceive the Canadian context as a "strange" and unsafe place. The mothers' need for safety, in turn, pressed them to search for ways to keep their daughters close. Their daughters sequentially searched for ways to understand their mothers' trauma and to stay connected with them. These attempts led to intense conflict or to greater understanding between mothers and daughters.

SALVADORIAN MOTHERS' LOSSES AND UNRESOLVED TRAUMA

Most Salvadorian mothers reported that they felt that their roles as mothers and caregivers had intensified because they did not have family members living near them. In particular, they felt the responsibility for raising their daughters rested solely with them. A mother of an adolescent daughter stated, "Here in Canada I have no family ... I have no one." A Salvadorian mother of three adolescent daughters, ages 14, 16, and 18, commented on the need to have extended family nearby:

> It is hard to raise your children here ... because most of us don't have
> extended family here. For us family includes everybody, like your

cousins, uncles, aunts, and so on. So if you have a problem with your child, you go to them for support or the children go to them for support.... The aunt or the uncle will help the kids understand what the mother is trying to teach them. But here where do I go? Where do they go? To no one, no one.... It is hard to learn to live without them living next door or down the block from you.... I miss them so much.

Another Salvadorian mother of two daughters, ages 15 and 17, observed:

My daughters and I feel lonely without family here. We have the need to find other Salvadorian people here, but the Salvadorian community here is so small and almost nonexistent. Well, there is no Hispanic community here. So we have tried to make friends with other people ... Canadian people.

The absence of family members became even more palpable because the daughters of these Salvadorian women were still going through the adolescent stage around "strange" people. A mother of an adult daughter reflected upon those years:

It was hard when my daughters were growing up because I didn't have anybody to go to. I mean you're trying to raise them to be good people like the way we were raised. But doing it here was not the same. Like I had to do it alone and with no support. They're older now. They're married and have their own families. They're starting to understand now with their own kids how hard it is. But I tell them that at least they have me and they have each other for support. I had no one.

For the women in the study, raising their daughters in their new country and being physically apart from extended family was extremely challenging. They had to process their own ambiguous losses—not seeing and relying on extended family members on a day-to-day basis and raising their daughters in new culture. Hence, the mothers found themselves dealing with multiple processes of mothering and migration. While they reflect on these experiences, their response is embedded with a sense of satisfaction on having raised good and responsible daughters and is linked to their success and identity of being good mothers.

Another part of the Salvadorian mothers' experience was that most of them in the study reported feeling anxious when they did not know their daughters' whereabouts. For example, they worried when their daughters came home from school five minutes late or went to the store alone. Other mothers reported experiencing intrusive thoughts, having poor concentration, and feeling hypervigilant. Others felt chronic headaches or a sense of loneliness and isolation. As one mother responded, she worries about her daughter constantly:

> *My husband died in the war. They killed him right in our house. My daughter was very little then.... It was hard. [It] still is very hard. I often think how he would have liked to see her all grown up now.... That makes me more impatient.... I mean, more impatient because I need to know where she is at all times. I get anxious when I don't know.... This annoys her and makes her even more angry.*

One mother of two teenage daughters reported her experiences:

> *[Witnessing the murder of family members] affects me still. I still have those memories, like flechazos [flashbacks] out of nowhere. Then an intense fear comes. Like fear that something really bad is going to happen to [my two daughters]. I bought them a phone so I can call them wherever they are, but when I cannot get a hold of one of them, because I know that they're always together, I get these intense headaches that kill me. I want to start running looking for them. I feel alone, all alone in the world until they're safe with me.... I know that I have vestigios de la guerra [vestiges from the war]. I don't have a sense of safety. I mean I feel like my daughters are not safe anywhere. I don't trust anyone around them. I feel like they'll be kidnapped or something bad is going to happen. I always have this sense that they're in danger. I know that it is because of what we went through in El Salvador and the way we lived [hiding from persecution by death squads] before we came to Canada.... We were in hiding, always running for our lives.*

As the mothers connected their own traumatic experiences of having witnessed the murder of their life partner or a loved family member to their need to know their daughters' whereabouts at all times, they become aware of their overwhelming concern to protect their daughters in the new country. Fear triggered the mothers' intense watchfulness and safeguard of their daughters. Hence, grief and fear deeply permeated the mothers' relationship with their daughters and, as a result, created tensions between them. While this legacy of loss, warfare, and trauma is not easy to resolve in the Salvadorian mother-daughter relationship, it does show the resiliency of Salvadorian mothers who brought their daughters to safety and their desire to construct new relationships in a different context.

ADOLESCENT SALVADORIAN DAUGHTERS: LOSSES, AND ANNOYANCE WITH THEIR MOTHER'S PROTECTIVE BEHAVIORS

Most Salvadorian adolescent daughters commented about the difficulties growing up without extended family in Canada. A 15-year-old girl stated her dilemma:

> I'd love to get to know them better. Well, my mom's mom, my aunt, my uncles, all my mom's family is down there [in El Salvador]. My mom doesn't have any family here. My dad's side of the family is down there as well. It [is] just the four of us here.

Another talked about missing her adolescence with her cousins in El Salvador:

> I miss all my cousins. Like, we all grew up together right up until we [she and her immediate family] came to Canada. I still remember us all going to school together. Hanging out at my aunt's place and my uncle's house. It was so different then.

Growing up without extended family was a significant loss for most Salvadorian adolescent daughters. They too, as their mothers, experience the ambiguity of having extended family members but not having them close enough to grow up and share their life with them as they would have if they had grown up in El Salvador.

In regard to their mother's vigilance and wanting to know where they were "at all times," some Salvadorian adolescent daughters referred to their mothers' behaviors as "annoying." One 14-year-old daughter, in particular, stated her frustrations:

> *My mom and I get into a lot of fights because she always wants to know where I am. She freaks out if I'm like five minutes late. Like who does that, right? She gets even more annoyed when I tell her, "Relax, I'm just five minutes late. I was talking with a friend. It's not like I was murdered or something!" Then she never stops talking. Sometimes I do it just to get her going.... It's funny [laughter] ... I'm sorry. I shouldn't be so sarcastic and laugh about her. Like I know she went through a lot in El Salvador. She lost family members.... So maybe she's afraid that something will happen to me. She tells me that. But I'm like, "Get over it!"*

In addition, a 16-year-old daughter noted her mother's overprotective conduct:

> *My mom is always on my back. It gets annoying. She questions me about everything. Who are you with? What time are you coming home? Who else is going to be there? Like, I don't know! I know it's because of what she lived through in El Salvador, but it JUST gets annoying sometimes.*

Adolescent daughters are still in their own developmental process. As such, they are asserting their independence from their mothers and are moving away from the Salvadorian interdependent mother–daughter relationships. Most of the adolescent daughters seemed to have little awareness about how their mothers' losses and traumatic experiences were at play and continued to profoundly influence their mothers' behaviors toward them. Those who acknowledged it tended to minimize or to disregard it very rapidly. This attitude may be due to various reasons. For instance, the daughters may wish to disconnect from their mothers' world of fear, sadness, and terror. In addition, socialization and peer relationships are of greater importance during adolescence than relationships with mothers.

ADULT DAUGHTERS: UNDERSTANDING OF THEIR
MOTHERS' AND THEIR OWN TRAUMA AND LOSSES

Salvadorian adult daughters reported some understanding about their mothers' "worries" about them. Therefore, they were mindful of telling their mothers where they were "at all times," even if it meant being teased by their peers or feeling "different." One adult daughter and a mother mentioned this issue:

> *Salvadorian moms are different. They're more protective, I guess because they want to know where you are at all times.... My friends don't understand this. They think that she's trying to control me, but I know it's not about that. I know that after everything we went through we got much closer.*

Most Salvadorian adult daughters also expressed awareness about their mothers' struggles to adapt to Canadian society and were therefore sensitive toward their mothers' need to ensure their safety. An adult and married daughter expressed her relationship with her mother:

> *Yes, I love my mother. I am very protective of her, like she is of me. We hang out together like every weekend. My mom and I talk like on the phone like three times every day. We go out for lunch at least once a week, and I know that my sister and my brother are the same way. She is the most important person in my life.*

Another adult and married daughter noted the complexity of the Salvadorian mother-daughter relationship. She talked about her dedication and commitment to her mother's emotional welfare:

> *Absolutely, I'm more appreciative of her. Like I almost feel that I owe my life to her and what she's done for us, like leaving El Salvador in the middle of the night. I don't want to give her grief or make things any harder for her. No, I don't want her to worry about me. No, I don't want to do anything that might upset her. No, I don't want to do anything that may impact our relationship, I mean in a negative way. She's done more than enough for us, like; I want to be there to support her. I want her to have the best life she can have.*

I want her to be happy, and I'll do anything to make her happy and nothing to upset her. So, if it means I still have to call her at all times telling her where I am, so be it. That's the least I can do.

Yet, another adult daughter talked about her reflections about her mother's losses and sacrifices:

I sometimes think, "Oh, my God. She's always talking about all her friends she left there [in El Salvador]." She's been saying, "Oh, my God. My friend called me today." I look at all those things and I go, "Oh, my gosh. I can never give her back what she did for me and us," and I guess sometimes I feel bad when I think, "Oh, my gosh. What would her life have been like if she had stayed there?" I always feel like I owe her everything, from the smallest thing to the biggest. She was very young when she came here [to Canada] and she put everything for herself on hold. It's never ever been about her or her needs. It's always been about us. I feel that she's missed out, you know ... Sometimes I think, "What could've happened if we'd stayed there? Where would we have been? Where would she have been?" I think about her career, like, "Where would she be in her career?" The job she has now doesn't even come close to what she had there. I think about all the friends she had. I think about the language barrier for her, how it's left her out in the cold. I look at things like that and then I wonder. Yeah, I wonder if it would have been different for her. I don't think that she regrets the decision that she made, but I wonder, "What did she miss out on? What did I miss out on?"

Heightened awareness about their mothers' losses, worries and sacrifices permeates the relationship between adult daughters and their mothers. Their *agradecimiento* (gratitude) seems to be at the core of their relationship and centered on what their mothers sacrificed to ensure their children's well being and safety. This finding concurs with what Falicov argued regarding the sacrifices of Latina mothers (199). For the mothers in this study, however, their sacrifices were not an effort to emulate the Virgin Mary. Rather these were coerced by the Salvadorian context of warfare, persecution, and terror, since these mothers had no other choice but to leave behind their loved ones, and their careers to bring themselves as well as their daughters to safety. In this context, their sacrifices depict their sense of agency, commitment to the welfare of their children, and resistance to oppressive circumstances.

ADULT DAUGHTERS' TRAUMATIC EXPERIENCES

Witnessing traumatic experiences was also a part of most adult daughters' lives before they left El Salvador:

I saw so much violence, like corpses on the streets. Horrible things that I'd rather not think about. I think all that affects me to this date. Ahhh, I have this constant feeling that I am going to lose my entire family. The people that you love the most.... My Canadian friends don't understand my relationship with my mother because they don't know what we, I lived through....

Another adult daughter talked about her own trauma in the following manner:

Yeah, I do remember ... I remember the bombs and the screaming. Yeah, I remember being very scared. Like we used to travel for the whole day running and hiding and there would be helicopters flying around us throwing bombs at the people on the ground. I was little then. I don't know how we're alive to tell the story. Every time I remember I feel really nervous about it and almost sick to my stomach.... We lived close to the police when the big thing happened like the big ofensiva que decían [the last battle, they said]. Well, we could hear everything that was going on.... We would go outside, like to the store, because we had to get some food because we didn't have anything to eat for days. We were so hungry. So we were coming back from the store and then there was like a lot of people running. There was shooting going on and we could see the bullets flying everywhere [she ducks when saying this]. That was really scary. There were bombs too. One of the bombs landed in our house. I don't know how we came out of that alive. It made a big hole in our house.... I couldn't sleep at night. When I came to Canada, I remember that I use to jump at every little noise I heard. It took me a while to recuperate because every little noise would make me

jump. I remember that I saw so many dead people outside after the
ofensiva. There were a lot of people dead. They killed a lot of people
[pause, and tears in her eyes]. They also burnt a lot of people alive.
It doesn't bother me anymore, but when I first came it did a lot ...
especially when I was a kid.

Much like their mothers, all the adult daughters in this study endured experiences related to warfare and trauma. These experiences serve as a unique bond between them and their mothers that contribute to their deep understanding of each other. In addition, they were acutely aware of how their collective history of loss, persecution, warfare, and trauma had shaped their relationships and their perceptions toward their mothers. This awareness highlights not only their vulnerabilities, but also their resilience to overcome a traumatic history that followed them across borders and deeply permeated their mother-daughter relationship in their new land.

CONCLUSION

Mothering in a new country and away from the support of extended family members is a difficult experience. The Salvadorian mothers in this study expressed the frustrations that resulted from not being able to share the responsibilities of mothering their adolescent daughters with their extended families as customary in their home country. They also talked about their traumatic experiences and losses prior to their migration. In addition, they discussed how they continue to struggle to put these memories behind as they continue to shape their current mother-daughter's relationships in Canada.

Although the anger and annoyance that Salvadorian adolescent daughters expressed toward their mothers may be considered normative of their stage of development, the findings indicate that the intensity of their negotiation is due to various reasons: (a) Salvadorian mothers' fears for their daughters' safety; (b) Salvadorian mothers' lack of support (i.e., extended family and community) in the settlement country; and (c) the fact that Salvadorian mothers were raising their daughters in a context different from that of their own upbringing. The conflict that occurs between Salvadorian mothers and their adolescent daughters tends to resolve itself as the daughters mature and become mothers themselves.

However, the tensions that exist between them during adolescence due to the mothers' "vigilance" are palpable. This tension has the potential to create long-term damage to the Salvadorian mother–daughter relationship and to deter them from their ultimate goal; that is, the survival of the family unit.

These relationships are governed by high levels of cohesiveness between the Salvadorian mothers and daughters, and by the adult daughters' appreciative attitude toward their mothers. Despite their cohesiveness though, there is tension in their communication patterns. Fear caused by past traumatic experiences is a key element in how these mothers and daughters relate to one another and try to adapt to living in the settlement country.

Practitioners working with members of the Salvadorian community (or with members of any other community that has experienced political warfare) need to understand how the communication and relational patterns between family members have been significantly impacted by the family's experience of loss, trauma, and political violence. Furthermore, special attention must be given to how family roles have changed or intensified as a result of multiple losses due to migration. Practitioners must also take into account the presence of fear as a strong mediating factor within the mother-daughter relationship.

[1]In the case of refugees women, taken-for-granted system of care refers to the rituals developed in their day-to-day activities like going to the market, talking with the neighbor, feeding the chickens or their pets, going to work, going to church, or caring for their children in familiar surroundings.

[2]Data collection took place between the periods of 2005-2006.

[3]The roots of grounded theory can be traced back in the fields of sociology and anthropology and to a movement known as symbolic interactionism.

WORKS CITED

2006 Census of Canada. Cumulative Profile-Canada. "Provinces and Territories Table." Web. 10 Oct. 2009.

Baron, Moises. "Addiction Treatment for Mexican American Families." *Bridges to Recovery: Addiction, Family Therapy, and Multicultural Treat-*

ment. Ed. Jo-Ann Kresta. New York: Free, 2000. 219-52. Print.

Carranza, Mirna E. "Salvadorian Mothers Navigating the Hazards of Acculturation in Canada." Dissertation, University of Guelph, 2007. Print.

DiQuinzio, Patrice. *The Impossibility of Motherhood: Feminism, Individualism and the Problem of Mothering*. New York: Routledge, 1999. Print.

Ely, Margot. *Doing Qualitative Research: Circles within Circles*. New York: Falmer, 1991. Print.

Falicov, Celia. *Latino Families in Therapy: A Guide to Multicultural Practice*. New York: Guilford, 1998. Print.

Figley, Charles R., ed. *Trauma and its Wake: The Study of Treatment of Post-traumatic Stress Disorder*. New York: Brunner, 1985. Print.

Herman, Judith. *Trauma and Recovery: The Aftermath of Violence from Domestic Abuse to Political Terror*. New York: Basic, 1997. Print.

Kusnir, Daniel. "Salvadoran Families." *Ethnicity and Family Therapy*. Ed. Monica McGoldrick, Joseph Giordano, and Nydia Garcia-Preto. New York: Guilford, 2005. 256–65. Print.

Peeke, Lori and Alice Fothergill. "Displacement, Gender, and The Challenges of Parenting after Hurricane Katrina." *National Women's Studies Association Journal* 20.3 (2008): 69-105. Web. 19 January 2008.

Rosenthal, Miriam K. and Dorit Roer-Strier. "Cultural Differences in Mothers' Developmental Goals and Ethnotheories." *International Journal of Psychology* 36.1 (2001): 20–31. Web. 12 May 2008.

Statistics Canada. "Immigrant Population by Place of Birth." *Provinces, Census, Divisions and Municipalities*. 1991. Web. 9 February 2008.

Strauss, Anselm, and Juliet Corbin. "Grounded Theory Methodology: An Overview." Ed. Norman K. Denzin and Yvonna S. Lincoln. *Handbook of Qualitative Research*. Thousand Oaks, CA: Sage, 1994. 273–85. Print.

Wang, Chia-Hui, and Jean S. Phinney. "Differences in Child Rearing Attitudes Between Immigrant Chinese Mothers and Anglo-American Mothers." *Early Development and Parenting* 7 (1998): 181–89. Web. 15 March 2008.

Yoda, Tomico. "The Rise and Fall of Maternal Society: Gender, Labor and Capital in Contemporary Japan." *The South Atlantic Quarterly* 99.4 (2000): 865-902. Web. 20 January 2008.

IV.
The Ties that Bind:
Literary and Cultural Representations of Latina/Chicana Mothers

Counternarratives in the Literary Works of Mexican Author Ángeles Mastretta and Chilean Author Pía Barros

MARY LOU BABINEAU

FEW EXPERIENCES HAVE DEFINED WOMEN CULTURALLY AND socially as much as that of motherhood. Although historically this has been true throughout most of the world, motherhood has been especially venerated within the context of Latin American societies where the idealization of this role has been so hegemonic that precious few spaces exist for the conceptualization of meaningful womanhood outside of this realm, or for the expression of dissatisfaction or regret with regards to childbearing and child rearing. Within the realm of Latin American women's literature, however, one does in fact find expressions of dissidence in powerful counter-narratives of motherhood.[1] This paper examines such counter-narratives in the literature of Mexican author Ángeles Mastretta and Chilean author Pía Barros, whose defiant protagonists give voice to the often silenced and unrecognized feelings and experiences of pregnant women and mothers. In their portrayal of the aversion and dissociation that these protagonists experience towards their own pregnant and post-partum bodies, as well as their strong feelings of isolation, alienation, and rejection towards their children, this literary production makes a valuable contribution to contemporary discourses surrounding Latin American mothering. As a result of their non-traditional and even controversial maternal representations, these narrative works represent significant transgressions of traditional patriarchal conceptions of motherhood, and they create necessary spaces for the exploration of the many complex layers that underlie what has historically been Latin American women's most revered and defining role.

The complex relationship between patriarchy and the institution of motherhood[2] has been widely explored and deconstructed by feminist-informed theorists and writers across many disciplines.[3] In so doing, these women have highlighted some of the predominant myths that have traditionally defined the experiences of pregnancy and motherhood in patriarchal societies. Liliana Trevizán, a scholar who has written extensively on literary theory and Latin American women's literature, argues that at the root of these myths is the often unexamined assumption that the two fundamental parts of reproduction are inseparable; that since women are biologically able to carry children, then they must also be the ones who are primarily responsible for their care and upbringing ("Deshilando" 29). This assumption has resulted in firmly-entrenched divisions of gender roles along productive/reproductive lines that have relegated men to the public realms of politics and culture, and women to the domestic spheres of home and family. Furthermore, being a mother has been socially constructed as the "normal" and "desired" state for women, her highest calling and greatest justification in life (Trevizán, "Deshilando" 28; Rich 34; Glenn 3). For women, consequently, motherhood and meaningful adulthood are perceived to be inseparable, and women's existence has historically been legitimized by their reproductive role. As the scholar of comparative literature América Luna Martínez and others[4] have underlined, it is through this division of gender roles and the idealization of motherhood that patriarchy has reduced women to bodies at the service of others (46).

From these assumptions and myths spring those that have come to define all good mothers. According to Fiona Green, whose research focuses primarily on feminist mothering and media representations of mothers, it is commonly accepted that the ideal mother is completely responsible for nurturing and caring for her family members, and that "she finds parenting to be the most meaningful aspect her life. Providing love and care for her family fills her with boundless happiness and self-fulfillment" (33). Diana Gustafson, a sociologist whose expertise lies in the areas of women's studies, health, and education, concurs with Green's views and emphasizes that the ideal mother is also characterized by utter self-negation; the ideal mother is especially selfless and she never hesitates to put her children's needs before her own (28). In Latin American societies this image of the ideal mother is rooted in the cultural tradition of *marianismo*[5] which has historically attributed such traits as moral superiority and spiritual strength to women, as well as an infinite capacity for humility and sacrifice. Modeled on the image of the Virgin Mary, she is imagined to be saintly, literally semi-divine. In such societies where myth and religion, social and legal institutions, family organization and popular culture work together to entrench and idealize motherhood and the mother-child bond, it is difficult to create spaces within which to articulate experiences of motherhood that do not conform to these rigid and at times oppressive dominant images and expectations.

Latin American women's literature has succeeded in creating these critical spaces. In their literary works, women authors such as Mastretta and Barros examine and question dominant discourses surrounding motherhood by representing maternal characters through non-tradi-tional, complex, and even controversial lenses. As Ralph Waldo Emerson famously affirmed, fiction reveals truth that reality obscures; as such it can be said that this literature deconstructs traditional images of Latin American mothers by scratching beneath the surface of appearances and transgressing the boundaries of traditional discourses surrounding motherhood. Catherine Pélage, who conducts research on Chilean women's literature at the Sorbonne, analyzes the role of transgression in the realm of women's literature. She argues that the concept of trans-gression in general has three important dimensions:

> *la primera, social, trataría de poner en tela de juicio las representa-ciones simbólicas y las opresiones vigentes; la segunda, psicológica, consistiría en borrar las censuras tradicionalmente interiorizadas por el 'segundo sexo' en general y por la autora en particular; la tercera, literaria, sería una forma de expresión acorde con dichos principios* (the first is social, as it attempts to question predominant symbolic representations and oppressions; the second is psychological, which consists in erasing the censorships that have tradition-ally been internalized by the 'second sex' in general and by the author in particular; the third is literary, which would be a form of expression that would reflect these principles). (66)

It can be argued, therefore, that contemporary Latin American women authors whose writing questions the idealized, traditional representa-tions of motherhood in their societies are realizing significant works of transgression. A very clear example of this can be observed in Rosario Ferré's critical work entitled "Frankenstein: una versión política del mito de la maternidad" ("Frankenstein: A Political Version of the Myth of Maternity") where she explores the connections between the greater socio-political context of patriarchy and dominant representations of motherhood, which have resulted in what she calls the tyranny of motherhood and myth of motherhood (35-37). Ferré begins to shine a light onto some of the darker, but nonetheless "normal" reactions that women have towards motherhood, including guilt and rejection—reactions that have only barely begun to be acknowledged (36). It is precisely from this perspective that Mastretta and Barros' literary representations of motherhood will be explored.

ÁNGELES MASTRETTA:
MOTHERING IN THE PATRIARCHAL STATE

Like Ferré, Mastretta explores the relationship between motherhood and patriarchy in her novel *Arráncame la vida* (*Tear this Heart Out*) (1985). The young Mexican protagonist Catalina Guzmán is swept away in marriage by Andrés Ascencio, a man twice her age, when she is barely fifteen years old. Mastretta's novel is set in the post-revolutionary years of the 1920s in Mexico and it follows Andrés' rise to power as Governor of Puebla and as an aspiring candidate to the presidency of the Republic. Their significant age difference, combined with Andrés' military rank, social class, and political position, create a power differential that makes it impossible for the very young and naive protagonist to fully consent to the decision to marry. Her naiveté in regards to the conditions and assumptions underlying her union with Andrés is apparent in the kinds of questions that she asks on her wedding day. She is curious, for example, as to why she must sign her name "de Ascencio" while her new husband does not reciprocate by signing his "de Guzmán," and Andrés' answer very clearly exposes the patriarchal ideology that shapes his expectations of her and their marriage. He explains: "*No m'ija, porque así no es la cosa. Yo te protejo a ti, no tú a mí. Tú pasas a ser de mi familia, pasas a ser mía*" ("No, my child, that's not how it works. I protect you, you don't protect me. You become a part of my family, you become mine") (19).

From the beginning, their marriage is marked by a stark division of gender roles: Andrés is an active public figure seeking power and fortune in the realm of politics, while Catalina's role is limited primarily to the domestic sphere. This division of roles entails the dependence of Catalina on her husband, and this significant power differential provides the context within which Catalina begins the journey of pregnancy and motherhood. As she has no significant power or agency, she certainly has no input as to whether or not she will have children. In fact, her youth and naiveté are such that she is not even certain of how women become pregnant. One day she wakes up with a feeling of exhaustion that she cannot overcome, and it is Andrés who first realizes and then informs Catalina that she is pregnant. Catalina reflects that she has no desire to be a mother and she describes her experience of pregnancy as burdensome and invasive:

> *La había cargado nueve meses como una pesadilla. Le había visto crecer a mi cuerpo una joroba por delante y no lograba ser una madre enternecida. La primera desgracia fue dejar los caballos y los vestidos entallados, la segunda soportar unas agruras que me llegaban hasta la nariz. Odiaba quejarme, pero odiaba la sensación de estar continuamente poseída por algo extraño.* (I had carried her for nine months like a nightmare. I had watched a hump grow on the front of my body and I could not manage to be a loving mother. The first misfortune was when I had to abandon horseback riding and form-fitting dresses; the second was enduring heartburn that went right up to my nose. I hated to complain, but I hated the sensation of being continually possessed by something foreign.) (39)

Catalina's feelings and perceptions surrounding pregnancy are not uncommon according to the renowned psychotherapist Dr. Estela Welldon who explains that, although women's bodies are designed to accommodate another living body, "the wonder is more than the static situation, marvellous though it is, of one body within another. The fact that the inner body is growing within the outer one is impossible to ignore, however disturbing or unwelcome it may be to the mother. Indeed, many women express strong feelings of revulsion about it, whereas others ... feel only gratified when pregnant" (26-27). Catalina's unwelcome journey into motherhood intensifies unexpectedly when, in the months following the birth of her first child, Andrés brings six more of his children to live with them. Catalina had known nothing of his children from previous relationships and, once again, she is forced to assume the role of mother without being consulted and without actively accepting this responsibility.

Nonetheless, although Catalina has no significant control over the circumstances surrounding her life as a mother, she refuses to be silenced or conform to societal expectations of how she should express herself or behave in this role. Instead, she insists on voicing her anger, her fears, and her resentment towards the roles that she is expected to assume as a mother in a patriarchal society. As a result, Catalina weaves a complex counternarrative surrounding pregnancy and motherhood that intensifies throughout the novel, and she often finds an outlet for expression within the private sphere of her closest friendships. It is within this context that some of the women in the novel create the necessary spaces within which to contest hegemonic patriarchal constructions of pregnancy and motherhood. This is the case, for example, when Catalina sympathizes with her pregnant friend, Bibi, who wonders aloud who might have come up with the notion that pregnant women are happy and beautiful. Catalina responds that it must have been men, and that she herself had spent most of her pregnancy crying with rage. Catalina's reaction to her friend's pregnancy is countercultural and defies dominant discourse, which is most commonly characterized by compliments and congratulatory expressions. Some of the more "traditional" wives of politicians in the novel reproduce this official discourse defining pregnancy and motherhood, providing a contrast to Catalina's transgressive words and attitude. For example, when the wife of one of Andrés' colleagues affirms that motherhood is very noble and that all women are beautiful when they are pregnant, Catalina responds:

> *Si quieres te digo que todas las mujeres embarazadas son preciosas, pero no lo creo. Yo nunca me sentí más fea* (If you want me to I will tell you that all pregnant women are beautiful, but I don't believe it. I [have] never felt uglier). (131)

Her comments are laughed off and dismissed as those of a woman who is just trying to be dramatic or difficult. These dismissive reactions serve to highlight the ambivalence inherent to patriarchal discourses around motherhood; in other words, while the role of motherhood is publicly venerated on the one hand, it is often diminished and dismissed on the other, especially in private and in response to women when they articulate the challenges and sacrifices inherent to this role.

This ambivalence characterizing hegemonic discourses relating to motherhood can also be observed in the contrast between Andrés' attitude towards motherhood in private and his political discourse in the public realm. Although he is clearly proud of having impregnated his wife, he is no longer interested in her sexually nor does he want to hear about her physical discomfort, doubts, or fears. At home, he effectively silences her complaints when he comments that pregnant women love to complain just so that they can feel important. In public, however, his rhetoric repeatedly affirms the importance of women and of the family unit to the country and the Revolution. In his political speeches, he especially emphasizes the importance of equality between husband and wife, at which time Catalina reflects that from that moment on she does not believe a single thing he says. As Andrés is closely tied to the power structures governing his state and country, his public discourse on the role of women and mothers in relation to these institutions is worthy of analysis, particularly as they quite obviously affect the protagonist's experience of motherhood. As the novel progresses, Catalina becomes painfully aware that her role as a woman/mother is secondary and subordinate to that of Andrés as man/father/head of state, and that as a woman her value is, in the words of Mary Louise Pratt, "specifically attached to her reproductive capacity" (51). Pratt, a well-known scholar of postcolonial women's literature, argues in her essay "Women, Literature and National Brotherhood" that women's role within the modern state is inseparable from mothering:

> What bourgeois republicanism offered women by way of official existence was what Landis and others have called "republican motherhood," the role of the producer of citizens. So it is that women inhabitants of modern nations were not imagined as intrinsically possessing the rights of citizens; rather, their value was specifically attached to (and implicitly conditioned upon) their reproductive capacity. As mothers of the nation, they are precariously other to the nation. They are imagined as dependent rather than sovereign. They are practically forbid-

den to be limited and finite, being obsessively defined by their reproductive capacity. Their bodies are sites for many forms of intervention, penetration, and appropriation at the hands of the horizontal brotherhood. (51)

Pratt's analysis of the relationship between motherhood and the modern state[6] provides a valuable framework within which to examine Catalina's experience of motherhood. As she comes to understand the emptiness of her husband's public rhetoric surrounding women and the family, Catalina begins to understand that her own value and function with the context of the patriarchal state is limited to that of producer of citizens and reproducer of men who, unlike her, do enjoy all the rights and freedoms as full citizens of the state.

As time passes, Catalina becomes increasingly aware of Andrés' political and criminal activities and, as a result, she is forced to consider her own position and possible contribution, as his wife, in benefitting from, and perhaps even helping him in his corruption and his greed. She hears many rumors of political corruption, abuses of power, and suspicious deaths of his political opponents and she concludes that, as his wife, she is his official accomplice. As she becomes increasingly tortured by her role in reproducing her husband and his ways, her perception of herself as a mother begins to deteriorate. This deterioration of her sense of competence as a mother is in great part determined by her increasing awareness that she cannot protect her children from their father's influence and criminal activities. This realization reaches its greatest intensity on the day that her five-year-old son expresses his thoughts to her about where people go after they die; he assures his mother that the dead do not become stars in the sky, as some believe, but rather that they are "in a hole" (87). When Catalina asks him why he believes this, he answers that he has heard his dad saying "dig that guy a hole," which means that they have to kill him. As she begins to vomit uncontrollably, Catalina recognizes that her limitations as a mother are closely tied to the corrupt patriarchal institutions:

No podían vivir en las nubes nuestros hijos. Estaban demasiado cerca. Cuando decidí quedarme decidí también por ellos y ni mode de guardarlos en una bola de cristal (Our children could not live in the clouds. They were too close. When I decided to stay I also decided for them, and there is no way to keep them in a bubble). (88)

Her response is to abdicate her role as mother, withdrawing from all of her mothering obligations and abandoning her children to the care of domestic servants. Given the context within which her dramatic final decision is made, it may be interpreted in several ways. It may be seen as a coping mechanism for her sense of guilt in not protecting her children from their father's crimes, or as an act of rebellion against her prescribed role in raising them in his image. However, two things are certain. First, Catalina's decision defies traditional social expectations defining "good" mothers and, second, her choice to distance herself from her children is intimately connected to her political, social, economic, and marital context.

PÍA BARROS:
MOTHERING THROUGH POST-PARTUM DEPRESSION

The relationship between the political sphere, patriarchy, and women's writing in Chile has also been highlighted by literary critics such as Cecilia Ojeda, Liliana Trevizán, Carmen Galarce, and Guillermo García-Corales who, in their critical essays and interviews with Chilean authors, explore the impact that the military dictatorship had on Chilean women and their writing.[7] Ojeda focuses specifically on the literary production of Diamela Eltit and Pía Barros, and she argues that the dictatorship greatly strengthened and reinforced patriarchal ideology because its primary objectives were legitimizing and normalizing a system of reasoning and cultural symbolization anchored in patriarchal values. This patriarchal system, asserts Ojeda, excluded women from public life, limited their roles to the domestic sphere only, and promoted the notion of feminine sexuality exclusively as a means of procreation (103). The Chilean women's movement, which strengthened in response to the authoritarian regime, adopted the motto "democracia en el país y en la casa" ("democracy in the country and in the home") which very clearly highlights the interdependent nature of what feminists have historically called the political and the personal—a link that Barros herself has made in conversations about her writing (Trevizán, "Escritoras" 581-82). In an interview with García Corales, Barros expresses her interest in exploring the ways in which women perform in relationships and become "others." In her opinion, this performance creates a state of alienation that is similar to the experience of living in a dictatorship where, in the context of constant vigilance, one is also forced to perform in order to conform to outside expectations and alter one's behavior, to the point that she compares it to schizophrenia (402). In response to these observations, Barros explains that in her short stories she attempts to scratch beneath the surface of appearances, and to rebel against imposed norms and institutions such as the canon and the family (400-01). In particular, she focuses on defying the symbolic and stereotypical representations of women that have traditionally been associated with sexuality, maternity, and domesticity.

Barros' collection of short stories entitled *A horcajadas* (1990) was published soon after the end of the military dictatorship, a time when spaces where being forged for the development of narratives that challenge the political, social, and cultural discourses that have traditionally defined women. In the short story "Artemisa," the myths surrounding maternity and maternal instinct are subverted through the psychological evolution of the protagonist Luisa after the birth of her first child. Luisa's reaction towards her baby defies societal norms and expectations for mothers:

> *Parecía un siglo, pero sólo dos meses antes se lo habían puesto en los brazos con un "Felicidades, señora" y ella lo había rechazado con asco, encogiendo los brazos. "Lléveselo"* (Though it seemed like a century ago, it was only two months earlier when they had put him in her arms saying "Congratulations" and she had rejected him with disgust, folding her arms. "Take him away"). (46)

As social anthropologist María Victoria Castilla emphasizes in her review of the interdisciplinary literature in which the concept of "good mothers" is defined, there are common assumptions upon which these definitions generally rest historically and cross-culturally. Castilla describes the most prominent foundational assumption as "women's natural ability to protect and love their children" (199). In contrast to this commonly-held perception of women's natural abilities, however, Luisa feels no motherly love when she looks at her baby boy and she feels unable to connect with him. He seems foreign and even inhuman to her as she compares his size and movements to those of a small animal, and she is repulsed by the way that he latches on to her nipple like dogs to their prey (Barros 46). As a result of her inability to feel love and tenderness at the sight of her newborn, she is unable to develop an attachment with her child; rather, she is overwhelmed by feelings of revulsion and rejection.

The aversion that Luisa feels towards her son is intimately connected to her feelings towards her own post-partum body. This aversion centers on her breasts, whose appearance and function have changed as a result of pregnancy and breastfeeding. Luisa perceives that breastfeeding has transformed her body into something that is completely foreign to her, a sort of a biological host at the mercy of a parasite. These feelings first arise in the hospital when, to her utter horror, a nurse forces her to breastfeed for the first time: *"[T]uvo que soportar a ese bicho adosado succionándola. Le dolía y asqueaba."* ("She had to endure that little beast sucking on her. It hurt and disgusted her") (46). Luisa's aversion to breastfeeding is of particular interest in light of Castilla's findings on the relationship between breastfeeding and hegemonic definitions of "good mothers." The motivation for her research, based on interviews with breastfeeding mothers, was the apparent contradiction between what she refers to as the "medicalization of motherhood" on one hand—which emphasizes breastfeeding as one of the most important determinants of physical and affective well-being in infants—and, on the other hand, the social sciences literature in which the mention of breastfeeding as constitutive of socially accepted definitions of "good mothers" is conspicuously absent. Castilla finds that breastfeeding does, in fact, constitute a part of the so-called "natural" essence of all women which allows them to love and care for their children:

> *[E]xisten comunes denominadores (amorosa, pendiente, entrega total) que se consideran elementos "naturales" (no aprendidos ni condicionados por la cultura o sociedad de las mujeres-madres). Y la lactancia, en su especificidad, constituye un claro ejemplo de ello.* (There are common denominators [love, concern, total dedication] that are considered to be "natural" elements (neither learned nor conditioned by the culture or society of the women-mothers). And breastfeeding, specifically, constitutes a clear example of this"). (207)

Given Castilla's findings about the unspoken assumptions regarding

the supposed universal, natural, and instinctive nature of breastfeeding for all mothers, Luisa's absolute repugnance towards this practice
certainly stands out as characteristic of an unnatural mother and, by
correlation, of an unnatural woman. Castilla's research leads her to
conclude that the curious absence of breastfeeding in social sciences
literature defining "good mothers" can be explained by the fact that it has
been naturalized as part of female gender constructions (213). In other
words, these gender constructions have attributed social reproduction
to women as a result of essentialist premises that define motherhood
based on biological conditions specific to women such as pregnancy,
childbirth, and breastfeeding. In expressing rejection and aversion towards breastfeeding, therefore, Luisa interrupts and calls into question
this essentialist and "naturalized" narrative of motherhood.

In addition to the disgust that she expresses towards the maternal
function of her breasts, Luisa also experiences strong feelings of loss
and nostalgia as a result of the changes that her body as undergone
throughout and after pregnancy and childbirth. She longs for the shape
and appearance of her stomach and breasts before pregnancy, and her
longing is rooted in her full awareness that this pre-pregnancy form
is that which is socially defined and admired as beautiful. As a new
mother, Luisa looks in the mirror and sees herself only as grotesque, a
perception that is further fueled by her husband's behavior towards her.
Marcos no longer seems to be attracted to her and he no longer treats
her as a sensual woman, but rather only as a mother—the mother of
his son who, in turn, has become his primary concern and obsession.
Marcos' transformed attitude towards his wife is clearly exemplified
when, on one particular evening, she prepares a romantic evening for
the two of them and welcomes him suggestively when he arrives home
from work. Marcos responds by interrupting her overtures to ask "*¿Y mi
hijo?*" ("'And my son?'") (48). Luisa feels that she has become invisible
and so it is not surprising that, when Marcos pressures her to continue
to breastfeed by telling her that it is beautiful, Luisa is not convinced;
she reacts instead by hiding her body and insisting that he not look at
her. Her reaction is a result of her awareness that, under his gaze, she
cannot exist as both a sexual being and a mother, but only as the latter. This awareness underscores the ambivalence towards mothers in
patriarchal societies where, while maternity is venerated on one hand,
the maternal body does not represent the socially predominant ideal

of attractiveness and desirability. Within this socio-cultural context it is not surprising that Luisa is horrified when she looks in the mirror in search of her pre-pregnancy form and instead finds the swollen curves of her post-partum body—a body that is rejected by her husband, not socially recognized as beautiful, and whose beauty even the protagonist herself is unable to see. Consequently, she feels shame and hides both her body and her feelings.

Although Luisa is clearly struggling on various levels and she resents many of the expectations of her as a new mother, she is continually silenced and her preferences are not given any consideration. It is clear that in becoming a mother her wishes, needs, feelings, and general well-being are unquestionably subordinate to those of her child. She is ruthlessly pressured to continue to breastfeed her son, first by the nurse and then, in subsequent months, by her husband. Luisa defies this imposed obligation and takes advantage of Marcos' absence from the home to stop breastfeeding, but when he returns he uses anger, guilt, and shame to gain her compliance. Marcos' intransigent insistence that Luisa continue breastfeeding underscores his lack of concern for her well-being; although both he and the nurse recognize that Luisa is suffering from post-partum depression, they only comment on her condition in passing, as though it were no more serious than a paper cut. No one addresses her grief, guilt, and anger and Luisa cannot find a voice to express them. Thus, she sinks deeper into a depression and her anger is directed towards her son with whom she is unable to bond.

Luisa's condition becomes more and more serious, and her perceptions appear to be increasingly disconnected from reality. She begins to suffer from overwhelming delusions that she is being devoured, figuratively but also literally, by her baby. On the one hand, she is completely overwhelmed by the endless demands of mothering a newborn and the perception that that her baby has taken over every last drop of her life and energy. However, this sensation of being overwhelmed appears to lead to delusions that she is being physically devoured by her son, and she suffers acute distress as a result of her perception that he is sucking not only on her nipples, but also on her arms, her knees, her back, and every inch of her skin. Symbolic of her sense of being physically devoured, Luisa sees nipples beginning to appear all over her body; they emerge under her left breast, then on her neck, and finally they cover her from head to toe:

Luisa despertó sola y horrorizada. Tenía el cuerpo cubierto de tetillas y de cada una manaba leche. El niño mostraba su hambre revolvién-dose inquieto en la cuna (Luisa woke up alone and horrified. Her body was covered with nipples and milk was oozing from each of them. The child was showing signs of hunger, turning over unsettled in his crib). (51)

In portraying this level of post-partum depression and perhaps even psychosis, Barros' short story subverts the patriarchal construction of motherhood which assumes that for all women, unilaterally, it is the most wonderful, joyful, and fulfilling role.

In conclusion, it can be asserted that the representations of pregnancy and motherhood in the literary works of Mastretta and Barros con-tribute to the full expression of the complexity of women's experiences throughout pregnancy and motherhood. These representations defy traditional discourses that shape the perceptions of mothering in the social, political, and cultural realms. In their writing these women authors endeavour to transgress dominant patriarchal ideology and discourse surrounding Latin American mothering and, consequently, they open creative and valuable spaces within which to explore the plurality of women's experiences. As a result of the highly uncomfortable and yet very authentic experiences that these authors depict, the works make an invaluable contribution in giving voice to the extremely diverse journeys of Latin American women as they embrace—or endure—pregnancy and motherhood.

[1]For example, in Rosario Castellanos' poems "De la vigilia estéril" and "Se habla de Gabriel"; Alfonsina Storni's poem "El hijo"; in Rosario Ferré's "La bella durmiente" and "La muñeca menor"; in Laura Esquivel's *Como agua para chocolate*; in Diamela Eltit's *Los vigilantes* and Ana María Shua's "Como una buena madre."

[2]Adrienne Rich makes an important distinction between mothering as a *potential relationship* of any woman to her reproductive abilities and children, and mothering as a *patriarchal institution* which, in ensuring that this potential relationship remains under male control, is often oppressive to women.

[3]See for example Barbara Katz Rothman's article tracing the history of

the relationship between patriarchal ideology and mothering back to the Book of Genesis. She argues that in a patriarchal kinship system children are born to men out of women, and that it is women's motherhood that men must control in order to maintain patriarchy.

[4] See the abovementioned article "Deshilando el mito de la maternidad" by Trevizán; see Ferré's "Frankenstein: Una versión política del mito de la maternidad" where she argues that because patriarchal ideology structures the world according to domination/dominated or master/slave, motherhood within this context implies slavery towards that which has been created (36); see Gustafson's "The Social Construction of Maternal Absence" where she examines the social construction of legitimate, meaningful womanhood as inseparable from motherhood, and motherhood as primarily marked by self-negation where mothers' needs are always subordinate to those of her children (26-30); see also Castilla's "La ausencia del amamantamiento en la construcción de la buena maternidad" ("The Absence of Breastfeeding in the Construction of Good Mothering") where she asserts that western sex/gender constructions define motherhood based on biological conditions that are specific to women such as pregnancy, childbirth, and breastfeeding. Consequently, constructions of motherhood have tended to be homogeneous throughout time and across cultures, and they dictate that women are primarily responsible for the care and well-being of children (189-90).

[5] See Stevens' in-depth exploration of the roots and evolution of *marianismo* in Latin America.

[6] See also Domínguez's *De donde vienen los niños: maternidad y escritura en la literatura argentina* (*Where Children Come From: Motherhood and Writing in Argentine Literature*) where, in her literature review on women and motherhood, she highlights that within the context of the modern state and its related political institutions, motherhood is often used as a resource to be exploited for political ambitions (21-22).

[7] See Trevizán's "Escritoras chilenas III: Novela y cuento" where she describes the role that the 1980s Chilean women's movement and literature played in developing a countercultural discourse that questioned all forms of authoritarianism; see Galarce's interview with Pía Barros where Barros discusses the relationship between repression, censorship, violence, and eroticism in her work; see also García-Corales' interview with Pía Barros where Barros refers to the impact that the dictator-

ship had on the *Generación del 80* (generation of the 1980s) of women writers in Chile.

WORKS CITED

Barros, Pía. "Artemisa." *A horcajadas*. Santiago, Chile: Mosquito Comunicaciones, 1990. 45-51. Print.

Castellanos, Rosario. *Meditación en el umbral: antología poética.* Comp. Julian Palley. México, D.F.: Fondo de Cultura Económica, 1985

Castilla, María Victoria. "La ausencia del amamantamiento en la construcción de la buena maternidad." *La ventana* 21 (2005): 189-218. Print.

Domínguez, Nora. *De donde vienen los niños: maternidad y escritura en la cultura argentina.* Rosario, Argentina: Viterbo, 2007. Print.

Eltit, Diamela. *Los vigilantes.* Buenos Aires: Editorial Sudamericana, 1994.

Esquivel, Laura. *Como agua para chocolate.* México: Planeta, 1989.

Ferré, Rosario. "Frankenstein: una versión política del mito de la maternidad." *Debate feminista* 3.6 (1992): 32-43. Print.

Ferré, Rosario. *Papeles de Pandora: cuentos.* New York: Vintage, 2000.

Galarce, Carmen. "Pía Barros: la generación del descanto y la pérdida de utopías." *Confluencia* 13.1 (1997): 221-27. Print.

García-Corales, Guillermo. "La lucha por la inclusión de la literatura femenina actual: el caso de Pía Barros." *Revista monográfica* 13 (1997): 394-405. Print.

Glenn, Evelyn Nakano. "Social Constructions of Mothering: A Thematic Overview." *Mothering: Ideology, Experience, and Agency.* Ed. Evelyn Nakano Glenn, Grace Chang, and Linda Rennie Forcey. New York: Routledge, 1994. 1-29. Print.

Green, Fiona. "Feminist Mothers: Successfully Negotiating the Tensions Between Motherhood as 'Institution' and 'Experience'." *Mother Outlaws: Theories and Practices of Empowered Mothering.* Ed. Andrea O'Reilly. Toronto: Women's Press, 2004. 31-42. Print.

Gustafson, Diana L. "The Social Construction of Maternal Absence." *Unbecoming Mothers: The Social Production of Maternal Absence.* Ed. Diana L. Gustafson. New York: Haworth, 2005. 23-50. Print.

Martínez, América Luna. "Maternidad y escritura femenina: una experiencia perturbadora." *La otredad: los discursos de la cultura de hoy, 1995.* Ed. Sivia Elguea Véjar. Mexico City: Universidad Autónoma

Metropolitana-A., 1997. 45-52. Print.

Mastretta, Ángeles. *Arráncame la vida*. 3rd ed. Madrid: Alfaguara, 1994. Print.

Ojeda, Cecilia L. "Entre simulacros y enmascaramientos: 'Cuando Santiago está a oscuras' y 'Cartas de inocencia' de Pía Barros." *Revista canadiense de estudios hispánicos* 23 (1998):110-17. Print.

Pélage, Catherine. "Pía Barros y Diamela Eltit: transgresión y literatura femenina en Chile." *Palabra y el hombre* 114 (2000): 59-77. Print.

Pratt, Mary Louise. "Women, Literature, and National Brotherhood." *Women, Culture, and Politics in Latin America: Seminar on Feminism and Culture in Latin America*. Berkeley: University of California Press, 1990. 48-73. Print.

Rich, Adrienne. *Of Woman Born: Motherhood as Experience and Institution*. 2nd ed. New York: Norton, 1986. Print.

Rothman, Barbara Katz. "Beyond Mothers and Fathers: Ideology in a Patriarchal Society." *Mothering: Ideology, Experience, and Agency*. Ed. Evelyn Nakano Glenn, Grace Chang, and Linda Rennie Forcey. New York: Routledge, 1994. 139-57. Print.

Shua, Ana María. *Como una buena madre*. Buenos Aires: Editorial Sudamericana, 2001.

Stevens, Evelyn P. "Marianismo: The Other Face of Machismo in Latin America." *Female and Male in Latin America: Essays*. Ed. Ann Pescatello. Pittsburgh: University of Pittsburgh Press, 1973. 89-101. Print.

Storni, Alfonsina. *Poesías completas*. 6th ed. Buenos Aires: Sociedad Editora Latino Americana, 1968

Trevizán, Liliana. "Deshilando el mito de la maternidad." *Una palabra cómplice: un encuentro con Gabriela Mistral*. Ed. Regina Rodríguez. Santiago: Isis Internacional and Casa de la Mujer La Morada, 1989. 27-35. Print.

Trevizán, Liliana. "Escritoras chilenas III: Novela y cuento." *Escritoras chilenas*. Ed. Patricia Rubio. Santiago: Cuarto Propio, 1999. 579-93. Print.

Welldon, Estela V. *Mother, Madonna, Whore: The Idealization and Denigration of Motherhood*. London: Free Association, 1988. Print.

Contesting the Meaning of Latina/Chicana Motherhood

Familism, Collectivist Orientation, and Nonexclusive Mothering in Cristina García's *Dreaming in Cuban*

YOLANDA MARTÍNEZ

MOTHERHOOD AND THE ACT OF MOTHERING ARE NOT EXCLUSIVE to biological mothers nor simply determined by gender. Not all women are mothers, while those who are mothers do not all mother; the father-mother dyad as the traditionally alleged norm in conceiving and raising children has to coexist with other discourses of parenting in the 21st century: homosexual parents, single mothers, divorced or separated couples, and foster and extended families. This recent parenting allows for greater flexibility in the exploration of the maternal discourse in the post-millennium as socially constructed and not biologically inscribed (Waterman 24; Glenn 3); yet, our social values that (re)position women within national mythologies are not easily dismantled (Mostov 89).

According to Patricia Hill Collins in *Black Feminist Thought: Knowledge, Consciousness, and the Politics of Empowerment* (1990), women are often romanticized as mothers in their personification of "devotion, self-sacrifice, and unconditional love" (116). Jean F. O'Barr, Deborah Pope, and Mary Wyer add that they are seen as being "endlessly loving, serenely healing, emotionally rewarding" (O'Barr et al. 14). Responding to the mythological concept of the "Ideal Mother," a mother is omnipotent and "sees, understands and fulfils her children's every need" (Leira and Krips 87); however, she can also be "demonized as smothering, overly involved, and destructive" (Glenn 11; Chodorow and Contratto 56-7). The existence of mothering myths further counteracts women's efforts to break away from Western discourses on "good mothering"; women's failed attempts to simulate the "magical fantasy mother" frustrate them in their fear of falling outside the paradigms that socially determine good or bad parenting; such myths propagate archetypal gender roles and therefore aide in the internalization of a fictitious image of "good motherhood," which may hinder both balance and harmony in mother-daughter relationships and women's sense of self-worth as mothers.

This essay explores the various concepts of the maternal in Cristina García's *Dreaming in Cuban* (1992) as a construct that challenges conventional motherhood imagery in order to offer new approaches to theorizing the Latina maternal experience. The portrayal of motherhood in García's novel offers new insights to conceptualize motherhood since Latina/Chicana families are "characterized by a unique constellation of features derived from their socially and historically specific context" (Segura and Pierce 64). Furthermore, *Dreaming in Cuban* is illustrative of how this "constellation" of a tumultuous history of politics in Cuba and in the Diaspora disrupts the mother-daughter dyad, further challenging other contemporary Latina/Chicana constructs such as "familism," *compadrazgo*, "collectivist orientation," and "nonexclusive mothering" (Segura and Pierce 64; Mirandé and Enríquez 98, 107).

THE LATINA/CHICANA (M)OTHER(ING) EXPERIENCE: FAMILISM AND THE *DEL PINO* WOMEN

Up until the 1950s, theoretical approaches to family and family values perceived the family as a conjugal nuclear institution in which the relationship between husband and wife was central to the rapport between mothers and children.[1] Although after the 1950s the concept of family values entered into a crisis, such a romanticized ideal of the family and the sexual division of labor persisted as a way of empowering men and disempowering mothers and children (Jagger and Wright 9). From the 1960s onwards, different perspectives on mothering have shown a continuous evolution in the conception of the various meanings of motherhood for different social agents: from the social psychology tradition to the psychoanalytic and feminist view of motherhood, passing through the "good-enough" mother or "optimal frustrator" and the anthropological tradition.[2] In particular, motherhood as an institution for unequal power distribution received early attention in Adrienne Rich's text *Of Woman Born* (1977), where she explains motherhood as an "institution, which aims at ensuring that ... all women shall remain under male control" (13). Similarly, in Jean F. O'Barr, Deborah Pope, and Mary Wyer's complication *Ties That Bind: Essays on Mothering and Patriarchy* (1990) the institution of motherhood is named as an authoritative voice of patriarchal culture that shapes women's subjectivity at home and abroad ("Introduction" 2; Chodorow and Contratto 56). Despite developments in conceptualizing motherhood, the "prevailing gender belief system" and the location of motherhood in a "societal context organized by gender" have stayed very much the same (Arendell 1193).

The concept of "family crisis" that Cristina García portrays in her novel addresses the impossibility of fulfilling the role of the "fantasy of the perfect mother" and the role of "natural" motherhood as explained by Adrienne Rich:

> [First, that] a "natural" mother is a person without further identity, one who can find her chief gratification in being all day with small children, living at a pace tuned to theirs; that the isolation of mothers and children together in the home must be taken for granted; that maternal love is, and should be, quite literally selfish; that children and mothers are the "causes" of each others' sufferings. (22)

Rich's definition of "natural" motherhood finds its counterpart in *Dreaming in Cuban* where discourses on the maternal as a state of bonding, identification, and dependency between mothers and daughters are additionally called into question by different political allegiances that highlight the emotional distance between family members across and within diasporic borders (De Abruna 87).

In an interview with Iraida H. López, Cristina García explains that in *Dreaming in Cuban* the positioning of three generations of women in a very close relationship with one another before and after the Cuban Revolution was used to examine "how women have responded and adapted to what happened to their families after 1959," and explore "the emotional and political alliances that form within families" (609). By placing women at the center in Cuba's history of political and socio-economic relations with North America, the author further questions traditional representations of family and motherhood by intertwining the private/domestic sphere with a public/political context. García also explains in this interview that by focusing on women the female characters have a voice of their own to recount their own personal (hi)stories of separation, alienation, and reconciliation outside the realm of male traditional history:

> Traditional history, the way it has been written, interpreted and recorded, obviates women and the evolution of home, family and society, and basically becomes a recording of battles and wars and dubious accomplishments of men. You learn where politics really lie at home. That's what I was trying to explore on some level in *Dreaming in Cuban*. I was trying to excavate new turf, to look at the costs to individuals, families, and relationships among women of public events such as the revolution. (López 610)

Referring back to Adrienne Rich's concept of "natural" motherhood, in Cuba, Celia del Pino is a character with a "further identity" who finds her "chief gratification" in the opportunities brought by the Revolution to women in the military since women can expand upon their previous traditional domestic role. She dedicates herself to the Revolution, volunteers to cut sugarcane for microbrigades, builds nurseries for infants, and becomes the judge in her neighborhood.[3] When asked about Celia, Cristina García explains that she wanted to show "how much revolution and political activism galvanized her [Celia]. For her, the Revolution means something she can put her energies, her intellect and her heart into. It stimulates her blossoming, her flowering, her fulfillment; she is able to reach her potential" (Carabí 21). Paradoxically, considering that the role of the mother prevails as the most notable contribution in post-revolutionary Cuba and that women's position is re-located as primarily a biological function, a role that "remains the same as in old, patriarchal, pre-revolutionary times" (Torrents 177), Celia is inevitably limited in reaching her "chief gratification," a "failure" which is epitomized in the lack of familism between the del Pino women.

The characters' commitment to different political systems is an essential component in defining their allegiance towards each other or their sense of familism. Their personal vendettas are the result of a personal and familial past of loss and abandonment, "a past infected with disillusion" (García, *Dreaming in Cuban* 117) which, in the form of political loyalties, leads to confrontation between family members, and isolation and alienation amongst them (Kevane 87). Celia is moved by her strong support for communism, patriotism, and loyalty to *El Líder*, and refuses to leave the island; Celia's daughter Lourdes, driven by her pursuit of the American Dream, migrates with her daughter Pilar to New York and leaves Castro's "island prison" behind (García, *Dreaming in Cuban* 173); Pilar criticizes her mother's support of North American values and yearns to go back to Cuba and to Celia; Lourdes's sister Felicia lacks commitment to the revolutionary cause, which becomes a source of great rancor between her and her mother (107); and Felicia's twin daughters, who grow up inculcated in Castro's Cuba, live in a boarding school away from their mother.

The lack of family ties is reinforced by the characters' geographical distance and thus, their inability to communicate physically; the tangible boundaries that separate them across the ocean convey an emotional and spiritual disconnection from each other: "[e]ach character lives within the confines of his or her personal obsessions, unable to reach out to the others" (Kevane 87). This physical and emotional estrangement is further complicated by the rejection of an inability to fulfill the maternal fantasy and "perfectibility" of the mother by the three generations of the del Pino women (Chodorow and Contratto 55). Lourdes describes how she feels rejected from her mother:

> She imagined herself alone and shriveled in her mother's womb, envisioned the first days in her mother's unyielding arms. Her mother's fingers were stiff and splayed as spoons, her milk a tasteless gray. Her mother stared at her with eyes collapsed of expectation. If it's true that babies learn love from their mothers' voices, then this is what Lourdes heard: "I will not remember her name." (García, *Dreaming in Cuban* 74)

After giving birth to her "porous baby," "with no shadow" (50), Celia is confined to a mental institution as a result of a nervous breakdown. She later tries to revive her troubled and disturbed relationship with her children Lourdes, Felicia, and Javier, who are "desolate, deaf and blind to the world, to each other, to her" (117). Yet, there is still an emotional divide with Lourdes, which Celia writes about in a letter to her lover Gustavo: "That girl [Lourdes] is a stranger to me. When I approach her, she turns numb, as if she wanted to be dead in my presence.... She still punishes me for the early years" (163). Similarly, Lourdes, whose "views are strictly black-and-white" (26), is continuously infuriated by her daughter Pilar's resistance to coercion and admits that she "has no patience for dreamers, for people who live between black and white" (129). Pilar, however, suffers from her mother's arbitrariness and inconsistency (140) and openly expresses her desires to escape to Cuba and see her grandmother Celia: "I feel much more connected to Abuela Celia than to Mom, even though I haven't seen my grandmother in seventeen years. We don't speak at night anymore, but she's left me her legacy nonetheless.... Even in silence, she gives me the confidence to do what I believe is right, to trust my own perceptions" (176).

The volatile mother-daughter relationships exemplified by the del Pino women cast aside the traditional and limited perception of mothering as "good" and "bad"; instead, these conflictive kinships support the codification of "mother" as "a complex and multiple signifier" within a Latina/Chicana discourse in which maternal woman to woman relationships are highly valued (Flores 700). Furthermore, motherhood is redefined according to specific social, political, and generic circumstances; and the act of mothering is contested, and potentially reformulated so that the mother-daughter dyad and motherhood constitute "a learning process" (Everingham 7).

Detachment and lack of familism between the del Pino women is also metaphorically represented in Celia undergoing a mastectomy. Her missing breast denotes a range of theories which, according to Kathryn Schwarz in her analysis of the Amazonian body and the breast as a point of sexual difference and escape from patriarchal structures, involves the denunciation of sexual politics, reproductive practices, aesthetics, and the violence wrought upon women's bodies by authoritative and oppressive discourses on gender roles (147-69). Moreover, Celia's mastectomy disrupts the terms of the erotic, aesthetic, and maternal conventions as does her rejection of pregnancy. The removal of the breast itself suggests that the female body is no guarantee of a maternal role: "Representations of the breast, and particularly of the maternal breast, are always at least as concerned with morality as with medicine, and the question of what obligation a mother has to nurse her child" (152). Swcharz adds that "the breast has more power than the womb or even the seed, excluding men from the child's formation; whether exposed for the sake of nursing or of fashion, the breast threatens always to signify an excess of female control" (152).[4] In the same vein, when examining fascination with the female breast from the seventeenth to nineteenth century, Nina Prytula's article "Great-Breasted and Fierce" highlights how the breast was primarily and ultimately associated with an idealized notion of maternity (173). These fictitious and allegorical maternal associations of the female breast as being nourishing and embracing, nurturing and protective, and unifying the mother and child are dismantled in the image of Celia. Celia's missing breast echoes her lack of control and the rupture of family ties, which divides the family politically, emotionally, and geographically. Likewise, the analogy of Celia's breast as a symbol of nurture goes beyond being symbolic of her dismembered family.

TRANSNATIONAL MATERNAL (DIS)CONNECTIONS: THE ABSENCE OF COLLECTIVIST ORIENTATION AND THE PRACTICE OF NONEXCLUSIVE MOTHERING

Many of the imaginary constructs of mothering and the ideal nuclear family are filtered through Western white middle-class ideology or "motherhood ideology" (Kaplan 121). When making a distinction between the relationship of white middle-class families and African-American to capitalist political economies, Patricia Hill Collins explains that unlike white middle-class women, for women of color, work and motherhood have never functioned as a dichotomy but as intertwining acts for supporting the family. Being both economically able to provide for the family and performing the maternal role was, and is "an integral part of motherhood" (Collins, *Black Feminist Thought* 49; "Shifting the Center" 46). Collins further asserts that, "women of color have performed motherwork that challenges social constructions of work and family as separate spheres, of male and female gender roles as similarly dichotomized, and of the search for autonomy as the guiding human quest" ("Shifting the Center" 47). The relevance of "motherwork" lies in being a deconstructing act of heterosexist mothering models that defy the perception of Latina/Chicana women as being "the hearth of the home; [to be] chaste, modest, honorable, clean, and, most importantly, to minister to the needs for her husband and children" (Mirandé and Enríquez 98).

Within a Latina/Chicana family context, Collins' concept of "motherwork" could be translated into what Denise A. Segura and Jennifer L. Pierce refer to when comparing Chicana/o family structure and European-American women as a "collectivist orientation" (64). They state that Chicana/o families "maintain and affirm a distinct culture characterized by familism, *compadrazgo*, and a sense of collectivist orientation that is devalued by the dominant culture's emphasis on individualism" (70). Along the same lines, Alfredo Mirandé and Evangelina Enríquez add that, "it is not uncommon for Chicanos to pool their resources to help members of the immediate family or other relatives" (108).

In *Dreaming in Cuban*, Lourdes del Pino is the character that best exemplifies the rejection of a collectivist orientation in favor for individual success. In her pursuit of the American Dream, Lourdes betrays her own people by selling out to North American interests, which is highlighted when she opens her second bakery in Brooklyn and plans to sell "tricolor cupcakes and Uncle Sam Marzipan" (136). Her commodification to the American global market and the mass production of food "also allows her to identify herself with an alternative community that is not Cuban" (Dalleo and Sáez 123): "She envisioned a chain of Yankee Doodle bakeries stretching across America to St. Louis, Dallas, Los Angeles, her apple pies and cupcakes on main streets and in suburban shopping malls everywhere. Each store would bear her name, her legacy: LOURDES PUENTE, PROPIETOR" (García, *Dreaming in Cuban* 171). Lourdes is not only complicit and a victim of her own fanatical consumerism, but she emphasizes the impoverishment of her own people who are suffering from severe food shortages as a result of the United States' embargo on Cuba's largest export crop, sugar: "Each glistening éclair is a grenade ... each strawberry shortcake proof—in butter, cream, and eggs—of Lourdes's success in America, and a reminder of the ongoing shortages in Cuba" (117). Lourdes' thirst for power is directly conveyed in her antagonism to Celia's Cuba and all that her mother embodies. As she foments "her own brand of anarchy closer to home" (177) by holding sessions at the bakery with Cuban extremists, Lourdes is "convinced [that] she can fight Communism from behind her bakery counter" (136) and "denounce the Communist threat to America" (171). Reflecting on her actions, Lourdes openly rejects the familial component of familism; in the face of arduous social and economic conditions, she refuses to establish long-distance attachment and unconditional loyalty to family members (Falicov 278; García, *The Mexican Americans* 102).

While examining the mother-daughter dyad from both a psychological and a sociological perspective, Alice Adams states that "[m]ost treatments of mothering, feminist or not, emphasized that the primary task of the prototypical middle-class daughter was to separate" (414). Similarly, in her book *Writing Mothers, Writing Daughters: Tracing the Maternal in Stories by American-Jewish Women* (1996), Janet Burstein stresses the confrontation of the daughter with two possible alternatives through the mirror motif: either behaving like her mother or separating from her—a choice also echoed in Adrienne Rich's idea of "becoming individuated" (236). While daughters sought to achieve economic and professional independence and autonomy, they also found themselves drawn towards the "gendered cultural imperatives" of domesticity and parenthood in which their mothers were trapped: "They stood, as it were, between mirrors that offered incompatible images of the world and themselves" (Burstein 115).

Faced with the impossibility of penetrating a mother's world, and in their need of "becoming individuated," daughters are forced to seek motherly affection elsewhere by bonding with other (fe)male figures or "othermothers" as defined by Simone A. James Alexander (7)—an extension of a Latina/Chicana version of *compadrazgo* or "fictive kinship system" (Williams 24). In *Dreaming in Cuban,* there is the almost inexistent extent of behavioral familism, that is, "the degree of interaction between both nuclear and extended family members" (García, *The Mexican Americans* 102). In particular, Lourdes and Felicia fail to see themselves as a continuation of their mother Celia, as well as Pilar of Lourdes; thus, the relationships fail to produce a "multi-object relational configuration of daughter/mother/aunt/grandmother/godmother/father" (Segura and Pierce 77). Instead, the strained mother-daughter relationship favors closeness primarily with the figure of the grandmother, as initially is the case between Celia and Pilar, probably because "the grandmother/granddaughter relationship is less tense than that of mothers and daughters" (77).

As Pilar separates from her mother Lourdes, she temporarily finds security, self-affirmation, and guidance in her grandmother Celia. The telepathic connection between Celia and Pilar is illustrative of "psychological familism," the existence of an "intergenerational bond between country and family" (Falicov 279). Pilar's memories are kept alive through the image of her grandmother, the representative of her Hispanic past left behind on the island. However, after Pilar visits Cuba and realizes that she belongs to New York *more* than Cuba, she also recognizes that she cannot be her grandmother's guardian of Cuban history or her granddaughter: "Everyday Cuba fades a little more inside me, my grandmother fades a little more inside me" (García, *Dreaming in Cuban* 138). As with the other female characters in the novel, Pilar and Celia's connection and gradual separation is further epitomized through the loss of language: while Celia criticizes that Pilar's Spanish "is no longer hers" (7), Pilar uses painting to "find a unique language, obliterate the clichés" (139); Lourdes speaks another idiom entirely, a language which is lost to the other Cubans in Cuba (221); Felicia utters empty words that keep her daughters "prisoners in her alphabet world" (121); and Felicia's daughters speak a coded language that Felicia cannot penetrate (120). The female characters' impossibility of rapport due to the loss of language opens instead alternative communication path liaisons between daughter/father and mother/son: Lourdes maintains conversations with her father's spirit and fantasizes about the son she miscarried in Cuba, whom she replaces at the end of the novel by taking Felicia's son Ivanito to New York with her; Felicia tries to contact his father through the ritual practices of *santería* and, for a while, finds comfort in her son in a world of poetry and coconut ice cream; and Luz and Milagros, fraught with mixed feelings of anger, resentment, and maternal need reconcile with their father as an act of contempt and defiance towards Felicia. They find in their father a "language more eloquent than the cheap bead necklaces of words their mother offers" (124). The stereotypical familial associations challenged by the father/daughter and mother/son connection in the novel sustain the paternalist scheme within the family system by which mothers are more likely to pamper and indulge their sons than their daughters (Mirandé and Enríquez 114); such transposition of dyads in childhood not only establishes the irreparable bonds between mothers and daughters that will pervade into adulthood, but it also questions the persevering view advocated by Latinas/Chicanas that "*la familia* is the basic source of emotional and physical support for the individual" (114).

CONCLUSION: SHAPING NEW MEANINGS
OF LATINA/CHICANA MOTHERHOOD

That the concept of motherhood is "the most profound life transit a woman undertakes, the deepest knowledge she can experience" is arguable in that such an ideological approach responds to a set of social, political, and cultural rules dictated by men for the benefit of men (O'Barr, Pope and Wyer 1): "Motherhood as an institution has been named by the authoritative voice not of women but of patriarchal culture" (2). Nevertheless, the concept of motherhood as the mechanism that defines women solely as reproducers and biological subjects of the nation still persists in Western and Eastern conservative societies today. The analysis of Cuban American writer Cristina García's novel *Dreaming in Cuban* demonstrates that myths on the fantasy of the perfect mother are not reduced to men's performativity, but that women themselves struggle to come to terms with their understanding of the maternal role, and thus, they might aid in their own subordination. Furthermore, Cristina García defies the "almost invariably stress" that Latina/Chicana narratives put on familism as a way of inclusiveness and interdependence between family members (Falicov 278). The fact that the del Pino women fail to overcome each others' political and personal agendas culminates in an absence of a sense of family coherence (Falicov 278) and a lack of family connectedness, that is, "the obligation to care for and support one another" (Mirandé and Enríquez 278). In an attempt to sustain cultural continuity and recreate cultural spaces, the characters move across "a psychologically complex experience of presence and absence" as in Pilar's psychological and physical connection with Cuba or Lourdes' physical and emotional disconnection with her mother/land (Falicov 276).

Dreaming in Cuban examines motherhood and mothering in terms of gendered and national formulations on female subjectivity. The novel not only responds to the feminist theories of "family crisis," but it also defies Latina/Chicana family concepts such as familism, *compadrazgo*, collectivist orientation, and nonexclusive mothering. The division of the del Pino family members and the impossibility of mothering are not unique to a specific nuclear family or given society; instead, it represents a cross-cultural phenomenon. These transnational geographies, however, can serve as physical and emotional spaces to collectively challenge traditional constructions of femininity towards new spaces that negotiate women's identities as mothers, and discourses on motherhood. On the one hand, *Dreaming in Cuban* confronts a prescriptive and normative Westernized comprehension of the nuclear family and motherhood as monolithic constructs. On the other hand, the novel displaces family components characteristic of Latina/Chicana family. These challenges are evident of the need for a new revaluation on sentimentalized notions of motherhood and family according to "unique constellations" that define specific and alternative family values and patterns, in particular on the roles of the maternal, and the meanings of mothering and motherhood.

[1]The idea of the nuclear family as "natural, normal and ideal" encompassed patterns of structured inequality in terms of power imbalance and class, race and gender-based inequalities (Jagger and Wright 2). Conservative constructs on the idea of family perceived this, above all, as an adoptive unit that mediates between the individual and society to provide the individual with personal growth and development, and for physical and emotional integrity. For a detailed analysis on modern sociological theories of family life and the diverse realities of contemporary family values, see Jagger and Wright.

[2]The three perspectives on mothering from the social psychology tradition, the "good-enough" mother and the anthropological tradition identify the needs of the child as natural, as given by biology. Whilst the first one places emphasis on the child as the shaper of the mother's behavior and the third one focuses on the diversity in which different cultures meet the child's needs, the "good-enough mother" learns to identify the child's needs and offers a nearly perfect care-giving environment. The psychoanalytic and feminist view of motherhood, however, is based on an act of mutual recognition by the mother and child and acknowledgment of autonomy and independence from each other (Everingham 11-12).

[3]Celia's commitment to the revolutionary cause brings to mind the figure of the female combatant, common icon of Cuban nationalism. As Stoner asserts: "[n]o other symbol so permeates Cuban nationalist lore than that of the stalwart and feminine combatant, willing to sacrifice her home, family, and wealth for her nation and its patriarchal leaders" (72).

[4]Rothman refers to the concept of "seed" to make the distinction between a patriarchal and "matrilineal" system. The seed is essential to draw on theories of blood ties, understood as a genetic connection that controls women as mothers, daughters and also sons, who grow out of man's seed.

WORKS CITED

Adams, Alice. "Maternal Bonds: Recent Literature on Mothering." *Signs: Journal of Women in Culture and Society* 20:2 (1995): 414-27. Print.

Alexander, Simone A. J. *Mother Imagery in the Novels of Afro-Caribbean Women*. Columbia: University of Missouri Press, 2001. Print.

Arendell, Terry. "Conceiving and Investigating Motherhood: The Decade's Scholarship." *Journal of Marriage and the Family* 62.4 (2000): 1192-1207. Print.

Burstein, Janet. *Writing Mothers, Writing Daughters: Tracing the Maternal in Stories by American Jewish Women*. Urbana: University of Illinois Press, 1996. Print.

Carabí, Angels. "People on the Edge See More. A Conversation with the Cuban-American Writer Cristina García." *Lectora: Revista de Dones i Textualitat* 1 (1995): 19-23. Print.

Cheal, David. *Family and the State of Theory*. Toronto: University of Toronto Press, 1991. Print.

Chodorow, Nancy and Susan Contratto. "The Fantasy of the Perfect Mother." *Rethinking the Family: Some Feminist Questions*. Ed. Barrie Thorne and Marilyn Yalom. Longman: New York, 1982. 54-75. Print.

Collins, Patricia Hill. *Black Feminist Thought: Knowledge, Consciousness, and the Politics of Empowerment*. New York: Routledge, 1990. Print.

Collins, Patricia Hill. "Shifting the Center: Race, Class and Feminist Theorizing about Motherhood." *Mothering: Ideology, Experience and Agency*. Ed. Evelyn Nakano Glenn, Grace Chang, and Linda Rennie Forcey. London: Routledge, 1994. 45-66. Print.

Dalleo, Raphael, and Elena Machado Sáez. *The Latino/a Canon and the Emergence of Post-Sixties Literature*. New York: Palgrave, 2007. Print.

De Abruna, L. Nielsen. "Twentieth-Century Women Writers from the English-Speaking Caribbean." *Modern Fiction Studies* 34 (1998): 85-96. Print.

Everingham, Christine. *Motherhood and Modernity: An Investigation into the Rational Dimension of Mothering*. Buckingham: Open University Press, 1994. Print.

Falicov, Celia J. "Ambiguous Loss: Risk and Resilience in Latino Immigrant Families." *Latinos Remaking America*. Ed. Marcelo M. Suárez Orozco and Mariela M. Páez. Berkeley: University of California Press, 2009. 274-88. Print.

Flores, Lisa A. "Reclaiming the "Other": Toward a Chicana Feminist Critical Perspective." *International Journal of Intercultural Relations* 24 (2000): 687-705. Print.

García, Alma M. *The Mexican Americans*. London: Greenwood, 2002. Print.

García, Cristina. *Dreaming in Cuban*. London: Flamingo, 1992. Print.

Glenn, Evelyn Nakano, Grace Chang and Linda Rennie Forcey, eds. *Mothering: Ideology, Experience and Agency*. London: Routledge, 1994. Print.

Jagger, Gill, and Caroline Wright, eds. *Changing Family Values*. London: Routledge, 1999. Print.

Kaplan, E. Ann. "Look Who's Talking, Indeed: Fetal Images in Recent North American Visual Culture." *Mothering: Ideology, Experience and Agency*. Ed. Evelyn Nakano Glenn, Grace Chang, and Linda Rennie Forcey. London: Routledge, 1994. 121-38. Print.

Kevane, Bridget. *Latino Literature in America*. Westport: Greenwood, 2003. Print.

Leira, Halldis and Madelein Krips. "Revealing Cultural Myths on Motherhood." *Daughtering and Mothering: Female Subjectivity Reanalyzed*. Ed. Janneke van Mens-Verhulst, Karlein Schreurs, and Liesbeth Woertman. London: Routledge, 1993. 83-113. Print.

López, Iraida H. "...And There Is Only My Imagination Where Our History Should Be: An Interview with Cristina Garcia." *Michigan Quarterly Review* 33.3 (1994): 605-17. Print.

Mirandé, Alfredo, and Evangelina Enríquez. *La Chicana*. Chicago: University of Chicago Press, 1979. Print.

Mostov, Julie. "Sexing the Nation/Desexing the Body: Politics of National Identity in Former Yugoslavia." *Gender Ironies of National-*

ism: Sexing the Nation. Ed. Tamar Mayer. London: Routledge, 2000. 80-110. Print.

O'Barr, Jean F., Deborah Pope, and Mary Wyer, eds. *Ties That Bind: Essays on Mothering and Patriarchy.* Chicago: University of Chicago Press, 1990. Print.

Prytula, Nina. "'Great-Breasted and Fierce': Fielding's Amazonian Heroines." *Eighteenth Century Studies* 35.2 (2002): 173-93. Print.

Rich, Adrienne. *Of Woman Born: Motherhood as Experience and Institution.* London: Virago, 1977. Print.

Rothman, Barbara Katz. "Beyond Mothers and Fathers: Ideology in a Patriarchal Society." *Mothering: Ideology, Experience and Agency.* Ed. Evelyn Nakano Glenn, Grace Chang, and Linda Rennie Forcey. London: Routledge, 1994. 139-57. Print.

Schwarz, Kathryn. "Missing the Breast." *The Body in Parts: Fantasies of Corporeality in Early Modern Europe.* Ed. David Hillman and Carla Mazzio. New York: Routledge, 1997. 147-70. Print.

Segura, Denise A., and Jennifer L. Pierce. "Chicana/o Family Structure Gender Personality: Chodorow, Familism, and Psychoanalytic Sociology Revisited." *Signs* 19.1 (1993): 62-91. Print.

Stoner, K. Lynn. "Militant Heroines and the Consecration of the Patriarchal State: The Glorification of Loyalty, Combat, and National Suicide in the Making of Cuban National Identity." *Cuban Studies* 34 (2003): 71-96. Print.

Torrents, Nissa. "Women Characters and Male Writers: A Cuban Approach." *Feminist Readings on Spanish and Latin-American Literature.* Ed. Lisa P. Condé and Stephen Hart. Lewiston, NY: Mellen, 1991. 173-92. Print.

Waterman, Barbara. *The Birth of an Adoptive, Foster or Stepmother Beyond Biological Mothering Attachments.* London: Kingsley, 2003. Print.

Williams, Norma. *The Mexican American Family: Tradition and Change.* Oxford: Altamira, 1990. Print.

The Telenovela *Alborada*

Constructions of the Latina Mother
in an Internationally Successful Soap Opera

PETRA GUERRA, DIANA I. RIOS, AND D. MILTON STOKES

THE MASS MEDIA HAVE BEEN EFFECTIVE IN RECYCLING IMAGES in popular entertainment productions (Berg 314). Viewers are exposed to formulaic, yet interesting representations of people, including stereotypes of mothers and mothering. At times, these stereotypes portray mothers who are callous or horribly neglectful of their children, or the opposite is portrayed—mothers live through their children so intensely that they have no life of their own. Telenovelas (Spanish language soap operas), such as the award-winning *Alborada*, provide various constructions of Latina mothers and Latina motherhood to inform large audiences through hyperbole. In *Alborada*, mothers are intimately engaged with the faults, indiscretions, fortunes, and destinies of those in their familial and social networks. In addition, they are subjected to the social class stratification and conventional gender roles of the time period, nineteenth-century colonial Panama and Mexico. As such, they have limited rights and are dependent upon men. Since women cannot also own land or valuables, they are compelled to raise their sons to positions of power so that they can enjoy privileges given only to men. These gender roles are presented in *Alborada* and other *telenovelas* as normative, as part of a necessary and acceptable ordering.

In our analysis of Latina mothers and mothering, we will primarily examine Latina/Chicana feminists Carla Trujillo, Gloria E. Anzaldúa, AnaLouise Keating, Aida Hurtado, Gabriela F. Arredondo, Rosa Maria Gil, and Carmen Inoa Vázquez to build our critique of traditional patriarchal systems of social order that are oppressive to women and are presented in the *telenovela* form of mass media. Chicanas and Latinas experience sexism and other discrimination through social, political, and economic systems, reflecting ideological and patriarchal values (Anzaldúa and Keating 306). The mass media is an integral part of an ideological system that reinforces established orders of power, and the oppression of less powerful segments of society, through its dissemination of select information about society that is deemed to be natural or simply regular (Demers 177; Gitlin 10). Telenovelas in general expose viewers to limited definitions of Latina mothers. Similarly, *Alborada* draws audiences into a highly romanticized spectacle of motherhood from the "desired" bygone days and stereotypical images of Latina women, which is problematic for audiences who accept these distortions.

Through our analysis of *Alborada*, we closely examine mother characters and related story elements, as well as discuss the impact of *telenovela* content on audiences. Secondly, we explore several constructions of the Latina mother in *Alborada* and how these constructions contribute to popular culture repertoire of Latina stereotypes in the mass media and motherhood (Berg 314). In our analysis, we look at *la madre marianista* or the marianist mother who suffers; the abused mother who is oppressed; the "good" mother and the "bad" mother who are kind and mean respectively. When examining these broad "good" and "bad" qualities of motherhood, it is important to note that these polarities misrepresent the nuances and intricacies of mothering since there are quandaries that real mothers, as well as other human beings, face in society that cannot always be neatly categorized as "good" or "bad." Furthermore, this essay explores the femme-macho mother who is alluring and brash. Variations of these nonexclusive constructions can be found in many Latin American *telenovelas*. For example, *El Pecado de Oyuki* shows a Marianist as a suffering mother who is also a maltreated "good" mother. *La Usurpadora* also features dichotomized "good" and "bad" mothers; one of whom is wrongly exploited while the other is a cruel, harsh mother who will stand up to men and not allow them to stop her from her underhanded machinations. Lastly, this essay presents critical discussions regarding how the constructions of Latina mothers and mothering often reinforce traditional women's gender roles and promote a traditional family ideal that is impractical. In contemporary socio-economic climates, such as in the U.S., women are needed in non-traditional roles outside the home as breadwinners or co-breadwinners along with their partners. Although *telenovelas* such as *Alborada* illustrate some ruptures in the fabric of traditional roles, in the end this television series supports a traditional illusion of domesticity to its viewers. Unfortunately, truncated media representations enforce erroneous views about Latina mothers and Latina mothering when in reality, motherhood and mothering is complex and dynamic.[1]

TELENOVELAS IN LATINA AND LATINO LIVES

Television's impact on viewers raises questions about the potential influences of content for Latinos and other audiences.[2] In particular, the overabundance of harmful stereotypes across various mass media and mediated images of Latina mothers provide inaccurate information to viewers about what to expect from Latina mothers and mothering. Extending ideas from the sociocognitive perspective of mass media impact, Albert Bandura in "Social Cognitive Theory of Mass Communication" suggests that these types of media representations, images and story elements, can serve as a reinforcement for some viewers' own ideas of mothering style, thus supporting flawed models of behavior as correct or ideal (138).

As a popular television genre, *telenovelas* have a wide proliferation among viewers. Nora Mazziotti discusses in "La Industria de la Telenovela: La Producción de Ficción en America Latina (The Industry of the Telenovela: The Production of Fiction in Latin America) that *telenovelas* facilitate audience emotional participation because they treat basic human problems and challenges involving love, honor, birthright, death, good, bad, reward and punishment (Mazziotti 14-16). Hence, the content of *telenovelas* invites audiences to vicariously experience the tensions and frictions within communities, families, and social networks; and this participation points toward a range of outcomes. Some scholars argue that certain *telenovelas* can encourage women to challenge restrictive gendered norms of their society (La Pastina 170); can encourage communication between friends and family across U.S.-Mexico borderlands (Mayer 484); and can provide ideas and inspiration for career goals (Rios 59). On the other hand, research indicates that television also influences viewers' creation of false realities (Gerbner et al. 30). In this latter sense, *Alborada* and other *telenovelas* contribute to television viewers' accumulated mental storehouse of mediated ideas and imagery about Latina mothers and motherhood that is erroneous and potentially detrimental when used as points of reference.

ALBORADA: PRODUCTION AND STORY

Alborada is a Mexican *telenovela* and was shown from December 2005 to April 2006 in the United States. This *telenovela*'s popularity led to several recognitions including the *TV y Novelas* award for best *telenovela* of the year in 2006, six *Bravo* awards, and the distinguished *Las Palmas de Oro* award from the National Circle of Mexican Journalists. There are many reasons why this television program was a success with viewers. Aside from the aesthetic beauty of scenery and costume, the program had interesting male and female characters, romantic tensions, and a main protagonist who is a mother and manages her motherhood through many life challenges. *Alborada* also resonates with elements of viewers' lives by depicting interpersonal issues such as relationship troubles, family conflicts, and other issues such as maintaining a family and defining one's place in the world.

Alborada tells the love story of Hipolita and Luis, and how their lives eventually come together as a result of numerous social gyrations, mishaps, and adventures. In spite of being a love tale, it also portrays different mothering styles of the women in the story. Various mothers, including Hipolita, struggle in their own way to thrive and advance during the socio-economic, systemic constraints of the 19th-century colonial era. For example, Doña Adelaida de Guzman, a domineering and greedy mother, controls her son's life and uses him to maintain her position in upper class society. She encourages her son Antonio to marry Hipolita, so that he can provide an heir to inherit the Guzman fortune, once Doña Adelaida's brother dies. Much to Doña Adelaida's consternation, her son Antonio has no interest in sex with his wife, thus never gives her the heir she much desires. Doña Adelaida's mistreatment and Antonio's indifference marks the beginning of Hipolita's difficult journey toward motherhood and a traditional happy family, away from the people who oppress her. The "goodly" Hipolita's quest to overcome mean-spiritedness and barriers in the world also becomes linked to the stereotypical motif of finding a Prince Charming in order to be a wife and mother.

The "bad" mother-in-law motif is personified through Doña Adelaida de Guzman's victimizing of Hipolita and her controlling, abusive, and self-serving nature. As this evil figure, she uses Luis Manrique y Arellano, an affluent Mexican commercialist, to give her an heir. She blackmails

Luis, who agrees to have sex with Hipolita for his freedom. By the time Luis is led to Hipolita, she has been drugged by her mother-in-law. Never having slept with her husband, Hipolita mistakes Luis for Antonio; and when she realizes this grave error, she panics and is overwhelmed by guilt. Luis is also embarrassed by his actions and when he attempts to apologize, he is interrupted by a noise outside the door—a sound which is likely made by Doña Adelaida in an attempt to kill him. He quickly leaves, but never forgets about Hipolita and the possibility that he might have fathered a child. Later, the pregnant, "good" mother Hipolita decides to risk the uncertainty of paternity for the sake of staying married and raising her child with a paternal figure.

LA MARIANISTA

Madonna-like constructions are common in Latin American-style popular media such as *telenovelas*.[3] Marian motifs, or motifs harkening la marianista, are easily identifiable for Latina/Chicana audiences who are culturally rooted in a European originated Catholic Mary, the parallel Indigenous woman called Tonantzin, and the syncretic Maria Virgen de Guadalupe (Burkhart 11). Linked to the common Marian motif are the qualities of inherent goodness and the challenges to maintain virtuosity when struggling with adverse conditions. This struggle is echoed as part of a larger theme known as good vs. evil or good overcoming evil. Within the Marianist context, a Marianism motif is presented when a virtuous mother, who is unfairly treated, suffers injustice until a favorable conclusion is met. For example, a virtuous mother is vindicated after withstanding years of agony at the hands of the more powerful. Also, a related motif is of a mother's separation from her child. This is illustrated when a virtuous estranged mother is reunited with her offspring after a heartbreaking period. Furthermore, because of this type of mother's "innate goodness," her foes are either converted to decency, die an unexpected death, or leave. The "good" woman's suffering is equivalent to achieving purity through endurance, while her vindication becomes equivalent to achieving a heavenly prize. The familiarity with the image and related motifs provide a level of comfort to viewer's expectations since a "good" woman (the main female character) leads the viewer through a maze of interpersonal relationships with a reward at the end. Marianism in general can be problematic in how it is interpreted and brought into women's lives. It is critiqued by Latina/Chicana scholars because "in the classic manner" the suffering of Mary means that women should accept repression (Trujillo 220). Conversely, Marianism can be reinterpreted and made useful and empowering to women who need to tap into a source of spiritual feminine power (Trujillo 220).

The *marianista* figure appears as the suffering mother in Yolanda Vargas Dulche's *El Pecado de Oyuki (Oyuki's Sin)*. This *telenovela* tells of a young dedicated mother, who is wrongly sent to prison for the murder of her husband. She suffers the Marianist qualities of being noble and having silent penitence, while her abusive brother, the true murderer, raises her daughter. After twenty years, the brother confesses to his crime and she is vindicated. Moreover, in *La Madrasta* (The Stepmother), Maria also depicts a Marianist as a long-suffering mother who is wrongly accused of murder and is sentenced to prison. She later reclaims her children when she is released and must work to build a relationship with her children. The Marian construction in *Alborada* is presented in the goodness qualities of Hipolita and her tearful, silent suffering from verbal onslaughts and other's wicked schemes. Her qualities underscore virtues lacking in other characters and contrast starkly with the highly avaricious mother characters such as the scheming mother-in-law Doña Adelaida de Guzman and the devious aunt Juana Arellano viuda de Manrique. In regard to the motif of separation, the "good" Hipolita was temporarily and unwillingly separated from her son, until she gained employment that enabled her to provide for him. Just like Maria in La *Madrasta*, Hipolita behaved as a caring mother who did not abandon her son, but worked to create a better place for him. In reality, many Latina mothers leave their children while they work, and feel that they are abandoning their children. According to Carla Trujillo, some scholars view Latina mothers as the center of the family, the ones who are the caregivers and the nurturers. Contemporary Latinas, Trujillo points out, are multi-dimensional women, workers, spouses, lovers, and mothers (104). Furthermore, they have the double burden of keeping a job and running a household, which can create guilt and anxiety among women who should look after themselves too (Trujillo and Rodríguez 117). It is not necessary to be a long-suffering mother, as is depicted in *Alborada*, in order to be an effective mother. As Latino communities support mothers by having more realistic expectations about their time and roles, they will also provide a foundation for them to secure time and space for their own mental and physical health.

At first glance, Marianism or *marianismo* offers positive ideals for girls and women who may one day be mothers, since this asks for charity, kindness, and tolerance—all of which are displayed by Hipolita. However, these ideals have been highly critiqued by Latina/Chicana scholars who see *marianismo* as supporting gender role constraints, subjugation of females, and excusing violence against females (Norat 236). The marianista, a woman who practices Marianism, is also expected to be obedient to male authority, passive, and self-sacrificing. According to David Sequeira in *The Machismo Marianismo Tango*, a Mariana accepts domination, dependence, and responsibility for all household chores (30). As Melba Sánchez-Ayendez posits, "Taking its cue from the worship of Mary, marianismo pictures its subjects as semi divine, morally superior and spiritually stronger than men. This constellation of attributes enables women to bear the indignities inflicted on them by men, and to forgive those who bring them pain" (242). Rosa Maria Gil and Carmen Inoa Vásquez in *The Maria Paradox: How Latinas Can Merge Old World Traditions with New World Self-Esteem* discuss what they call the "Maria paradox," in which they see Latinas conflicted by old world traditions and contemporary dreams (15). They argue that the successful managing of the "Maria paradox" can allow Latinas and other women to build a healthy self-esteem as they thrive in society. A part of a successful balancing of the "Maria paradox" for a mother, then, would include a healthy balance between emotional (e.g. self-esteem, love, interdependency) and physical (e.g. food and shelter) needs for herself and family.

The balancing of needs for self and those of others is represented in *Alborada* to some degree, but it is undermined. The character Hipolita lives in an old-world context and must define her life to a certain level of self-determination within the oppressive familial, religious-cultural system of the era. *Marianismo* dictates that she be subservient to her husband Antonio, who has no amicable or sexual interest in her. Moreover, with no physical contact with her husband, she cannot have children with her lawful husband. She is therefore retained as a non-mother virgin and is initially blocked from becoming the traditional mother assumed by *marianismo*. She is also forced to submit to elders such as her abusive mother-in-law Doña Adelaida, who manipulates her movements and deceives her to produce an heir. According to the traditional *marianismo,* girls are raised to be "good" women of the house and to make their husbands happy and have children.[4] They are also expected to follow their dreams through their children and family and to become dependent on them for emotional and financial sustenance.

Given the many barriers and contradictions in her life, the road for Hipolita is difficult. Her only option for emotional survival is to leave her oppressive situation and to remake herself as a single woman. Therefore, she needs to hide the impregnation by Luis Manrique y Arellano, and temporarily venture outside her immediate family system and elite class structure. For a while, Hipolita redefined herself and her motherhood by incorporating the Marianist qualities of kindness and beneficent strategies. Having no income, she gladly toils as a washer-woman, works as a maid for a convent, withstands misunderstandings and insults from members of the elite who see her as socially inferior, and withstands affronts from men who want to take sexual advantage of her. Despite her troubles, Hipolita does not become bitter toward those who oppress her. As Evelyn Stevens states, Hipolita appears to be "the ever-loving, always forgiving surrogate of the Virgin Mary" (60). Though she toils independently for a significant part of the story, at the end, Hipolita falls back into a romanticized, traditional motherhood and wifely role with her Prince Charming, Luis Manrique y Arellano, and the child that was conceived one night. Through sacrifice, labor, and humbleness, she constitutes love and virtue and represents the qualities of traditional Marianism.

THE ABUSED MOTHER

Another Marianist motif is demonstrated in *Alborada* through Asunción, Hipolita's mother, who suffers and passively accepts her subjugated gender roles as a wife and mother. Her pain starts when she abandons Hipolita to protect her social reputation from rumors of having a baby without being married. As discussed by Patricia Zavella, having a baby out of wedlock would be a physical manifestation of defiance of social controls over women's sexuality, a breach of social class mores, and an act of sin (229-33). Aida Hurtado adds in "The Politics of Sexuality in the Gender Subordination of Chicanas" that women who "save their virginity until marriage are [the only ones] to enter the revered status of wife, and eventually mother and grandmother" (398). Asunción's guilt opens her to lifelong verbal condemnations from her husband Francisco who reminds her that she was not a "good" woman when he married her because she was not a virgin. As a cruel and conniving man who controls everyone, he also declares Asunción as "damaged" and uses this as an excuse to physically abuse her. Asunción accepts his abuse as deserving punishment for her previous relationship with a married man. His mistreatment also causes her to withdraw, thus she has no voice in the marriage, nor does she stand up for her children. Following traditional, cultural, and religious normative thinking, she accepts suffering as a human necessity and as part of being a "good" mother whose self-denial leads to a form of salvation. According to the Mujeres Latinas en Acción, an organization that provides assistance to women and tracks information on domestic violence, "Women who are deeply religious may believe a violent spouse is their cross to bear" (Facts and Statistics). Traditional modes of thinking are controversial among Latina/Chicana feminists such as Aida Hurtado, Carla Trujillo, and Anna NietoGomez. These scholars acknowledge qualities of nurturance as favorable, but would not support conditions that would cause a woman to be abused and subjected to violence (Hurtado 384-88; Trujillo 220-21; NietoGomez 48-50). Unfortunately, Marianist qualities as modeled by the abused Asunción send harmful messages to viewers regarding what "good" wives and mothers should do.

THE GOOD MOTHER AND THE BAD MOTHER

Definitions of the mother in our mass mediated culture have been deliberated by various interdisciplinary scholars whose sociological and feminist frameworks would pose that "good" versus "bad" mothers is a highly inaccurate dichotomy, obscuring a multiplicity of ways in which mothers actually exist and in which mothering occurs.[5] Therefore, counter to a romanticized "good" mother who must be romantically partnered with a man or is awaiting her Prince Charming, "good" mothers can be found in many forms—single mothers, lesbian mothers, working mothers. Furthermore, the dominant definition and ideal of motherhood that the media presents is reflective of patriarchal needs to maintain societal power over women's roles by illustrating the right or correct way to be a mother. These so-called "correct" ways mean maintaining and continuing traditional gender roles. As Gloria Anzaldúa discusses in an interview with Ines Hernández, because of historical parenting expectations, modern day mothers are labeled "bad" when they become part of the labor force in order to contribute to their family needs (191). In addition to the limits that patriarchy places on motherhood, patriarchal-defined tradition disparages single mothers and is rejecting of lesbian mothers. Therefore, any challenges to the "traditional" definitions of motherhood are unacceptable (Trujillo 181).[6]

At one point in *Alborada*, Hipolita challenges the traditional parenting style when she is forced to seek employment to provide for her family. Unlike her mother Asunción, who permanently gave her away, Hipolita left baby Rafael with her maid and enters a convent as a menial worker. While Hipolita leaves her son in the care of a loving guardian, she may still fall outside the "club" of "good" motherhood (Johnson and Swanson 22). The delineation is complex though, as Hipolita must balance her responsibilities to maintain her family in their upper class lifestyle and to emotionally care for them as well. Deirdra Johnson and Debra Swanson examine this predicament when they state that "the construction of motherhood, particularly in the form of dominant ideologies, may have little correspondence to the lived social realities of mothers" (22). For many working mothers, physical separation—albeit temporary—from their children is a complicated situation and speaks more to the harsh reality of survival not "good" or "bad" motherhood.

THE FEMME-MACHO

When describing common character roles of women actors in El Teatro Campesino, a well-known Chicano theater guild, Aida Hurtado stated that the virgin or whore, a common "bipolar" role, was available to women artists who were known to be sweet off stage or sexy and rough in real life (387). The femme-macho, a third role that falls between the Madonna/whore binary, was also available to women actors. Femme-machos are often villainous because of their "inherent deviant" nature; and are sexually ambivalent and attractive to men because they exude power and strength (387).[7] In *Alborada*, Juana Arellano viuda de Manrique, the baby-switching villainess, is the femme-macho mother. She represents a unique kind of motherhood through the lack of soft, generous, self-sacrificing qualities commonly associated with a *marianista* or long-suffering virginal mother. Doña Juana is also what Hurtado calls "men's challenge" (387), since she is ruthless, boorish, and masks her emotions to manipulate others. As Hurtado describes, "The femme-macho can be sarcastic, funny, outrageous, aggressive, mean, or belligerent, but she cannot be tender, loving (except in a political or abstract sense), frightened, or insecure. In fact, the femme-machos are always in mortal combat with men to emasculate them and overpower them" (388). Representing the femme-macho, Juana exercises a lack of common sensitivities and circumvents the patriarchal heir structure by stealing her nephew and replacing him with her own infant. Thus, her son Diego becomes a count and inherits her brother's wealth. Later, when Diego's brain is affected by syphilis and he begins to deteriorate, he is given a poison by Juana to ease his pain. Juana also takes the poison to join Diego in death. For Juana, this is the most merciful act she could do in order to protect her son. According to Rosa Maria Gil and Carmen Inoa Vázquez, "When we look at the Latin woman's caretaking qualities, we are confronted with the compulsion to be selfless ... selflessness really means not being there for yourself but for other people" (81). As a "good" mother, Juana makes an extreme sacrifice. Yet, her immoral characteristics such as stealing and lying make her more of a "bad" mother. Contrary to what is expected of a traditional Marianist-like woman, Juana defies the social order to show other complex representations of mothering.

CONCLUSION

Telenovelas may have an accumulated impact on their audiences that can lead to positive action and/or to unrealistic expectations, since mother and mothering images tend to be limited to particular types, and then connected to common motifs and themes that support the status quo of patriarchal order. However, there are discerning viewers who do not accept the distorted motherhood representations offered by *Alborada* and other *telenovelas*. What is significant is that "...television consumption—whether it is the frequency, recency, or the content features of viewing—may serve to enhance the accessibility of particular constructs" (Shrum 53). Our main concern is that *telenovela* viewers are confronted with this incongruency between their complex reality and television's "fictional reality" of motherhood and must accept or reject this fairytale model of mothering based on punishment or social sanctions.[8] The different mothering styles discussed by scholars such as Anzaldúa, Hurtado, Trujillo, Stevens, and Martínez reflect necessary revisions for outmoded conceptualizations of Latina/Chicana mothers. In addition, more critical discussion is needed on the particular representations of mothers and mothering in *telenovelas* and issues facing Latinas/Chicanas.

[1]See Santiago-Rivera, Arredondo, Gallardo-Cooper; and Torres and Rivera.
[2]See Wilson et al. for further explanation of how television has impacted Latino and other ethnic minority viewers.
[3]See Gruzinski and MacLean for further explanation of the Madonna-like constructions.
[4]See Rodríquez who argues that traditional mothers are also the ones expected to educate their children about social, cultural, and religious values.
[5]Further interdisciplinary understanding of motherhood is available from McCann and Kim; Ladd-Taylor and Umansky; Glenn, Chang, Forcey; Kaplan.
[6]Carol R. McCann and Seung-Kyung Kim suggest that in order for Latino/Chicano societies to advance forward, false dichotomies must be unlearned and men must be taught that they should not think of themselves as "superior and therefore culturally favored over *la mujer* (the woman)" (184).
[7]Hurtado coined the term "femme macho" and wrote extensively about this term.
[8]See Bandura for social learning theory.

WORKS CITED

Anzaldúa, Gloria, and AnaLouise Keating. *Interviews/Entrevistas*. New York: Routledge, 2000. Print.
Arredondo, Gabriela F. *Chicana Feminisms: A Critical Reader*. Durham: Duke University Press, 2003. Print.
Bandura, Albert. "Social Cognitive Theory of Mass Communication." *Media Effects: Advances in Theory Research*. Ed. Jennings Bryant and

Dolf Zillman. Hillsdale, NY: Erlbaum, 2002. 121-53. Print.

Berg, Charles Ramírez. *Latino Images in Film: Stereotypes, Subversion, Resistance.* Austin: University of Texas Press, 2002. Print.

Burkhart, Louise M. *Before Guadalupe: The Virgin Mary in Early Colonial Nahuatl Literature.* Austin: University of Texas Press, 2001. Print.

Demers, David. *The Media Essays: From Local to Global.* Spokane: Marquette, 2003. Print.

"Facts and Statistics." *Illinois Statistics.* Web. 27 Aug. 2009.

Gerbner, George et al. "Growing up with Television: The Cultivation Perspective." *Media Effects: Advances in Theory and Research.* Ed. Bryant Jennings and Dolf Zillman. Hillsdale, NJJ: Erlbaum, 1994. Print.

Gil, Rosa Maria, and Carmen Inoa Vázquez. *The Maria Paradox: How Latinas Can Merge Old World Traditions with New World Self-Esteem.* New York: Putnam, 1996. Print.

Gitlin, Todd. *The Whole World is Watching: Mass Media in the Making and Unmaking of the New Left.* Berkeley: University of California Press, 2003. Print.

Glenn, Evelyn Nakano, Grace Chang and Linda Rennie Forcey. *Mothering: Ideology, Experience, and Agency.* New York: Routledge, 1994. Print.

Gruzinski, Serge, and Heather MacLean. *Images at War: Mexico from Columbus to Blade Runner (1492-2019).* Durham: Duke University Press, 2001. Print.

Hernández-Avila, Inés and Gloria E. Anzaldúa. "Quincentennial: From Victimhood to Active Resistance." *Interviews/Entrevistas.* Ed. Gloria E. Anzaldúa and AnaLouise Keating. New York: Routledge, 2000. 177-94. Print.

Hurtado, Aida. "The Politics of Sexuality in the Gender Subordination of Chicanas." *Living Chicana Theory.* Ed. Carla Trujillo. Berkeley: Third Woman, 1998. 371- 82. Print.

Johnson, Deirdre D., and Debra H. Swanson. "Invisible Mothers: A Content Analysis of Motherhood Ideologies and Myths in Magazines." *Sex Roles* 49.1 (2003): 21-33. Print.

Kaplan, E. Ann. *Motherhood and Representation: The Mother in Popular Culture and Melodrama.* New York: Routledge, 1992. Print.

La Pastina, Antonio C. "Telenovela Reception in Rural Brazil: Gendered Readings and Sexual Mores." *Critical Studies in Media Communication* 21.2 (2004): 162-81. Print.

Ladd-Taylor, Molly, and Lauri Umansky. *"Bad" Mothers: The Politics of Blame in Twentieth-Century America*. New York: New York University Press, 1998. Print.

Mayer, Vicki. "Living Telenovelas/Telenovelizing Life: Mexican American Girls; Identities and Transnational Telenovelas." *Journal of Communication* 53.3 (2003): 479-95. Print.

Mazziotti, Nora. *La Industria de la Telenovela: La Producción de Ficción en America Latina*. Buenos Aires, Argentina: Editorial Paidós, 1996. Print.

McCann, Carole R., and Seung-Kyung Kim. *Feminist Theory Reader: Local and Global Perspectives*. New York: Routledge, 2003. Print.

NietoGomez, Anna. "La Chicana-Legacy of Suffering and Self-Denial." *Chicana Feminist Thought: The Basic Historical Writings*. Ed. Alma M. García. New York: Routledge, 1997. 48-50. Print.

Norat, Gisel. "Women Staging Coups through Mothering." *Feminist Mothering*. Ed. Andrea O'Reilly. Albany: State University of New York Press, 2008. 219-241. Print.

Rios, Diana I. "U.S. Latino Audiences of 'Telenovelas'." *Journal of Latinos & Education* 2.1 (2003): 59-65. Print.

Rodríguez, Jeanette. *Our Lady of Guadalupe: Faith and Empowerment Among Mexican-American Women*. Austin: University of Texas Press, 1994. Print.

Sánchez-Ayendez, Melba. "Puerto Rican Elderly Women: The Cultural Dimension of Social Support Networks." *Women in the Later Years: Health, Social, and Cultural Perspectives*. Ed. Lois Grau and Ida Susser. Binghamton, NY: Haworth, 1989. 239-52. Print.

Santiago-Rivera, Azara L., Patricia M. Arredondo and Maritza Gallardo-Cooper. *Counseling Latinos and La Familia: A Practical Guide*. Thousand Oaks, CA: Sage, 2002. Print.

Sequeira, David. *The Machismo Marianismo Tango*. Pittsburgh: Dorrance, 2009. Print.

Shrum, L. J. "Media Consumption and Perceptions of Social Reality: Effects and Underlying Processes." *Media Effects: Advances in Theory and Research*. Ed. Jennings Bryant and Mary Beth Oliver. New York: Routledge, 2009. 50-73. Print.

Stevens, Evelyn P. "Machismo Marianismo." *Society* 10 (Sept. 1973): 57-63. Print.

Torres, José B., and Felix G. Rivera. *Latino/Hispanic Liaisons and Visions for Human Behavior in the Social Environment.* New York: Haworth Social Work Practice, 2002. Print.

Trujillo, Carla Mari. *Living Chicana Theory.* Berkeley: Third Woman, 1998. Print.

Wilson, Clint C. et al. *Racism, Sexism, and the Media: The Rise of Class Communication in Multicultural America.* Thousand Oaks, CA: Sage, 2003. Print.

Zavella, Patricia. "Talkin' Sex: Chicanas and Mexicanas Theorize About Silences and Sexual Pleasures." *Chicana Feminisms: A Critical Reader.* Ed. Gabriela F. Arrendondo. Durham: Duke University Press, 2003. 228-53. Print.

Malinches, Lloronas, and Guadalupanas

Chicana Revisions of *Las Tres Madres*

CRISTINA HERRERA

IN HIS STUDY ON ARCHETYPES AND THE COLLECTIVE UNCONSCIOUS, Carl Gustav Jung discusses the mother archetype in the form of the "goddess, and especially the Mother of God, the Virgin, and Sophia" (81). The mother archetype appears in a number of forms, and each image may have a positive or negative meaning attached to it (81). Jung defines the archetype as a recurring motif that may appear in literature, folklore, or myth (Wehr 28). Those archetypes that are closely tied to gender may be symbolic of socially-defined, rigid gender roles (37). Because of the existence of archetypes, woman has been split into the impossible binary of virgin/whore. According to the Chicana feminist writer Ana Castillo in *Massacre of the Dreamers: Essays on Xicanisma* (1994) and others, this binary of woman has a profound effect on Mexican and Chicana women, the majority of whom are Roman Catholic (69). They argue that the binary of virgin/whore has been perpetuated by the Catholic Church in an attempt to enforce patriarchal authority upon women (119). The Catholic Church's polarization of the "good" woman symbolized by the Virgin Mary and the "bad" woman as seen in the figure of Eve forces women to "choose" between the two confining roles (116). "Good" women cannot be sexual or rebellious, while "bad" becomes synonymous with sexuality.

Without a doubt the mother archetype in her various forms pervades Mexican folklore, songs, and other oral traditions, making the maternal image very common and familiar to a majority of Mexicanos/as and Chicanos/as. According to María Herrera-Sobek in *The Mexican Corrido* (1990), the mother archetype appears throughout Mexican folklore in the form of the "Good and Terrible Mother" and "the Mother Goddess," once again highlighting the polarities of the mother figure (xix). The realities of motherhood are contrasted with the Mexican culture's tendency to elevate the self-sacrificing, self-abnegating mother. As Ana Castillo explains, Marianismo, that is, veneration of the Virgin Mary creates the impossible notion of the virgin mother (119). Marianismo, above all else, is an "invented concept," argues Castillo, used to enforce practices that confine women to narrow possibilities for self-determination (119). However, as Castillo reminds us, mothers are not virgins and because of this fact, society has stigmatized mothers (182). Her non-virgin female body is tied to sex, and because sex is "bad," the mother becomes denigrated; she is thus simultaneously elevated and denigrated (183).

Chicana motherhood must be studied within the context of the good/bad mother dichotomy inherent within Mexican culture. As scholars such as Norma Alarcón, Tey Diana Rebolledo, and others have argued, the confining binaries of virgin/whore and good/bad mother represented by the mythic and historical figures of La Malinche, La Llorona, and La Virgen de Guadalupe have become so embedded in the Mexican/Chicano cultures that many Chicana writers use this theme in their literature to illustrate how this destructive binary of women inhibits women's self-realization. Yet the three mothers of Chicana/o culture, La Virgen de Guadalupe, La Malinche, and La Llorona, find themselves re-constructed in the works of Chicana writers in ways that stray from traditional masculine representations that view women as "others," the most famous voiced by Mexican writer Octavio Paz: "Woman is another being who lives apart and is therefore an enigmatic figure" (66). Chicanas, however, overturn Paz's relegation of woman (and mothers) as inferior by instead developing well-rounded, complex female characters. In challenging patriarchal authority, Chicana writers depict mother-daughter relationships outside the good/bad dichotomy (Gonzales 155). As Chicana feminist theorist Gloria Anzaldúa argues in *Borderlands/La Frontera: The New Mestiza* (1987):

> Ambiguity surrounds the symbols of these three "Our Mothers." ...In part, the true identity of all three has been subverted—*Guadalupe* to make us docile and enduring, *la Chingada* to make us ashamed of our Indian side, and *la Llorona* to make

us long-suffering people. This obscuring has encouraged the *virgen/puta* (whore) dichotomy. (53)

She points out that what we know of "our mothers" has been rendered through a patriarchal, masculinist ideology, making any revisionary attempts a frustrating, challenging task. Because the legends surrounding *las tres madres* have been tainted by patriarchal discourse, it is this male-oriented perspective that is reinforced from one generation to the next by the mothers themselves. Patriarchal doctrine has been responsible for the construction of this impossible binary in which the three mothers have been placed.

Chicana writers redefine their relationships with whom Anzaldúa has called *las tres madres* of Mexican culture by depicting them as feminist sources of strength and compassion. Chicana writers are left with a bind: how can they defend La Raza yet fight their culture's gender limitations? How can they be *femenistas* while rejecting the *malinchista* label? These writers use their perspectives as modern women to challenge the dualistic confinement of their cultural foremothers, *las tres madres*. By understanding this shift from traditional (patriarchal) representation to feminist Chicana revision, we may clearly see its influence on the mother-daughter dynamic. In re-thinking the duality of mothers and challenging this traditional context of motherhood, Chicana writers strive to create a complex rendering of the mother-daughter bond. Reclaiming the three mothers is a symbolic reclaiming of the maternal relationship. For it is only by modifying their cultural foremothers that contemporary Chicanas may come to terms with their own maternal relationships. By challenging patriarchal representations, Chicana writers re-construct their relationship as symbolic daughters of these mythic mothers.

LA VIRGEN DE GUADALUPE

La Virgen de Guadalupe, an apparition of the Virgin Mary, is a symbol of Mexican Catholicism and is considered the patron saint of Mexicanos and Chicanos. In traditional Mexican folk songs and ballads, Guadalupe is held as a sacred, benevolent, yet ultimately passive figure (Herrera-Sobek 33). As the patron saint of Chicanos/as, Guadalupe symbolizes those traits deemed appropriate for women, namely unselfishness and idealized motherhood (Rebolledo 53). According to *The Mexican Corrido*, in 1531 while on his way to Mexico City to seek help for an ill uncle, an Indian named Juan Diego sees an apparition in the form of the Virgin Mary on the hill of Tepeyac. The beautiful Virgin instructs Juan Diego to inform the bishop of her wish to have a church built in her honor on the hill of Tepeyac (1990: 34).

Significant to the story of La Virgen is her appearance on the hill of Tepeyac, known to be the worshipping ground of Tonantzín, a pre-Columbian Nahuatl goddess (Rebolledo 50). Tonantzín is an aspect of Coatlicue/Serpent Skirt, a fertility and earth goddess, recognized as being the oldest of the Nahuatl deities and is seen as both benevolent and destructive (50). Gloria Anzaldúa has been at the forefront in revising Guadalupe from the chaste, "perfect" mother sanctified by the Catholic Church to the feminist, brown mother goddess. She identifies Guadalupe by her Indian name, Coatlalopeuh, "she who has dominion over serpents," choosing to highlight La Virgen's Nahuatl ancestry (49). Guadalupe as Coatlalopeuh embodies maternity and sexuality, a far cry from Catholicism's idealization of virgin mother. This vision of Guadalupe as the brown mother goddess has been the most symbolic, critical gesture carried out by contemporary Chicana writers and theorists. Guadalupe/Tonantzín, the brown mother, represents for Chicanas/Guadalupanas a commonality, a shared maternal kinship that evokes indigenous, not Catholic, values. As Anzaldúa argues, the Spaniards' conquest of Mexico served to "desex" Guadalupe by "taking *Coatlalopeuh*, the serpent/sexuality, out of her. They completed the split begun by the Nahuas by making *la Virgen de Guadalupe/Virgen Maria* into chaste virgins and *Tlazolteotl/Coatlicue/la Chingada* into *putas....* Thus *Tonantsi* became *Guadalupe*, the chaste protective mother, the defender of the Mexican people" (49-50).

The chaste and desexed Virgen upheld by patriarchal Mexican Catholicism as an ideal role model for women becomes problematic for Chicana feminist writers and theorists who find this image unrealistic, confining, and misogynistic. The question remains, how exactly can contemporary Chicanas who comprise multiple sexualities model themselves after a virgin mother? As Anzaldúa argues, it is only by challenging dualistic modes of thinking intended to confine women that Chicanas and mestizas may learn "to see *Coatlalopeuh-Coatlicue* in the Mother, *Guadalupe*" (106). It is the symbolic reclaiming of Guadalupe as mother goddess, this reinsertion of sexuality and the rejection of virgin mother that allows contemporary Chicanas to honor and revere the woman who is emblematic of their *mestizaje*. Acknowledging the indigenous Coatlalopeuh who lives in Guadalupe provides Chicanas with the necessary tools to liberate themselves and their own mothers from the destructive potential of duality.

In her essay entitled "Guadalupe, the Sex Goddess," Sandra Cisneros explains how La Virgen symbolized the culture's role model for her, the other option being "*puta*hood" (48). But by researching La Virgen's Indian ancestry, Cisneros discovered Guadalupe's ties to Tlazolteotl, goddess of fertility, and other Nahuatl deities, thereby sealing Guadalupe's role for Cisneros as "Guadalupe the sex goddess, a goddess who makes me feel good about my sexual power, my sexual energy, who reminds me I must, [...] write from my *panocha*" (49). Unlike the Mexican Catholic Virgin who upholds the virtues of chastity and submission, Cisneros views Guadalupe in a subversive role, as an emblem representing freedom of sexuality. In fact, Rosario "Chayo," the protagonist in "Little Miracles, Kept Promises" from Cisneros's *Woman Hollering Creek* (1991) collection of short stories, may be read as a fictional account of the writer's discovery of La Virgen's Nahuatl ancestry: "When I learned your real name is Coatlaxopeuh, She Who Has Dominion over Serpents, when I recognized you as Tonantzín ... I wasn't ashamed, then, to be my mother's daughter..." (128). Prior to learning Guadalupe's indigenous background, Chayo aligned her with female complicity and submission. The traditional image of La Virgen as desexed and perfect, upheld by her mother and the Catholic Church, makes Chayo affirm to herself that "I wasn't going to be my mother or my grandma. All that self-sacrifice, all that silent suffering. Hell no. Not here. Not me" (127). She cannot reclaim her mother until she reclaims Guadalupe. By remodeling the image of La Virgen as a figure of fierce yet compassionate strength, Chayo is then able to re-connect the bond through the maternal line, discarding her shame as her mother's daughter. Reconstruction rather than rejection of her cultural foremother allows Chayo to negotiate gender and sexual politics within the Mexican/Chicano culture.

Chicana lesbian theorist Carla Trujillo further transcends the traditional representation of La Virgen by reconstructing her as a significant figure in Chicana lesbian desire. Rather than simply reject Guadalupe as a Mexican Virgin Mary, she asserts that Chicana lesbian theorists instead choose to "[reclaim] and [reconstruct] la Virgen in our own way and not as historically ascribed" (219). Trujillo redefines La Virgen as a role model of acceptance and love: "She loves unconditionally, accepting us in our differing sexualities" (222). Roman Catholicism holds a condemning stance toward homosexuality, and Guadalupe has been closely tied to this religion. In order to re-inscribe La Virgen outside (Mexican) Catholic doctrine, we must "unlearn the 'puta/virgin dichotomy' and reincorporate Tonantzín into La Virgen's religious iconography" (qtd. in Trujillo 224). Condemned by a homophobic Catholic Church, Chicana lesbians seek a loving goddess that embraces their sexuality, in contrast to an authoritative male God constructed by Christianity. Chicana artists work to reconstruct Guadalupe not as the passive, chaste virgin, but as the "bodily representation of desire" (226). Doubly oppressed by a rigidly heterosexual Church and patriarchal culture, Chicana lesbians seek refuge in the mestiza goddess who accepts all people regardless of their sexuality.

LA MALINCHE

La Malinche, derogatorily deemed the "traitor" and *chingada madre* of the Mexican people, has also been reconfigured by Chicana writers outside of traditional misogynistic representation. This is no small task, given that historically, she has been portrayed in Mexican culture as a "sellout" or *vendida*. *La chingada madre* refers to Malintzin Tenepal, the Indian woman sold into slavery to serve as Hernán Cortés's translator upon his arrival to the Americas and who later gave birth to his son Martín (Leal 227). Yet as various Chicana scholars have explained, a Chicana revision of La Malinche has not overturned traditional and often misogynistic views of her. Perhaps the most widely-known analysis of La Malinche is that by Octavio Paz, who in his essay entitled "The Sons of La Malinche" ("Los Hijos de la Malinche") in *The Labyrinth of Solitude and Other Writings* (1985), argues that Mexican males suffer anxiety from being descendents of *la chingada madre* (87). La Malinche has been derogatorily named *La Chingada* because of her supposed affair or rape by the Spaniard Cortés. For Paz, the term *chingar* suggests a cruel masculinity that commits violence upon a woman's body. This "active, masculine" *chingón* asserts his male dominance by "ripping open," by violating the passive *chingada* (77). *La chingada* therefore represents a passive sexuality, she who is being done to, in contrast to the male-defined *chingón*, he who is actively doing.

The concept of *la chingada madre* underscores the Mexican culture's "cult of virginity, [whereby] Chicanas have to maneuver to be less rather than more *chingada*" (Hurtado 395). Mexican and Chicana women learn at a young age the severe consequences of being labeled *chingada*. Paz and other Mexican male nationalists view Malintzin as culpable for the Spanish Conquest of Mexico, believing she willingly "gave" herself to Cortés (Pérez, "Sexuality and Discourse" 53). Because of her actions, "the Mexican people have not forgiven La Malinche for her betrayal" (Paz 86). As the symbolic "bastard son" of the white Spaniard, Paz and other males "must repudiate *la india y la mestiza* for fear that he could be like her, a weak, castrated betrayer of his people" (Pérez, "Sexuality and Discourse" 55). According to Emma Pérez and other Chicana theorists, this outright hatred and distrust of the Indian woman transcends into an illogical fear and hatred of all women, particularly those accused of overt or even covert sexuality.

For Chicana writers, to accept Paz's reading of La Malinche as a mere *chingada* and therefore a culpable, willing victim not only reinforces a patriarchal history of Mexico, but it also shapes contemporary relationships between women and men as inherently unequal. While Paz and other male writers shun and even reject lineage from La Malinche, Chicana writers embrace a return to *la madre/la india* by closely examining and celebrating La Malinche's (and thus their own) indigenous origins. Rather than negate La Malinche's role as a violated, powerless victim, which by default positions all Chicanas as such, Chicanas see her as instrumental in the survival and creation of a mestizo population. To accept their "violated" mother, Chicanas must work to re-imagine La Malinche's role in the shaping of Mexican history and resist the negative connotations associated with her.

Contemporary Chicana scholars have been instrumental in granting Malintzin a legitimate place in Mexican/Chicano history as a cultural foremother. As modern women and as daughters of La Malinche, Chicanas seek to establish a feminist revision, one that acknowledges their ancestral mother as a powerful, active symbol of Chicana feminism. Emma Pérez in *The Decolonial Imaginary: Writing Chicanas Into History* (1999) challenges La Malinche's place in Chicano/a history: "Where ... is the space for the story about women such as La Malinche? How has her legend been imagined, by whom and for whom? Our written Chicana history is often infected with judgments and moralizing" (xv). Given that La Malinche's place in history is full of "judgments and moralizing," it is up to contemporary Chicanas to provide a revisionary history for their ancestral mother.

The Chicana feminist scholar Norma Alarcón has also played a pivotal role in establishing a contemporary feminist revision of the myth of La Malinche, offering an interpretation of Malintzin's relationship with her mother who is partially responsible for selling her daughter into slavery:

> Because the myth of Malintzin pervades not only male thought but ours too as it seeps into our own consciousness in the cradle through their eyes as well as their mothers', who are entrusted with the transmission of culture, we may come to believe that indeed our very sexuality condemns us to enslavement. An enslavement which is subsequently manifested in self-hatred. All we see is hatred of women. We must hate her too since love seems only possible through extreme virtue whose definition is at best slippery. (183)

According to Alarcón, Mexican mothers teach their daughters to abhor sexual women. Malintzin's mother, in her role in her daughter's "enslavement" to sexuality holds a complex space whereby the mother holds most of the blame for her daughter's enslavement, although ironically both mother and daughter are equally subservient to patriarchal traditions (Alarcón 185). Thus, a question that arises is why would a mother subject her daughter to a life of slavery? "*Traitor begets traitor*," explains Moraga, stating that although Malinche's mother commits what we would consider a treacherous act, she "would only have been doing her Mexican wifely duty: *putting the male first*" (93). Stating "*I come from a long line of Vendidas*," Moraga articulates how the "sell-out" label is transferred from generation to generation of Mexican and Chicana women (108). The pervasiveness of the legend makes it nearly impossible for Chicanas not to "suffer under Malinche's name" (92). Moraga contends that this "legacy of betrayal" is passed on from mother to daughter. Although early Mexican male scholars would explain the first betrayal of the mother, followed by Malinche's "betrayal" of her people as evidence of the seemingly inherent unreliability of women, it is in fact the existence of a patriarchal culture that privileges males that is responsible for creating such acts of betrayal. The mother's betrayal of her daughter is a result of this "wifely duty" that perpetuates mothers' favoring and privileging of sons over daughters (95). Patriarchy thus determines that mothers reinforce a system which in turn betrays their own daughters.

Rather than negate her existence as simply the raped mother of the mestizo race, Chicana writers have embarked on a mission to transform Malintzin into "the powerful mother—not the phallic mother feared by modernist, patriarchal nationalists, but an enduring mother, a cultural survivor who bore a mestizo race" (Pérez, *The Decolonial Imaginary* 123). Most often, the transformation of La Malinche has been predominantly visible in Chicana poetry, one example being Carmen Tafolla's poem, "La Malinche." This poem follows the tradition of a Chicana feminist re-interpretation of La Malinche that rejects her actions as simply betrayal. Casting off the label "La Chingada," La Malinche assertively tells her readers:

> But Chingada I was not.
> Not tricked, not screwed, not traitor.
> For I was not traitor to myself—
> I saw a dream
> and I *reached* it.
> *Another world*.........
>
> la raza. (198-99)

La Malinche overturns the traditional rendering of "La Chingada" and voices her belief that in being true to herself and considering the fate of her people, she envisions a new possibility, "another world," a mestizo race. As speaker of the poem, La Malinche openly challenges traditional Chicano history that portrays her as a denigrated betrayer to her people. Because La Malinche's history has been mostly male-defined, it is significant that Tafolla uses the first-person pronoun "I." Speaking in the first-person narrative suggests an active, not passive voice, one that determines her own place in history.

Overturning the slogan *hijos de la chingada*, Chicana writers have adopted their role as *hijas*, articulated by Anzaldúa: "*Sí, soy hija de la*

Chingada. I've always been her daughter" (39). This acceptance of *la india* legitimizes an indigenous female ancestry that is subordinated by a masculine-oriented agenda of Mexican history. As *hijas de la chingada*, Chicana writers create a unique relationship with their mythic mother that sets her up not as a *chingada* but as an active, powerful mother of all mestizas/os. By giving voice to Malintzin, Chicana writers refuse to follow the pattern set by Mexican male nationalists seeking to promote a male-defined consciousness that negates her role to traitor and whore. Aligning herself with La Malinche, the Chicana feminist pioneer Anzaldúa takes a stand against the "sell-out" title that has been given to Malintzin: "Not me sold out my people but they me" (43). She subverts the long-standing tradition that has labeled Malintzin and other strong, Chicana women "sell-outs" and shifts the blame of betrayal by questioning the role present-day Chicanos/as play in reinforcing this dangerous legacy. In recontextualizing La Malinche's story, Chicanas also create a deeper insight into their experiences as brown women living in the 21st century. It is through the conscious task of restoring Malintzin's good name that Chicanas can envision new possibilities for themselves as mestizas, contemporary descendants of a powerful mother.

LA LLORONA

Although La Malinche has been linked to the legend of La Llorona, La Llorona is the infanticidal mother like La Malinche in that she is the rejected and "inferior" mother. The weeping woman also holds an entirely different function in the Mexican and Chicano cultures. There are several versions of La Llorona, although the basic story line remains the same: a rich Spaniard courts an Indian woman and she bears his children. When he informs his lover that he intends to return to Spain to marry a rich woman and take his children with him, she goes to the river and drowns his children. La Llorona dies from grief and is told by "the master of the gate" that she may not enter into heaven until she retrieves her dead children; this is why it is said that children must not go to bodies of water after dark, as La Llorona may mistake them for her own children (Gonzales 160). The tale follows the tradition of the motif of the long-suffering mother, for La Llorona is said to roam at night in search of her drowned children as her punishment for infanticide. The "bad" mother, La Llorona is punished for drowning her children, which then serves as a threat to women to be "good" mothers. This is particularly evident in cultures that stress the self-sacrificing merits of motherhood. Escaping punishment is the father of La Llorona's children, and as the legend makes clear, patriarchy has made it impossible for La Llorona to exert any power other than by murdering her lover's offspring.

Although not deemed a "sell-out" like La Malinche, La Llorona has equally been negatively portrayed as the quintessential "bad mother." Yet Chicana writers resist this comparison, instead focusing on La Llorona's ties to ancient Nahuatl deities. In writings by Chicanas, "the Llorona of Chicana feminists no longer figures as enemy or as victim. Chicana border feminism, feminismo fronteriza, narrativizes the weeping woman's hysterical laments into historically based, residual memories of the disastrous encounter between sixteenth-century indigenous America and European conquerors" (Saldívar-Hull 126). The legend becomes symbolic of the historical gendered violence suffered by women during times of conquest. La Llorona specifically functions within the context of the Spanish Conquest as emblematic of the despair of losing one's offspring as a result of the threats of colonization. Naomi Quinónez's poem, "La Llorona," also narrates a sympathetic rendering of the weeping woman, a mother who acts out of compassion for her children that would otherwise live painful lives as mixed-blood offspring:

> La madre grieves
> > at bringing children into a world
> that may destroy them
> and will kill them. (156)

Long negated as a ruthless child-murderer, La Llorona in Quinónez's version imagines her as a selfless, compassionate brown mother who acts not simply out of vengeance over lost love; rather, the killing of her children serves as an instinctual response to deprive them from living in a harsh world. Works by Chicanas, particularly Sandra Cisneros's "Woman Hollering Creek" (1991), Helena María Viramontes's "The Cariboo Café" (1995) and Alma Luz Villanueva's poetry and her *Weeping Woman* collection stray from traditional Chicano folklore that represents La Llorona as a woman to be feared. Their works are free of indictment, challenging our culture's castigation of La Llorona as simply a child murderer.

The story of La Llorona has a critical role in discussing mother-daughter dynamics, given the fact that many mothers use the legend to control and protect their daughters. Mothers are often the "transmitters" of culture, according to Anzaldúa, using tales such as "La Llorona" to teach their daughters those rules created by patriarchy (38). Indeed, the tale has traditionally been used as a scare tactic for misbehaved children, yet the mother figure holds additional significance as well. The legend enforces "good" motherhood via marriage and subservience to male domination; "bad" women like La Llorona get punished for having adulterous sex and for not following orders. Mothers socialize their daughters through the telling of this legend, discouraging premarital sex and otherwise "rebellious" behavior. As Anzaldúa adds, "Through our mothers, the culture gave us mixed messages: *No voy a dejar que ningún pelado desgraciado maltrate a mis hijos.* And in the next breath it would say, *La mujer tiene que hacer lo que le diga el hombre.* Which was it to be—strong, or submissive, rebellious or conforming?" (40). It is because of these "mixed messages" ("I as a mother will not allow any disgraceful man to mistreat my children, yet the woman must do what a man says") that Chicana daughters are left with a bind. Do they follow their mothers' advice to be submissive and face a lifetime of oppression, or should they rebel against their mothers by instead choosing to reject a life of subservience to men?

In response to the traditionally narrow interpretation of La Llorona, Chicana writers have presented the weeping woman as a sympathetic figure, seen, for example, in Anzaldúa's "bible" of Chicana Studies, *Borderlands.* Anzaldúa details in her chapter "Entering into the Serpent" a deserted church near her hometown in South Texas where it was believed a woman could be seen at night floating around in a white dress. Anzaldúa's surrounding community believed this woman to be La Llorona, but she aligns her with "*Cihuacoatl,* Serpent Woman, ancient Aztec goddess of the earth, of war and birth, patron of midwives, and antecedent of *la Llorona*" (57). Cihuacoatl wails and screams like La Llorona, leading Anzaldúa to believe that this "Daughter of Night, [travels] the dark terrains of the unknown searching for the lost parts of herself" (60). In Anzaldúa's analysis, La Llorona searches for "lost parts" that have been robbed from her by a patriarchal system that has branded her a sinner and "bad" woman. This shift from the traditional perspective that relegates the weeping woman to a ruthless infanticidal mother to Anzaldúa's vision of her as goddess and patroness of midwives is subversive in its efforts to overturn La Llorona's common rendition. Transforming La Llorona from child murderer to goddess offers a unique perspective that allows contemporary Chicanas/Mexicanas to conceive of the possibility of liberating this mythic mother from the context of traditional, misogynistic narrative.

The legend of La Llorona has served as a strong influence in writing by Chicanas. Moraga credits the story of La Llorona for having a deep impact on her "writer's psyche" (142). Additionally, she envisions La Llorona as an iconic "sister" for all Chicanas and Mexicanas, particularly for herself as a Chicana lesbian, given that her sexuality is condemned by a patriarchal, heterosexist environment: "Any way you slice it, we were both a far and mournful cry from obedient daughters. But I am convinced that La Llorona is every Mexican woman's story, regardless of sexuality. She is sister to us all" (145). Moraga's reclaiming of La Llorona as an iconic sister forces present-day Chicanas to re-examine their lives and choices.

Examining the complexity of La Llorona's crime of infanticide, Moraga asks a pointed question: "...could infanticide then be retaliation against misogyny, an act of vengeance not against one man, but man in general for a betrayal much graver than sexual infidelity: the enslavement and deformation of our sex?" (145). Ironically, her question overturns the label of "betrayer" onto men, subverting the long-held tradition that holds women in this unflattering light. It is men, through the systematic oppression of women, according to Moraga, who have betrayed women and not the other way around. This argument ties into Anzaldúa's statement cited earlier, "Not me sold out my people." Because women have traditionally been defined solely in relation to men and children, they "wander not in search of our dead children, but our lost selves, our lost sexuality, our lost spirituality, our lost sabiduría" (147). La Llorona's search for her dead children may in fact be a psycho-sexual search for her integral female self denied to her by a patriarchal and confining construction of motherhood. La Llorona's tale, then, is symbolic of the lost female self who is confined within rigid patriarchal customs.

Chicanas offer a unique perspective of these three maternal figures, and in so doing they establish a new relationship with their cultural fore-mothers. As symbolic daughters of these mothers, Chicanas destabilize masculinist narratives that seek to invalidate the mother-daughter bond. The three mythic mothers as archetypal figures have been used in Mexican culture to define "appropriate" (La Virgen) and "inappropriate" (La Malinche and La Llorona) models of motherhood and womanhood. The presence of these female archetypes puts a strain on the mother-daughter relationship given that the archetypes reinforce the limited categories of women and mothers as either good or bad. It is only by applying a mestiza feminist vision to La Virgen, La Malinche, and La Llorona that mothers and daughters may succeed in defining their relationship outside a narrow framework.

WORKS CITED

Alarcón, Norma. "Chicana's Feminist Literature: A Re-Vision Through Malintzin/or Malintzin: Putting Flesh Back on the Object." *This Bridge Called My Back: Writings by Radical Women of Color*. Ed. Cherríe Moraga and Gloria Anzaldúa. Watertown, MA: Persephone, 1981. 182-90. Print.

Anzaldúa, Gloria. *Borderlands/La Frontera: The New Mestiza*. San Francisco: Aunt Lute, 1987. Print.

Castillo, Ana. *Massacre of the Dreamers: Essays on Xicanisma*. New York: Plume, 1994. Print.

Cisneros, Sandra. "Guadalupe the Sex Goddess." *Goddess of the Americas/La Diosa de Las Américas: Writings on the Virgin of Guadalupe*. Ed. Ana Castillo. New York: Riverhead, 1996. 46-51. Print.

Cisneros, Sandra. "Little Miracles, Kept Promises." *Woman Hollering Creek and Other Stories*. New York: Vintage, 1991. 116-29. Print.

Cisneros, Sandra. "Woman Hollering Creek." *Woman Hollering Creek and Other Stories*. New York: Vintage, 1991. 43-56. Print.

Gonzales, María C. "Love and Conflict: Mexican American Women Writers as Daughters." *Women of Color: Mother-Daughter Relationships in 20th Century Literature*. Ed. Elizabeth Brown-Guillory. Austin: U of Texas P, 1996. 153-71. Print.

Herrera-Sobek, María. *The Mexican Corrido: A Feminist Analysis*. Bloomington: Indiana University Press, 1990. Print.

Hurtado, Aída. "The Politics of Sexuality in the Gender Subordination of Chicanas." *Living Chicana Theory*. Ed. Carla Trujillo. Berkeley: Third Woman, 1998. 383-428. Print.

Jung, Carl G. *The Archetypes and the Collective Unconscious*. 2nd ed. Trans. R. F. C. Hull. Princeton: Princeton University Press, 1959. Print.

Leal, Luis. "Female Archetypes in Mexican Literature." *Women in Hispanic Literature: Icons and Fallen Idols*. Ed. Beth Miller. Berkeley: University of California Press, 1983. 227-42. Print.

Moraga, Cherríe. *Loving in the War Years: lo que nunca pasó por sus labios*. Cambridge: South End, 2000. Print.

Paz, Octavio. *The Labyrinth of Solitude and Other Writings*. Trans. Lysander Kemp. New York: Grove, 1985. Print.

Pérez, Emma. *The Decolonial Imaginary: Writing Chicanas Into History*. Bloomington: Indiana University Press, 1999. Print.

Pérez, Emma. "Sexuality and Discourse: Notes from a Chicana Survivor." *Chicana Critical Issues*. Ed. Norma Alarcón, et al. Berkeley: Third Woman, 1993. 45-69. Print.

Quinónez, Naomi. "La Llorona." *In Other Words: Literature by Latinas of the United States*. Ed. Roberta Fernández. Houston: Arte Público, 1994. 156. Print.

Rebolledo, Tey Diana. *Women Singing in the Snow: A Cultural Analysis of Chicana Literature*. Tucson: University of Arizona Press, 1995. Print.

Saldívar-Hull, Sonia. *Feminism on the Border: Chicana Gender Politics and Literature*. Berkeley: University of California Press, 2000. Print.

Tafolla, Carmen. "La Malinche." *Infinite Divisions: An Anthology of Chicana Literature*. Ed. Tey Diana Rebolledo and Eliana S. Rivero. Tucson: University of Arizona Press, 1993. 198-99. Print.

Trujillo, Carla. "La Virgen de Guadalupe and Her Reconstruction in Chicana Lesbian Desire." *Living Chicana Theory*. Ed. Carla Trujillo. Berkeley: Third Woman, 1996. 214-31. Print.

Villanueva, Alma Luz. *La Llorona and Other Stories*. Tempe, AZ: Bilingual Press, 1994. Print.

Viramontes, Helena María "The Cariboo Café." *The Moths and Other Stories*. Houston: Arte Público Press, 1995. 65-79. Print.

Wehr, Demaris S. "Religious and Social Dimensions of Jung's Concept of the Archetype: A Feminist Perspective." *Feminist Archetypal Theory: Interdisciplinary Re-Visions of Jungian Thought*. Knoxville: University of Tennessee Press, 1985. 23-45. Print.

About the Contributors

Mary Louise Babineau is an Associate Professor of Spanish at St. Thomas University in Fredericton, New Brunswick, in Canada. She has published articles on U.S.-Latino literature in the journals *Hipertexto* and *Border-Lines,* and her book chapter entitled "Lost Daughters of the Caribbean: Constructions of Identity by Hispanic and Francophone Women in the Caribbean Diaspora" will appear in an edited collection on Caribbean literature to be published by Rodopi in 2012. She is the recipient of teaching awards from both Arizona State University and St. Thomas University

Mirna Carranza has a Ph.D. in Family Relations and Human Development from the University of Guelph and is an Associate Professor at McMaster University. Her research interests include immigrant and refugee families and their process of acculturation as family units. She is also interested in studying issues of grief, warfare, and the impact of these on parenting practices.

Ana Castillo is a Chicana poet and writer and her work focuses on feminism and identity. Her texts include the collections of poetry, *My Father Was a Toltec and Selected Poems, 1973-1988* (1995) and *I Ask the Impossible* (2001); the novels, *My Daughter, My Son, The Eagle, The Dove* (2000) and *The Guardians* (2007); and the collection of short stories *Peel My Love Like an Onion* (1999).

Angie Cruz is the author of two novels, *Soledad* (2001) and *Let It Rain Coffee* (2005). Her shorter works have been published in the *New York*

Times, Indiana Review, and *Callaloo.* She teaches creative writing at Texas A&M University, where she lives with her husband and toddler.

Junot Díaz is the author of *Drown* (1996) and *The Brief Wondrous Life of Oscar Wao* (2007). He has received numerous awards, including the National Book Critics Circle Award and the Pulitzer Prize. He is the fiction editor at the *Boston Review* and teaches at the Massachusetts Institute of Technology.

Helyne Frederick is a doctoral student at Texas Tech University. She received her Master's degree in Human Development and Family Studies at Texas Tech University in 2008. Her research focuses on risk-taking behaviors among minority and immigrant youth, with particular emphasis on the sexual behaviors and attitudes of adolescents and young adults.

Petra Guerra earned her Ph.D. from Washington State University. She is an Assistant Professor of Communication at the University of Texas-Pan American. Her teaching includes public relations, health communication, media law, and ethics. She conducts research on the media's role in the lives of adolescents, children and women, and sex education in public schools.

Cristina Herrera received her Ph.D. in English from Claremont Graduate University in Claremont, California. Currently, she is an Assistant Professor in the Department of Chicano and Latin American Studies at California State University, Fresno. Her research focuses on mothers and daughters in literature by contemporary Chicanas and Latinas.

Laura Ruth Johnson is an Assistant Professor in the College of Education at Northern Illinois University in Dekalb, Illinois, where she teaches graduate courses in qualitative research. She primarily conducts qualitative and ethnographic research within Chicago's Puerto Rican community, with a focus on the experiences of young Puerto Rican mothers. She also expresses her sincere and everlasting gratitude to the mothers who participated in her study, as well as the staff of the Puerto Rican Cultural Center, Chicago.

Yolanda Martínez is a Spanish language tutor at the University of

Birmingham. She has published articles on Hispanic women writers in journals including *Wadabagei, New Mango Season, and Letras Femeninas* and is the author of the short story "Pan de Manteca" (*Letras Femeninas*). Her scholarly interests include racial, sexual, and socio-cultural representations of the female body and sexuality in the visual arts, and the global translatability of smell as a socio-cultural construct of female identity.

Richard Mora is an Assistant Professor in the Sociology Department at Occidental College. Using qualitative methods, he studies motherhood, masculinity, adolescence, and youth violence.

Gilda L. Ochoa teaches Chicana/o-Latina/o studies and sociology at Pomona College. She is the author of *Learning from Latino Teachers* (2007) and *Becoming Neighbors in a Mexican American Community* (2004) and co-editor of *Latino Los Angeles* (2005). She has also written articles on critical pedagogy and Mexican American women's activism.

Diana I. Rios earned her doctorate from the University of Texas at Austin. She is an Associate Professor of Communication Sciences/Institute of Puerto Rican and Latino Studies (PRLS) at the University of Connecticut and is the Interim Director of PRLS. Her research and teaching include media representation of gender, sexuality, and ethnicity/race; and women in higher education.

Anne R. Roschelle is an Associate Professor of Sociology at the State University of New York at New Paltz and is the author of numerous articles on work and family in Cuba and the intersection of race, class, and gender with a focus on extended kinship networks, family poverty, and homelessness.

Mayra Santos-Febres started publishing poems in 1984 in such international journals and magazines as *Casa de las Américas* (Cuba), *Página doce* (Argentina), *Revue Noir* (France), and *Latin American Revue of Arts and Literature* (New York). In addition to being a poet, she is also an essayist and novelist. Her novels include *Sirena Selena vestida de pena* (2000), *Cualquier miércoles soy tuya* (2002), and *Sobre piel y papel* (2005). She has taught at Harvard University and Cornell University and received the Guggenheim award in 2009. She currently teaches at the University of Puerto Rico, Río Piedras.

Dorsía Smith Silva is an Assistant Professor of English at the University of Puerto Rico, Río Piedras. She is the co-editor of the *Caribbean without Borders: Caribbean Literature, Language and Culture* (2008) and *Critical Perspectives on Caribbean Literature and Culture* (2011). Her work has appeared in several journals, including *Journal of the Association for Research on Mothering*, *Journal of Caribbean Literature*, and *La Torre* and her primary interests are ethnic mothering and mother and daughter relationships. She is currently working on a book about motherhood and ethnic societies.

D. Milton Stokes is a doctoral student at the University of Connecticut, Storrs in the department of Communication Sciences. His research and teaching interests include public health and mass media.

Michelle Téllez works as an Assistant Professor in the division of Humanities, Arts and Cultural Studies at Arizona State University. She specializes in women of color feminist theory, globalization studies, Chicana/Latina studies, social movements and border studies.

Elizabeth Trejos-Castillo is an Assistant Professor of Human Development and Family Studies, Texas Tech University. Her research interests include parenting and the etiology of risk-taking and problem behaviors across ethnic minority and immigrant youth. Recent publications include articles in the *Journal of Youth & Adolescence*, *Handbook of Parenting*, and *Journal of Adolescent Health*.